DIVERSITY AND TEACHING
TEACHER EDUCATION YEARBOOK I

DIVERSITY AND TEACHING
TEACHER EDUCATION YEARBOOK I

EDITORS
MARY JOHN O'HAIR   SANDRA J. ODELL
Texas Tech University   *Western Michigan University*

under sponsorship of the Association of Teacher Educators

HARCOURT BRACE JOVANOVICH COLLEGE PUBLISHERS
Fort Worth   Philadelphia   San Diego   New York   Orlando   Austin   San Antonio
Toronto   Montreal   London   Sydney   Tokyo

Publisher	*Ted Buchholz*
Acquisitions Editor	*Jo-Anne Weaver*
Project Editor	*Laura Hanna*
Production Manager	*Cynthia Young*
Book Designer	*Brian Salisbury*

Address Editorial Correspondence To:
Harcourt Brace Jovanovich College Publishers, 301 Commerce Street,
Suite 3700, Fort Worth, TX 76102

Address Orders To:
Harcourt Brace Jovanovich College Publishers, 6277 Sea Harbor Drive,
Orlando, FL 32887
1-800-782-4479, or 1-800-433-0001 (in Florida)

Printed in the United States of America

Library of Congress Catalogue Number: 92-73113

ISBN: 0-15-500498-0

3 4 5 6 7 8 9 0 1 2   090   9 8 7 6 5 4 3 2 1

TABLE OF CONTENTS

IV. DIVERSE ISSUES IN SCHOOL CURRICULA   237

THE ETHICAL RESPONSIBILITIES OF MEETING STUDENTS' DIVERSE NEEDS

A FOREWORD

D. JOHN MCINTYRE is Professor in the Department of Curriculum and Instruction and Director of the Teaching Skills Laboratory at Southern Illinois University at Carbondale. He is the 1992-1993 President of the Association of Teacher Educators. He has been honored with the ATE Research Award, and has been named as one of 70 Outstanding Leaders in Teacher Education.

When diversity was chosen as the theme for the 1993 annual conference, it marked the Association of Teacher Educators' continued dedication to the goal of meeting the needs of all students in all classrooms and in all situations. *Webster's New World Dictionary* defines diversity as a quality, state, fact, or instance of being different; or a variety or multiformity. Given this definition, the editors of *Diversity and Teaching: Teacher Education Yearbook I* have chosen to view diversity as a multidimensional concept. In addition to cultural pluralism and multicultural education, issues such as global perspectives, curriculum, program development, research, field experiences, and innovations in teacher education are addressed as they relate to diversity.

It is no secret that today's student population is the most diverse of any other that has ever adorned our classrooms. Today's teachers are responsible for classrooms that represent a rainbow of colors, languages, backgrounds, and learning styles. Data indicate that by the year 2010, nearly 40 percent of school age children will be persons of color. In the states of California, Texas, Arizona, New Mexico, and Florida, minority students will be the majority (Hodgkinson, 1989). Minority students already constitute a majority of students in 23 of the 25 largest school districts (Gay, 1989). In addition, it is said that 184 different languages are represented by the children in the Los Angeles public schools (Hodgkinson, 1989). These demographic data are also confounded by the many diverse approaches to learning that students bring to the classroom.

Kurth-Schai (1991) states that since we live in a world where difference often results in seclusion and discrimination, practicing a pedagogy of inclusion is an ethical responsibility of teaching. She further states that children's lives are affected by the prevailing attitudes toward the array of factors which constitute human diversity. In addition, John Goodlad (1990) argues that it is morally wrong that opportunities to gain access to the most generally useful knowledge are maldistributed in most schools, with poor and minority children and youths on the short end of the distribution. Unfortunately, society and our schools too often view any deviation from a "perceived norm"—whether that "norm" be ethnicity, culture, language, behavior, learning, and so on—as a problem rather than as an opportunity to celebrate the potential for learning from each other.

Goodlad (1990) asserts that it is likely that most future teachers will progress through their general education requirements and academic majors, perhaps to the level of their master's degree, without thinking about these inequalities in schooling. ATE agrees with Goodlad that this is an intolerable situation. It is unfathomable for our profession to permit future teachers to remain ignorant and unconcerned about these inequities, about this lack of effort to meet the needs of our diverse student population. This innocence must be shaken at its roots.

ATE also believes that the practice of inclusion is an ethical responsibility for all teachers, teacher educators, and the Association of Teacher Educators. In that light, *Diversity and Teaching: Teacher Education Yearbook I* is a compilation of articles that attempts to inform and alert teacher educators to the multidimensionality of diversity in our schools. Mary O'Hair and Sandra Odell are to be commended for editing a book that can make a difference in our profession. The authors are to be commended for sharing their insights and scholarly work in an effort to shed the ignorance surrounding diversity. Share this book with your fellow teacher educators, with your cooperating teachers, and with your students. Help ATE make a difference!

D. John McIntyre
ATE President, 1992–1993

REFERENCES

Gay, G. (1989). Ethnic minorities and educational quality. In J. A. Banks & C. A. Banks (Eds.). *Multicultural education: Issues and perspectives* (pp. 167–188). Boston: Allyn & Bacon.

Goodlad, J. (1990). The occupation of teaching in schools. In J. Goodlad, R. Soder, & K. Sirotnik, (Eds.). *The moral dimensions of teaching* (pp. 3–34). San Francisco: Jossey-Bass.

Hodgkinson, H. (1989). *The same client: The demographics of education and service delivery systems.* Washington, D.C.: The Institute of Education.

Kurth-Schai, R. (1991). The peril and promise of childhood: Ethical implications for tomorrow's teachers. *Journal of Teacher Education, 42*(3), 196–204.

INTRODUCTION
LINKING RESEARCH AND PRACTICE:
A REFLECTIVE APPROACH

MARY O'HAIR is Assistant Professor in Educational Psychology and Leadership at Texas Tech University. She has published articles in teacher education, instructional supervision, and organizational communication. Specific research interests include preparing teachers and administrators for intercity settings, power and politics in schools, and change/action research.

SANDRA J. ODELL is Associate Professor in Education and Professional Development at Western Michigan University. She has published articles on teacher induction, mentoring and teacher development. She maintains a career-long research interest in teacher development in the context of collaborative university/school district programs.

Convincing teachers and teacher educators of the need to link research and practice is not difficult. By the time preservice teachers enter the profession, they know enough about teaching and learning to appreciate the critical role that new and current knowledge play in helping them succeed in the classroom. However, teachers often feel isolated from current research on teaching and seek inclusion in the intellectual turbulence surrounding teacher education research. To sustain this inherent interest in new knowledge, teachers and teacher educators need books that encourage classroom research on critical issues in teaching and that help researchers and practitioners learn from one another. Thus, *the first objective of the yearbook is to present current research on the topic of diversity and teaching in a meaningful way for teachers and teacher educators.*

In addition, we understand that many teachers may find it cumbersome to interpret and apply research findings, on diversity and teaching or on any topic. This yearbook is designed to assist teachers in applying new knowledge in two specific ways. First, the yearbook combines educational theory, methodology, and specialized knowledge to improve teaching and teacher education and to seek answers to real-world problems. Second, respondents (experts) in teacher education interpret research results and provide a reflective framework to assist teachers in turning research into classroom practice. Accordingly, *the second objective of the yearbook is to apply new knowledge on diversity and teaching to classrooms.*

Finally, the yearbook framework emphasizes reflective inquiry for teachers and teacher educators by stressing observation, analysis, and interpretation.

We believe that researchers and practitioners are dependent on each other in making new and existing knowledge meaningful for classroom practice. Most teachers need guidance in reflecting about the complex interactions between research and practice and most researchers need guidance in reflecting about what implications research has for practice. By design, the yearbook offers such guidance. *The third objective of the yearbook is to provide a reflective approach to understanding research related to diversity and teaching.*

These three objectives—presenting current research, linking research and practice, and adopting a reflective approach to research, teaching, and learning—distinguish the yearbook from other books on diversity and teaching.

A NEW PERSPECTIVE

Yearbooks are not new to the Association of Teacher Educators (ATE). During the 1960s, several yearbooks were published by Wm. C. Brown in association with ATE. By design, the 1960s yearbooks were collections of articles that were generally read only by teacher educators in higher education; such collections were rarely disseminated to their colleagues in schools. The new yearbook series is based on the premise that "all educators are teacher educators" and therefore we must broaden the readership and authorship range to include all instructional leaders: teachers, professors, administrators, researchers, and others representing disciplines outside the field of education. Whereas the 1960s yearbooks focused solely on scholarship as the production of knowledge, the new yearbooks adopt a triadic definition of scholarship: a topic overview and framework of existing knowledge (respondents), the production of new knowledge (research reports), and the interpretation, synthesis, and application of new knowledge (respondents). This triadic approach provides a unique framework designed to assist teachers and teacher educators in synthesizing, interpreting, and applying research to their classrooms.

The new yearbooks address fundamental issues in teacher education by encouraging *all* teacher educators, both school and college based, to participate. Walter Doyle (1990), in describing directions for teacher education research wrote: "The signs are clear that there is a readiness within the research and teacher education communities to enlarge the vision of what teacher education can be and what knowledge can inform the enterprise" (p. 20). To assist the Association of Teacher Educators in enlarging the vision, professional organizations such as American Educational Research Association Division K, Association for Supervision and Curriculum Development, American Association of Colleges for Teacher Education, and International Communication

Association have been asked to participate actively in the development and conceptualization of the new teacher education yearbooks. The Communication Division of the yearbook provides an excellent example of what other disciplines (that is, instructional communication) have to offer the field of teacher education. Future goals include having a liaison from each organization to serve as a member of the *Teacher Education Yearbook* editorial board.

Collectively, the yearbook expands perspectives on teacher education. As described by Carl Glickman (1992) in reference to the field of supervision, times are changing: "To be blunt: as a field, we may no longer need the old words and connotations. Instead, we might be seeing every talented educator (regardless of role) as an instructional leader and supervisor of instruction. If so, indeed, the old order will have crumbled" (p. 3). As editors of the yearbook, we believe that teacher education is in transition. Teacher educators *are* instructional leaders who take risks to ensure the quality of teachers and teaching. The yearbook provides an avenue for dialogue, risk taking, and innovation.

HOW TO USE THE YEARBOOK

The yearbook is designed for use by all teachers and teacher educators. It can be employed alone as the main textbook in college courses or staff development programs designed to examine teaching contexts, processes, communication, and curricula or it can be used with a more traditional textbook to accomplish the same objectives. In addition, the yearbook may be adopted for undergraduate and graduate-level courses focusing on action research, multicultural education, communication education, and communities and schools.

In the past, college textbook authors and publishers often neglected the research needs and interests of school-based teacher educators. When asked by the yearbook editors to describe the importance of linking research and practice in his school district, Ray McNulty, Superintendent of Windham Southeast Supervisory Union, Brattleboro, Vermont, stated:

Schools must be viewed as educational centers where practitioners, researchers, children and others learn alongside one another. In the past linking educational research to actual classroom practice did not seem like a natural connection for most classroom teachers. When I would challenge teachers with "What I'm reading supports us doing X in the classroom and you seem to be doing Y, what are your reasons?", they would generally cite experience in the classroom as grounds for their actions and state that the research findings I quoted were conducted by university faculty or graduate students with their own agendas and rarely address real classroom problems. How could I make current research meaningful for classroom teachers and improve learning in the classroom? In response, I set out to incorporate into our school system a missing piece in our staff development program—action research.

With the help of a building principal, creative teachers, and a university willing to bend rules to fit the client learner needs, something we always ask our teachers to do for their students, we designed a course to support our efforts and meet our goals. It may be helpful to describe what this action research component of our staff development program is not. It is not experimental research. It is not data gathering for someone else's research project. What it can be described as, is a way for teachers to look at, reflect upon, and make changes in their own classroom practice. The success of our program can be summarized by one of the teachers who said, "This professional development model allowed me to do something I never seem to have time for, study my own teaching and class." The *Teacher Education Yearbook* series would assist us in stimulating thought and action on meaningful research and provide a dissemination outlet for the practitioner researcher.

EFFECTIVE ORGANIZATION

Research reports in four divisions are published in the yearbook. The four divisions consist of Diverse Contexts for Teaching, Diverse Processes in Studying Teaching, Diverse Perspectives on Communication, and Diverse Issues in School Curricula. Research reports were blind reviewed and ranked per division based on commonly accepted criteria for social science research. Each division employed a respondent(s) who reacts to the research reports selected, provides readers with a global understanding of the research topics, develops an organizational framework to help identify key concepts and trends, and states implications for reflective classroom practice.

APPRECIATION

As editors of this book, we have been involved in various forms of teacher education research and practice for several years. Although we had not collaborated on any major project prior to this yearbook, our shared interest in adding to the knowledge base in teacher education was keen, and we recognized the need for a teacher education yearbook series.

The original impetus for the project came when Mary John O'Hair sought to publish a proceedings of the research reports presented at the ATE

1993 Los Angeles conference. She contacted Sandra Odell, Conference Program Chair, and Dee Wolfe Eicher, Planning Committee Co-Chair, to discuss the possibility. In the course of the discussions, the yearbook concept emerged. Through the assistance of Gloria Chernay, ATE Executive Director; Jo-Anne Weaver, acquisitions editor, Harcourt Brace Jovanovich; and College of Education at Texas Tech University, we found sponsors for the work that appears in this book.

Many people have played critical roles in the development of this yearbook. We particularly wish to thank John McIntyre, President of the Association of Teacher Educators. John is truly a visionary leader of the Association. When presented with the idea of the yearbook, he immediately supported the concept and helped to conceptualize the final product. Also, the ATE Executive Board, Communications Committee, and Research Committee are appreciated for their swift endorsement and continual support of the yearbook.

Several others have played key roles in the project. We appreciate the involved and talented efforts of our editorial board members. From the beginning Martin Haberman and Robert Houston supported the vision of the project and recognized the risks involved in leaving the beaten path. They were enthusiastic about producing a book that is truly different. Their sincere support and guidance were helpful. Others supported the project by participating in the conceptualization, reviewing, or writing process: Dave Byrd, University of Rhode Island; Renee Clift, University of Illinois; Cherry Goodman, Texas Southern University; Edith Guyton, Georgia State University; Francisco Hidalgo, California State University, San Bernadino; Leslie Huling-Austin, Southwest Texas State University; Terry James, University of Central Arkansas; Elaine Jarchow, University of Nevada, Las Vegas; Elaine McNiece, University of Central Arkansas; and Ronald Opp, Texas Tech University.

Few authors could hope for a more involved and talented publishing team. Jo-Anne Weaver, acquisitions editor, Craig Johnson, marketing manager, and Laura Hanna, project editor, have made valuable contributions.

LASTLY

One editor recently described preparing an edited book as similar to savoring a gourmet meal in a fine restaurant rather than the drudgery of preparing the meal yourself at home (Miller & Knapp, 1985). Of course, this analogy rests on the assumption that you could prepare a gourmet meal of similar quality at home. It is our view as editors that our job consists of coordinating and arranging the dinner rather than participating in the actual culinary toil.

Appetizers consist of the respondents' overviews and frameworks. The main course involves research reports and implications, and the dessert focuses on respondents' applications for reflective practice. Bon appetit!

REFERENCES

Doyle, W. (1990). Themes in teacher education research. In W. R. Houston (Ed.). *Handbook of research on teacher education* (pp. 3–24). New York: Macmillan.

Glickman, C. D. (1992). Introduction: Postmodernism and supervision. In C. D. Glickman (Ed.). *Supervision in transition* (pp. 1–3). Alexandria, VA: Association for Supervision and Curriculum Development.

Miller, G. R., & Knapp, M. L. (Eds.). (1985). *Handbook of interpersonal communication*. Beverly Hills, CA: SAGE.

DIVISION I

Diverse Contexts for Teaching

Contexts: Overview and Framework

MARTIN HABERMAN
University of Wisconsin-Milwaukee

MARTIN HABERMAN has been directly or indirectly involved in every major development in American teacher education over the last thirty years. The National Teacher Corps was based on his intern teaching model. He has helped to develop teacher education programs focused on preparing teachers for children in poverty for numerous universities. The certification laws of several states and the selection procedures of numerous urban school districts have been influenced by his extensive research, writing and demonstration efforts.

THE WORLD CHILDREN IN POVERTY BRING TO SCHOOL

Many teachers can recall growing up in poverty themselves. They believe this helps them empathize with poor children they may teach today. For some teachers this may be true. But today's poverty is unlike poverty in former

1

times. The cumulative effect of growing up in poverty today produces school-age children who, in many critical ways, do not resemble textbook children.

Textbook children are what teachers trained in traditional programs of teacher education are taught "normal" children are like. In child development courses future teachers are required to read texts, see films, and even observe children. There is a year-by-year analysis of what "normal" one-year-olds, two-year-olds, three-year-olds, are supposed to be like. How *all* children behave, think, and perceive the world is laid out in terms of a "normal" universal development, year by year.

The expectations for children who then come to preschools and regular schools, administered as they are by middle-class professionals, is based on these textbook expectations. What middle-class youngsters of a given age do is regarded as "normal" behavior. "Normal," meaning typical, is then transformed by the experts who write the texts and make the films into "normal," meaning desirable behavior. The word *normal* which began with the meaning of "frequently observed" is thus changed into "behavior considered healthy." After all, who would not want to be or have a child who is a "normal" one-year-old, and so on? Thus future teachers are trained by seeing, on film, in texts, or even in person, "normal" children year by year.

There is more than a minor problem with such teacher training. The assumption that child development is supposed to proceed in the same way and at the same year-by-year rate in all groups and cultures and under all life conditions is dangerously naive. Children develop by interacting with specific people in particular environments. What is "normal" in one set of circumstances will not be "normal" in another. In fact, given the facts of life in growing up in urban poverty today it is clearly unreasonable to expect children to resemble the textbook models future teachers are trained to regard as normal. The important point is that the urban poor are quite normal. *They are making perfectly reasonable responses to those who raise them and to the life conditions under which they live and grow.*

A second and even more dangerous weakness in the way future teachers are trained in traditional teacher education programs relates to their apparent "kindness." This "kindness" is essentially a rejection of the child's development and plays out in the following manner. After accepting some grand, overall, universal theory of how all normal children are supposed to develop and the year-by-year rate of this development, future teachers are then taught exceptions. Many children have handicapping conditions: some are brain damaged; others have physical, emotional, or mental handicaps. And oh yes, there are also many in poverty who do not grow "normally" and who do not pass through the year-by-year growth stages that all "normal" children pass through. From this initial misconception of one universal growth pattern flows all kinds of "kindness." Headstart, Jumpstart, Get Smart, and a wide range of programs all begin with the youngest ages who can be put into some form of school on the basic assumption that these youngsters are not "normal." From toddlers on to preschoolers, these very young children are dealt with on the basis of their inadequacies. Beginning with such perceptions, day-care workers, teachers, and even parents frequently believe they are making a kindly, humane effort to give children with some abnormal deficiencies a better chance to compete with normal children later on. *Schooling, of any level for any child, which begins with the basic assumption that the child is a deficient human being, will prove to be miseducative and lead to more negative than positive achievements.*

To define the child as abnormal in order to begin a program or school is quite the opposite of "kindness" or "humanity" regardless of the stated motives of those who initiate such efforts. The human learner (and even laboratory rats) are extremely sensitive to the perceptions of those who would teach them. There is no basis in theory or in fact for believing that children who grow up in poverty are making anything other than normal responses to their treatment and environment.

The normal world which children in poverty bring to school is frequently at odds, therefore, with their teachers' expectations. It is not possible to provide neat general patterns of how children in poverty perceive their world. There are, however, several themes which have been identified in recent years that sensitive teachers can watch for and learn from. Following are some of the perceptions and behaviors identified by day-care and early childhood teachers who work with low-income children. These patterns are not found in all poor children. In many cases they help us understand why poverty today has a different impact than when many adults experienced poverty as children.

LACKING TRUST

Growing up without any adult(s) they can trust is currently an experience for many urban children. Trust is not a commodity that is readily available. Neither is it easily taught. I can recall a creative day-care center in which an imaginative teacher of five or six two-year-olds tried to actually give trust lessons. These were children without parents who were being cared for by various foster parents. Since the foster parents also worked outside the home, the children were in day care. This teacher would walk the toddlers around the block each morning. The teacher had prearranged that various individuals such as a newsdealer, a shopkeeper, a janitor, and several other adults would be present without fail at the same place each morning. As the youngsters made their daily walk they would be greeted by the same people in the same place. Each child was picked up and given a big hello by these adults. The teacher's hope was that she could actually teach the children to trust adults by having this experience of seeing and being greeted by the same adults at least once a day. This "curriculum" aimed at teaching something which we would hope would naturally be present in the lives of children but can no longer be assumed. More and more children are growing up without such experience and without a teacher seeking some sort of substitute way of teaching it. It is normal—to be expected—that children who grow up without adults in their lives they can trust will be somewhat suspicious—even fearful—of adults.

SUFFERING VIOLENCE AND ABUSE

Another condition that is more characteristic of children in poverty today than in former times is the higher degree of violence and abuse present in their immediate lives. A direct result of the drug culture is the increase in crime and violence. Children are frequently surrounded by death and those in the process of dying in violent and traumatic ways. There is also a much greater incidence of child abuse. Children are both the indirect victims of sharing the more violent lives of those they live with and the direct recipients of all forms of physical abuse. Growing up under these conditions will naturally lead children to be suspicious of adults and to learn strategies of self-protection. If one does not readily see adults as desirable and useful but as potentially dangerous, it is not likely that one would come to associate learning and positive experiences with adults. What are the consequences of avoiding adults rather than seeing them as guides and models?

HAVING LESS HOPE

Today's poor are characterized by less hope than in former times. In the past, low-income families expected to get out of poverty. If they did not see this goal as realizable for themselves in their own lifetimes, they were generally confident their children would have better lives. Today's urban poor are characterized as No Hopers. It is no accident that Jesse Jackson used "Keep Hope Alive" as his motto. The despondency that is common in most urban ghettos and barrios reflects a general economic outlook that was not the American scenario in former times. Individuals with little hope for themselves or their children communicate a different life view than those who perceive themselves as only temporarily poor. No Hopers are frequently perceived by others as lacking initiative, ambition, and drive. Such explanations seek to attribute lack of hope to some internal state and ignore the real barriers the poor face in trying to make a better life for themselves and their children. The feeling that "nothing I do will make any real difference" is not a perception that supports initiative. Learning is dependent on the willingness to take action in one's own behalf.

LIVING UNDER BUREAUCRACIES

The poor develop a series of learned behaviors in the process of interacting with the bureaucracies and organizations that control their lives. The welfare department, the criminal justice system, the health care they receive are quite similar to their experiences with utilities, insurance companies, employers, banks, and various branches of government including housing, police, fire, sanitation, and postal service. It is a set of learnings which carry over to schools. People in poverty become skilled at dealing with systems which can both hurt them and provide them with rewards. These skills of "massaging" bureaucracies do not involve trusting bureaucracies and organizations. Quite the contrary. If one lives in poverty one lives in an environment where fire insurance is unavailable; where car, life, and health insurance are triple what others pay; where sanitation services are poorer; and where few in the community ever report success in dealing with any of the organized arms of the larger society. Facing these conditions, it is quite normal to develop a feeling of being "done to." This means that all the organizations by which society conducts its business represent a threat rather than a service to individuals and families. It is only by skillful manipulation that the poor learn to turn some of these bureaucracies to their advantage and not be exploited by them. With this background of life experiences, it would be "normal" for various groups in poverty to regard the school as another dangerous threat to themselves and their children.

It is truly amazing that so many poor people still begin by assuming their local schools are there to help them. It is only after some experience with schools that many begin to suspect their schools in the same way they regard the other social institutions. The common motive the poor ascribe to employees of the welfare system or a housing authority or the electric company or any other bureaucracy is that the people who work there are merely earning a living and do not perform their services because they are humanitarians seeking to help them. Indeed, poor people anticipate being mistreated by those who work in bureaucracies and believe their jobs require them to be unfair. This background of experience provides the normal expectations which many poor people come to hold for schools and teachers. Their suspicions of schools and teachers are natural. What is unnatural is the relatively large number of the poor who are still willing to trust schools and teachers in spite of their life experiences.

BEING DONE TO

Living in poverty is living in a state of being done to. It is a system of top-down directiveness. It is, quite simply, a life of living with authoritarianism. The sporadic efforts of the federal government and private foundations at community organization and neighborhood development are attempts to empower neighborhoods and families. Such programs seek to demonstrate to the poor that they can exert some measure of control over their lives. There have been occasional successes, particularly in the area of politics. Every urban area has some elected officials who are genuine representatives of their constituents in poverty. Generally, however, projects at the neighborhood level cannot control economic development or the creation of jobs which are at the root of poverty. The forces which control jobs, safety, health care, housing, and even schools are beyond neighborhood control. It becomes normal and natural, if one grows up and lives in urban poverty, to see life in power terms. To view the system in which one lives as an authoritarian one is a natural consequence of experiencing nothing but directiveness from external authorities. What are the effects on children and youth who grow and develop with parents and neighbors who perceive themselves as helpless to control or even influence anything of importance in their lives?

The long-term effect of participating in an authoritarian system is to derive satisfaction from participating in the chain of command. To order and mandate the lives of those who are smaller, weaker, and younger is a logical consequence. We sometimes forget that developing in an authoritarian system produces not only people who seek to continue the chain by giving orders to others but also people who come to enjoy taking orders. Authoritarians learn to derive satisfaction from the taking as well as the giving of orders. What this means for many youngsters who grow up in urban poverty is that it is natural (normal) to respond to others in terms of power. Who controls me? What benefits do I derive from compliance? Whom do I control? What benefits will they derive? And some of these benefits may well be things like the absence of pain or punishment.

What does this add up to? Thus far we have traced five themes which characterize the lives of many who live in urban property. This is not to say that all poor people experience these forces to the same degree or that their children will all respond to these forces in precisely the same way. We have sketched typical forces which engender normal responses in both the adults and children who live under these conditions. To what might these five forces add up? How might they interact and influence a youngster growing up? What might be normal responses to these life conditions?

Lacking trust in any adults might naturally lead one to be suspicious of their motives and their actions. Appearing to be shy or withdrawing from adults might be a perfectly normal response. Not expecting or seeking safety or the solution to one's problems from adults might be another reasonable response. The second force cited was the violence typical of urban life today. If those around us are potentially dangerous and life-threatening, then interacting with them is to be avoided whenever possible. The perception of No Hope is the third force which characterizes urban life for those in poverty and is frequently mistaken for a lack of initiative. If one sees no viable options it seems useless to expend effort. The fourth force cited relates to the impact of living under mindless bureaucracies. It becomes natural, normal—even desirable—to give the bureaucracy what it wants rather than to respond in sensible or honest ways. It is only be responding to the bureaucracy on its own terms that any benefits can be derived. This teaches children who grow up under such conditions to initiate and reveal as little as possible and provide only what is being asked of them as their normal response. The fifth force cited relates to the culture of authoritarianism. The giving and taking of orders becomes the normal way of life. One's power becomes one's self-definition.

Taken together, the outstanding attribute one can be expected to develop normally as a result of these and other forces is frustration. Feelings of deep frustration are characteristic of both adults and children who grow up and live with the experience of urban poverty. And the one result we can be certain to derive from this abiding frustration is some form of aggression. For some it is overt and clear. For many others it takes the form of passive resistance. And for many others it is turned inward on oneself, leading to suicide and to the multiple ways poor people demonstrate a reckless abandon for their own bodies.

Children in poverty frequently begin school with a wait-and-see attitude. They are uncertain and mistrusting of adults, surrounded by family and friends being "done to," living with violence, and having learned how to give and take orders are some of their skills. How the schools build on this set of realities for children in poverty will be discussed in the next section. Does the school seek to change what these children bring to school or does the school deepen and enhance these themes?

Before proceeding to an analysis of how teachers connect with the experiences many children in poverty bring, a few clarifications are in order. The analysis of poverty themes, although strongly negative, omitted the forces of prejudice and discrimination. Racism directed at Blacks and bias against Hispanics and other ethnic groups exacerbates all the effects of poverty. It would be like taking the forces which act on all the urban poor and raising their impact to the fifth power. Teachers and schools must recognize and deal with children who have been brutalized by the forces of poverty *and* the impact of growing up in a larger society that still practices racism, sexism, ethnocentrism, handicappism, ageism, homophobia, and religious discrimination.

Finally, there will be some who will reject the preceding analysis because it has neglected the strengths and values which characterize many children and youth who grow up in poverty. There can be no question that many aspects of children's lives—even in desperate poverty—demonstrate real strengths. Even a cursory look at their games, songs, and sports and at the cooperative groups they naturally create on their own reveals some of these strengths. Many of these positive life experiences can be, and are, later built upon by outstanding teachers. When one considers the total impact of growing up in poverty, however, there is little to recommend it. Any strengths quickly pale when compared to the debilitating and life-threatening forces which must be faced on a day-to-day basis. Those with life choices who see great strength in *other* people living in poverty are free to join them. They may be surprised to find poor people most willing to trade places with them.

FOUR RESEARCH REPORTS

What follows is a set of four papers that focus on various aspects of teaching in diverse contexts. The first study, authored by researchers from four midwestern universities, addresses the factors that veteran teachers in three urban contexts identify as critical for successful teaching. The second study is an evaluation of the impact that a three-day workshop has on student teachers' beliefs about learners labeled high- and low-ability, the use of stereotypes, and providing equal opportunities for learning challenging subject matter. The third research report focuses on the impact of field experiences in preparing teachers to work in diverse contexts. Finally, in Division I, the fourth paper raises fundamental issues about the micropolitics of schools and classrooms and advocates broadening the focus of teacher preparation to include organizational and social issues that impact teaching.

CHAPTER 1

Reflections of Urban Education: A Tale of Three Cities

SUZANNE PASCH
University of Wisconsin-Milwaukee

MARVIN PASCH
ROBBIE JOHNSON
Eastern Michigan University

STEVEN ILMER
JOANN SNYDER
ELLA STAPLETON
Wayne State University

AWILDA HAMILTON
PAUL MOORADIAN
Kent State University

SUZANNE PASCH is Associate Professor of Educational Psychology and Director of the Center for Teacher Education at the University of Wisconsin-Milwaukee. Her primary research interests are related to the application of principles of learning and development to urban teacher education and urban school reform.

MARVIN PASCH teaches Curriculum and Instruction in the Department of Teacher Education at Eastern Michigan University. His previous teaching experience includes ten years at Cleveland State University and thirteen years in secondary school social studies.

ROBBIE JOHNSON is Associate Dean of the College of Education at Eastern Michigan University. She is responsible for admissions to the college, all field placement experiences, competency testing and certification. Her previous professional experiences include teaching at the University of Cincinnati and teaching positions in Cleveland, Indianapolis, and Greater Cincinnati schools.

STEVEN ILMER is Associate Dean for Research, College of Education, Wayne State University. His primary grant development, research and teaching interests are in urban education, school restructuring, special education and educational technology.

JoANN SNYDER is Assistant Professor in Teacher Education and currently Director of Student Teaching, College of Education at Wayne State University. Formerly, she was a teacher and administrator with the Detroit Public Schools. Her areas of professional expertise are curriculum and teacher preparation.

ELLA STAPLETON is on the staff at Wayne State University. She was formerly a consultant to William Glasser's Schools Without Failure and served as a teacher, counselor, assistant principal, principal and area assistant superintendent in the Detroit Public Schools.

AWILDA HAMILTON is Assistant Professor, Teacher Development and Curriculum Studies and Director of the Teaching Leadership Consortium Project at Kent State University. Her focus is recruiting and retaining minorities from community colleges.

PAUL MOORADIAN is Assistant Professor of Educational and School Psychology at Kent State University and Director of Cuyahoga Community College/Kent State University Collaboration. He is involved in minority teacher recruitment through the community college.

ABSTRACT

The study describes the variables that 88 urban teachers and administrators in Milwaukee, Detroit, and Cleveland identify as critical to teaching success in urban contexts. Subjects were specifically asked to discuss the impact of physical environment, access to resources, characteristics of students, and other factors that might affect the success of teachers in urban settings. Responses related to descriptions of teaching success were analyzed by identifying themes and subthemes related to pedagogical, personological, and contextual issues. While a variety of factors were viewed as important, those related to knowledge of the urban community and individual teacher traits had particular salience. Implications for the preparation of urban teachers, for staff development efforts in urban schools, and for urban school organization are discussed.

INTRODUCTION

This study is part of a larger program of research designed to analyze the nature and needs of urban education and urban teacher education as viewed by teachers and administrators in the metropolitan areas of Cleveland, Detroit, and Milwaukee. The collaborative authors of the study are associated with three urban teacher education projects whose major thrust is to increase the number of minorities preparing to become teachers.[1]

The genesis of this collaborative effort was the result of a spirited discussion concerning the philosophy and direction of the teacher education curriculum at one of the urban projects. In a policy-making meeting, the two viewpoints listed below were energetically defended and emphasized polarized viewpoints regarding the constitution and form of urban education:

1. The curriculum to meet the needs of prospective urban teachers must be distinct and separate from existing curriculum to prepare teachers. If urban teacher education students are mainstreamed into a substantial number of existing courses or if an entirely new program is not developed, it demonstrates a lack of commitment to the special knowledge, skills, attitudes, and contextual demands placed on urban teachers.

2. The curriculum to prepare urban teachers is essentially identical to the curriculum followed by students in quality teacher education programs at multiple sites with the exception that required field experiences occur in urban schools. There are no significant differences in the knowledge base needed by successful urban teachers as compared to teachers in other settings, and all teachers operate within differing contexts. Thus, few, if any, specialized classes for urban teacher education students are necessary.

After many rounds of argument and counterargument, a recommendation was made to postpone a final decision on the form of the professional program until more information was gathered on the issues that framed the debate. When representatives of the three programs met, they found similar discussions had occurred at each site. Thus, the rationale for this study was established.

A great deal of attention has been focused in recent years on the problems and challenges of the urban schools and many opinions regarding the solution to those problems have been offered, yet little attention has been directed toward garnering the views of the teachers and school administrators most immediately and integrally involved with teaching in urban schools. For example, in their two widely read reports, *An Imperiled Generation: Saving Urban Schools* and *Working in Urban Schools*, Corcoran, Walker, and White (1988) focused attention on the physical, organizational, and relational conditions that affect performance of urban educators. However, in neither case did the investigators focus attention on the educators themselves, nor did they solicit recommendations for preparing the next generation of urban teachers. The need for this information and the likelihood of its contributing to the design of effective teacher education efforts across the continuum of practice underlies the work reported here. Specifically, the framework for this study is derived from a belief that urban teachers and administrators have much to tell teacher educators about the needed characteristics and components of a worthy and effective initial and continuing certification teacher education program.

RESEARCH QUESTIONS AND OBJECTIVES

The study addresses five questions concerning teachers and teaching in urban schools:

1. What are the essential knowledge base, critical skills, and attitudes needed by urban teachers if they are to be successful?
2. How does the physical environment in which a teacher works impact an urban teacher's success?
3. How does the urban teacher's access to and use of resources impact a teacher's success?
4. How do the characteristics of urban students impact an urban teacher's success?
5. What differences and similarities are there between the nature and needs of urban education as compared to education in nonurban settings?

Objectives derived from those questions were to:

1. Generate responses from a sample of urban teachers and administrators using a personal, structured interview with each respondent that stimulated them to answer the research questions.
2. Develop themes and subthemes into which the responses could be classified in order to provide order and meaning to the data.
3. Produce generalizations of importance to both understanding the nature and needs of urban education and providing implications for the preparation of urban teachers.

4. Provide evidence that supports one of the two positions in the urban teacher education debate that spawned the study.

METHOD

INSTRUMENT

The three-city research team collaboratively developed a semistructured interview questionnaire that included demographic information on race/ethnicity, sex, number of years in urban teaching, current position, and educational experience along with seven questions asking respondents to identify factors which would be necessary for successful urban teaching. The seven items listed in Table 1–1 reflected various aspects of urban teaching including knowledge base, critical teacher skills and attitudes, student characteristics, physical environment, access to resources, and other factors which affect teaching success.

RESPONDENTS

A total of 88 respondents were selected by project participants in each of the three cities or by their public school partners. The sample of 30 respondents each in Detroit and Milwaukee and 28 in Cleveland consisted of experienced urban teachers and/or school administrators who were part of the

TABLE 1–1
Questionnaire Items for Description of Urban Teaching Analysis

Instructions: We are interested in knowing what factors you think are necessary to become a successful urban teacher. In responding to the following items, please provide as much detail and specificity as possible.

1. Describe the critical knowledge base urban teachers need if they are to be successful.
2. Describe the critical skills urban teachers need if they are to be successful.
3. Describe the critical attitudes urban teachers need if they are to be successful.
4. Describe how the physical environment in which you teach/work impacts your urban school and classroom(s).
5. Describe how your access to, and the nature of, available resources affect your teaching success.
6. Describe how the characteristics of your students affect your teaching success.
7. Are there other specific factors that affect your teaching success in an urban setting?

ongoing collaborative partnership relationships between public schools and universities or community colleges at each site. Each participant had more than three years of urban teaching experience. A description of the demographic characteristics of the sample is included in Table 1–2.

TABLE 1–2

Demographic Characteristics of the Interview Sample

	CLEVELAND (N = 28)	DETROIT (N = 30)	MILWAUKEE (N = 30)	TOTAL (N = 88)
Gender				
Male	9	5	10	24
Female	19	25	20	64
Race				
African American	17	12	12	41
American Indian	0	0	1	1
Caucasian	11	18	15	44
Hispanic	0	0	2	2
Years Experience				
1–10	4	2	5	11
11–20	14	13	10	37
21–30	10	15	15	40
Position				
Teacher	19	23	25	67
Administrator	9	7	5	21

As Table 1–2 indicates, 73 percent of the 88 respondents were women and 27 percent men, figures consistent with the approximately 70 percent female and 30 percent male composition of the national teaching force (Dorman, 1990). This sample, however, does not reflect national averages with respect to the percentage of minorities represented in teaching. While the current teaching force, including administrators, is about 6 percent minority and 5 percent African American, the respondents comprising this sample are split equally between minority and majority populations, with 47 percent being African American. The sample is, therefore, more representative of the communities they serve than of the teaching corps to which they belong. The average years of experience was sixteen years with a range of four years to thirty-three years. The age range was from thirty years to fifty years.

TABLE 1-3
Themes and Subthemes Used to Analyze Descriptions of Urban Teaching

THEME CATEGORY	SUBTHEMES OR DESCRIPTIONS	REPRESENTATIVE QUOTATIONS
Subject Matter	Any reference to specific content/subject matter for teaching	"No matter where or who you teach, you have to know your subject . . ." (H.S.)
Pedagogy	High expectations Classroom management/Discipline Focus on the individual child Communication skills Planning/Implementing instruction	"With many classes, there is so much absence that on a day-to-day basis you're not teaching the same kids, so each lesson has to be individual . . . You need to know how to present your material in smaller chunks." (H.S.)
Learner Needs and Characteristics	All children can learn Knowing the child Individual characteristics Urban learners Enjoying, respecting, caring for and about children	"Most of my students don't anticipate becoming adults. Especially my male students . . . So I think they take chances they shouldn't take." (Middle School) "They're real willing to speak their minds . . ." (Elem.)
Society/Home/Community/Culture	Home, family environment Knowing the urban community Hindering conditions Facilitative conditions Teacher's knowledge, comfort with diversity, cultural differences	"Last year we had so much gunfire in our neighborhood that before we could take kids out for Phy. Ed., we had to get school board security to walk around . . ." (Elem.) ". . . it's painful to see the death of innocence in children who are still so very young . . . you find that many of them don't dream." (Middle School)

continued

Category	Quote
Teacher Traits Empathy Nonjudgmental/Open-minded Positive attitude Patience/Long view/Durability Loving/Humane/Fair Flexible Self-confident	"In a way, it's a lot like selling. You make a lot of contacts before you make a sale. You can't get discouraged about the contacts that don't pan out." (H.S.) ". . . it's very important that a teacher be well-adjusted . . . and when they walk into that door and see the children that this day belongs to them." (Elem.)
Classroom/School Conditions Physical Organizational Relational	"Certain labs are not run because we don't have the equipment . . ."(H.S. Science) ". . . you can make your own classroom such an inviting and happy and joyful place that it blocks all the blight outside." (Elem. Special Ed.)
Funding/Resources/Materials Lack of resources (Laments, complaints, difficulties) Locating and using resources (People, community, material)	"There are a lot of good resources in the community . . . but our students can't afford it . . . we have to go out and find donations to help cover that for our students." (Reading Specialist)
Administration Any reference to need for provision of support, resources by building or district-level administrators	"A lot of times . . . administration is not sensitive to the problems you have in your classroom . . . . Administrators are talking at one level and not understanding what we're dealing with." (Elem.)
Collegiality Any reference to team-building, collaboration, partnerships	". . . urban teachers need more joint planning time . . . to truly work as a team and not segregate themselves by racial groupings . . . gender, or subject area . . . together we can know so much more about the kids." (Elem.)

PROCEDURE AND ANALYSIS

Interviews were conducted individually and lasted approximately 30 minutes. All respondents were interviewed on-site in their schools by the authors or by trained interviewers working with them. Interviewers were themselves all experienced urban educators. Subjects were given a copy of the questions to refer to during the interview. Each interview was audiotape recorded. The audiotapes were then transcribed verbatim at the respective universities for analysis. Subject identity was masked for purposes of analysis.

After the interviews were completed and transcribed, the research team met again to review the interview content and to practice the qualitative method to be applied to transcript analysis. A slightly modified version of Spradley's (1979) domain analysis was used to analyze the ethnographic data. Researchers first read each interview in its entirety for familiarity. Then each transcript was re-read and critical content was highlighted. Only specific, major ideas or phrases which captured the essence of each response were highlighted. There was no attempt, however, to limit artificially the number of critical responses made to each item; as many major ideas as emerged in each question were included. Researchers reviewed several of the transcripts from the other sites for reliability. After all transcripts were highlighted, the segments were organized onto a summary sheet by interview question for each respondent in the sample. This enabled a complete review of all major responses by question.

Following the practice session, the research team returned to the individual sites and applied the procedure generated at the meeting. The next step involved the further extraction and assignment of major themes from the content of each response by question. Members of the Detroit/Ypsilanti team had agreed to assume responsibility for initial identification of themes. Each site then used those themes as guidelines and added others, as needed, to reflect the responses that had been generated at that site. In this manner, each response per question per respondent was categorized according to the themes previously suggested or developed at that site. As appropriate, sub-themes were also identified within the major theme domains.

At this point, the research teams met again to review the interview items and to compare the thematic categories; to coordinate, refine, and validate the final thematic coding scheme; and to make any remaining decisions regarding issues of analysis. At this session, a final set of nine major themes was identified along with corresponding subthemes. These themes and examples of subthemes and representative quotes appear in Table 1–3.

It was also decided that the first three items of the interview related to knowledge base, skills, and attitudes, as shown in Table 1–1, should be collapsed since respondents had not differentiated between the three items for the first

TABLE 1-4

Frequency of Responses by Themes for Descriptive Questionnaire Items Across Sites

Items	I Subject Matter	II Teaching Skills/ Pedagogy	III Learner Needs	IV Home, Community, Culture, Society	V Personal Traits	VI Classroom, School Conditions	VII Funding, Materials, Resources	VIII Admin- istration	IX Collegiality	Total
Knowledge Base	50	218	144	117	200	6	5	0	5	745
Physical Environment	0	14	10	47	2	111	25	2	0	211
Resources	0	8	1	4	0	5	149	6	1	174
Student Characteristics	1	34	71	32	26	10	7	3	0	184
Other Factors	1	17	21	32	23	19	26	33	10	182
TOTAL	52	291	247	232	251	151	212	44	16	1496

TABLE 1-5

Proportion of Responses by Themes for Descriptive Questionnaire Items Across Sites

Items	I Subject Matter	II Teaching Skills/ Pedagogy	III Learner Needs	IV Home, Community, Culture, Society	V Personal Traits	VI Classroom, School Conditions	VII Funding, Materials, Resources	VIII Admin- istration	IX Collegiality	Total
Knowledge Base	0.07	0.29	0.19	0.16	0.27	0.01	0.01		0.01	1
Physical Environment		0.07	0.05	0.22	0.01	0.53	0.12	0.01		1
Resources		0.05	0.01	0.02		0.03	0.86	0.03	0.01	1
Student Characteristics	0.01	0.18	0.39	0.17	0.14	0.05	0.04	0.02		1
Other Factors	0.01	0.09	0.12	0.18	0.13	0.10	0.14	0.18	0.05	1
TOTAL	0.03	0.19	0.17	0.16	0.17	0.10	0.14	0.03	0.01	1

TABLE 1-6

Frequencies and Proportions of Descriptive Responses by Theme and Subthemes across Items

THEMES AND SUBTHEMES	MILWAUKEE		DETROIT		CLEVELAND		COMBINED	
	Frequency	Proportion	Frequency	Proportion	Frequency	Proportion	Frequency	Proportion
I. Subject Matter	13	0.02	17	0.04	22	0.05	52	0.03
II. Pedagogy	134	0.22	63	0.15	94	0.20	291	0.19
1. High Expectations	7	0.05	10	0.16	9	0.10	26	0.09
2. Classroom Management/ Discipline (Organization)	35	0.26	15	0.24	23	0.24	73	0.25
3. Focus on Individual/ Individualizing Instruction	19	0.14	6	0.10	9	0.10	34	0.12
4. Communication Skills (Listening, Clarity)	26	0.19	11	0.17	19	0.20	56	0.19
5. Planning and Implementing Instruction								
5a. Hands On/ Active Learning	7	0.05	7	0.11	13	0.14	27	0.09
5b. Multiple Methods and Strategies	20	0.15	8	0.13	15	0.16	43	0.15
5c. Responding Appropriately during Instruction	7	0.05	4	0.06	3	0.03	14	0.05
5d. Reflection/Self-Evaluation	13	0.10	2	0.03	3	0.03	18	0.06
III. Learner Needs and Characteristics	86	0.14	88	0.21	73	0.15	247	0.17

Category	n	%	n	%	n	%	n	%
1. All Children Can Learn	13	0.15	13	0.15	14	0.19	40	0.16
2. Knowing the Child	10	0.12	22	0.25			32	0.13
2a. Individual Characteristics	23	0.27	8	0.09	29	0.40	60	0.24
2b. Urban Child	29	0.34	19	0.22	16	0.22	64	0.26
3. Enjoying, Caring, Respecting Children	11	0.13	26	0.30	14	0.19	51	0.21
IV. Society/Home/Community/Culture	100	0.16	59	0.14	73	0.15	232	0.16
1. Home Environment (Home/Parent Characteristics)	35	0.35	17	0.29	24	0.33	76	0.33
2. Need to Know Urban Community	5	0.05	16	0.27			21	0.09
2a. Conditions Hinder Development	26	0.26	15	0.25	29	0.40	70	0.30
2b. Conditions Facilitate Development	2	0.02	4	0.07	3	0.05	9	0.04
3. Teacher Knowledge/ Comfort with Diversity	32	0.32	8	0.14	17	0.23	57	0.25
V. Teacher Traits	96	0.16	83	0.20	72	0.15	251	0.17
1. Empathy	5	0.05	11	0.13	4	0.06	20	0.08
2. Non-Judgmental/ Open-Minded	15	0.16	9	0.11	12	0.17	36	0.14
3. Positive Attitude	15	0.16	18	0.22	20	0.28	53	0.21
4. Commitment/Dedication	16	0.17	8	0.10			24	0.10

continued

5. Patience/Long View/ Durability	13	0.14	8	0.10	8	0.11	29	0.12
6. Loving/Humane/Fair	17	0.18	8	0.10	14	0.19	39	0.16
7. Flexible	9	0.09	10	0.12	11	0.15	30	0.12
8. Self-Confident	6	0.06	11	0.13	3	0.04	20	0.08
VI. Classroom/School Conditions	60	0.10	34	0.08	57	0.12	151	0.10
1. Physical	31	0.52	14	0.41	27	0.47	72	0.48
2. Organizational	18	0.30	8	0.24	12	0.21	38	0.25
3. Relational	11	0.18	12	0.35	18	0.32	41	0.27
VII. Funding/Resources/ Materials	91	0.15	57	0.14	64	0.14	212	0.14
1. Lack of Resources (Laments, Difficulties)	32	0.35	7	0.12	34	0.53	73	0.34
2. Using Resources (People, Community, Material)	59	0.65	50	0.88	30	0.47	139	0.66
VIII. Administration	22	0.04	9	0.02	13	0.03	44	0.03
IX. Collegiality	8	0.01	5	0.01	3	0.01	16	0.01
Totals	610	1	415	1	471	1	1496	1

stage of analysis. This created a five-question format for the descriptions of successful urban teaching that consisted of knowledge base; physical environment; resources; student characteristics; and for other factors added by respondents.

After the procedures described above were applied to individual interview protocols, each research team tallied the themes and subthemes and displayed the results by question across respondents. The data were then compiled separately for each site and in a composite for the three urban sites together. Data on the distribution of responses by theme and questionnaire items were recorded both in terms of raw response frequencies and, for equating purposes, by row-wise proportions.

RESULTS AND DISCUSSION

Tallied response frequencies and response proportions are presented for the total group of respondents across research sites, since examination of the data for individual sites indicated that the results were strikingly similar. Response frequencies by theme for the five questionnaire items used in this analysis are shown in Table 1–4. Proportions for those responses are presented in Table 1–5. While these data provide an interesting view of how teachers respond when asked directly about various aspects of urban teaching, it is the distribution of responses among themes and subthemes across items that permits a more detailed analysis of urban teaching as seen through the eyes of experienced practitioners. The frequencies and proportions of descriptive responses by theme and subthemes across items and respondents are presented in Table 1–6. In this table, the patterns of response are shown for each site individually and for the group as a whole.

Thematic Analysis.   The rank order of the nine major themes that emerged from the data analyses across the three interview sites, in terms of their relative frequency and percentage of the total responses, was as follows: Pedagogy/Teaching Skills ($f = 291$, 19.5 percent); Personal (Teacher) Traits ($f = 251$, 16.8 percent); Learner Needs and Characteristics ($f = 247$, 16.5 percent); Society/Home/Community/Culture ($f = 232$, 15.5 percent); Funding/Materials/Resources ($f = 212$, 14.2 percent); Classroom/School Conditions ($f = 151$, 10.1 percent); Subject Matter ($f = 52$, 3.5 percent); Administration ($f = 44$, 2.9 percent); and Collegiality ($f = 16$, 1.1 percent).

The highest proportion of responses for the combined group was for the Pedagogy/Teaching Skills theme, with Personal Traits, Learner Needs and Characteristics, and Home/Community/Culture/Society differing little from each other and following closely behind the first theme in terms of response percentage. Indeed, the relative importance of the themes as descriptions of teachers' success indicates that the combination of the themes ranked one through four accounts for 68.3 percent of the total responses. The themes ranked five and six, combined, represent an additional 24.3 percent of the total responses. Finally, the themes ranked seven, eight, and nine combined account for only an additional 7.5 percent of the total responses.

When the responses for the nine themes are reorganized to reflect the Pedagogical, Contextual, and Personological emphases generated by the teachers, the rank order derived from Table 1–5 reveals a pattern that seems to reflect accurately the essence of the respondents' statements:

1. **Contextual**
   Home/Community/Culture/Society, Classroom/School Conditions, Funding/Resources/Materials, and Administration ($f = 639$, 42.7 percent)

2. **Personological**
   Learner Needs and Characteristics, Teacher Traits, Collegiality ($f = 514$, 34.4 percent)

3. **Pedagogical**
   Subject Matter and Teaching Skills/Pedagogy ($f = 343$, 22.9 percent)

When aggregated into these three domains, the data suggest that urban teachers view the context inside and outside the workplace as the single most critical factor influencing success in urban teaching. While this finding may surprise no one, the data do provide empirical support for this aspect of common wisdom and, in this sample at least, demonstrate the strength of this conviction. Further, and equally important, the data also argue that urban teachers describe success in personal terms and view it as related to being personally durable and capable.

Perhaps as interesting as the themes the respondents emphasized are those they did not. While the respondents clearly indicated that pedagogy/teaching skills represents a very important dimension of their success (that is, as one teacher put it, ". . . For urban children, I think the most practical and most modern innovations in education are necessary"), the theme of subject matter knowledge was ranked low in terms of its contribution to influencing success in urban teaching. This may have been due to respondents' frequently stated assumption that subject matter knowledge is important for everyone or to the mixed distribution of teachers and administrators from all levels of teaching (although no separate pattern emerged in the Milwaukee data when this theme was examined for differences between elementary and secondary). But it may also reflect the straightforward belief that content is, indeed, not seen to be as important as teaching skills and knowledge about the students being taught and the contexts in which that teaching occurs. This is an interesting question, particularly in light of recent work describing the essential nature of the interaction between teaching and subject. These data do not suggest that subject matter is unimportant; rather, they support the need for teaching to be viewed in the context of community, personal abilities and feelings, and the ability to establish an environment conducive to learning.

Finally, these respondents did not view the role that other people play in influencing success to be as significant as the role of the environment and the individual teacher's effect on environment. Thus, Administration and Collegiality also were low in terms of response percentages. From some of the comments made by several respondents (that is, "there is just not enough time to plan with other teachers") this may be a function of the sheer magnitude of the task of teaching in urban schools. They may have neither the time nor energy left to work with others or they may not have had the opportunity to develop confidence that such work will be beneficial. This is another interesting question to further research, since some of the respondents' comments indicate there is considerably more to learn about their views regarding both their administrators and their colleagues.

Examination of Subthemes.   The subthemes presented in Table 1–6 provide additional insights into the interpretation of the themes and domains. First, it should be noted that not only for the nine themes but also for subthemes, the data may be characterized more by their similarities across sites than their differences. This is a powerful result, demonstrating the high degree of agreement that exists among these urban educators in the identification of factors significant to urban teaching. While this is self-report data and subject to limitations, it is, nonetheless, the case that in this study educators characterized by their years of experience, and selected by university and public school colleagues for their willingness and ability to reflect on general attributes of successful urban teaching, view it in remarkably similar ways across sites.

Some additional insights related to the themes are revealed through subtheme analysis. Major points include the following:

1. Across sites in almost identical proportions, organization and management skills, communication skills, emphasis on instructional planning, the ability to use flexibly a variety of instructional strategies, and a focus on the needs of individual learners contributed to the role that Pedagogy plays in influencing success in urban teaching.
2. Knowing the child one is teaching, especially in terms of understanding that child's background, contributes significantly to the theme of Learner Needs, although caring for children and believing that all children can

learn—"Every student is a unique individual and should be given an opportunity to be taught and to learn"—are also important variables.

3. The abilities to understand the urban community, recognize its strengths, and be knowledgeable about and comfortable working with multiculturally diverse learners are viewed as contributing critically to the role that the Home/Community/Culture/Society context plays in influencing success. Of equal note, however, is the fact that at all three sites, educators characterized conditions in the urban community as hindering success more often than facilitating it.

4. When Personal Traits of teachers are examined in terms of subthemes, it is a positive attitude that is viewed by these respondents as vital; loving, humane, fair treatment of children and the ability to interact with them in nonjudgmental ways are also seen as essential personal traits.

5. Aspects of the physical environment of the school and its classroom contribute most to the theme of Classroom/School Conditions, with respondents making statements that range from "It's extremely important that urban schools are attractive and have many things that provide a sense of ownership and belonging for children" to "Teachers in an urban setting feel that they're not in control of their environment, and by the environment I mean the classroom."

6. Although at all sites the respondents complained about a lack of resources or inequities in their distribution, the subthemes of the Funding/Resources/Materials theme indicate that successful urban teachers are nevertheless quick to pursue strategies necessary to procure resources through their own initiatives, often accepting this as part of the challenge of urban teaching.

7. Despite difficulties, it is also apparent that these urban educators who have elected to remain in urban schools for more than three years, and most for considerably longer, believe that urban teaching is a rich and rewarding undertaking.

SUMMARY AND IMPLICATIONS OF THE STUDY

This study was undertaken in part to help identify and define success among urban teachers by asking a group of experienced urban educators currently working in urban schools in Cleveland, Detroit, and Milwaukee to share their insights. Data were collected and analyzed from interviews on characteristics, factors, and conditions of urban teaching which help to explain teachers' descriptions of their success. This study seeks to extend current knowledge in the professional literature with respect to the conditions of urban teaching and, concomitantly, the dynamics of the urban school as a workplace. Specific findings from this study will be discussed in terms of their implications for urban schools and their implications for preservice teacher education and professional development across the career.

IMPLICATIONS FOR URBAN SCHOOLS

For urban schools, the findings reported in this study suggest strongly that schools and school leaders take every opportunity to recognize the impact and positive influence of personological variables upon teachers' success. Among groups of teachers, promoting participatory decision-making and collaborative, problem-solving strategies in addressing school issues may serve to reinforce the importance of personological traits. Staff development and in-service programs should similarly be designed to address the challenges of teaching in urban schools. More efforts also need to be undertaken to recognize the dedication and commitment that many experienced teachers as individuals bring to their work.

At the same time, funding/resource inequities and poor teaching/classroom conditions in urban schools cannot be ignored and must be effectively addressed given the impact these factors have on students and teachers. In light of the premium that respondents placed on the importance of a positive attitude, it is only reasonable to wonder how much burden can continue to be assumed, even by positive, committed people, before their level of effectiveness is affected. Additional thought and resources must be channeled to urban schools to encourage the development and retention of a high-quality teaching corps.

IMPLICATIONS FOR TEACHER EDUCATION ACROSS THE CAREER

The findings from this study hold important implications for the preparation of beginning teachers in urban schools and for the development and retention of qualified teachers for urban schools across the career. The pedagogical, contextual, and personological thematic domains that emerged in this study provide directions for these efforts.

First, preservice teachers need to acquire the foundational skills, particularly with regard to strategic learning and pedagogical/instructional methods, upon which they will be able to build with experience the kind of teaching repertoires necessary to address students' different learning needs.

Second, preservice teachers need to know the urban community from the perspectives of both experience and reflection. With respect to one of the questions raised at the outset, the data in this study do *not* provide any support for the notion that beginning urban teachers would benefit more from a teacher education program which provides separate professional preparation "tracks" for urban as opposed to nonurban teachers. The data *do* indicate that a critical differential training factor for urban teachers is the provision of early, ample, and carefully supervised field work experiences in *urban* school settings and in urban communities. However, the data also strongly support the notion that urban field experiences alone are not sufficient.

Rather, these respondents make a strong case for teacher education programs that provide excellent academic and clinical preparation, pay particular attention to helping beginning teachers understand and support the learning of students who may differ from themselves, and allow time and opportunity for teacher candidates to learn to reflect on the experiences they have in urban schools. This seems to argue for both preservice programs that provide a number of field-based experiences at different developmental points and for continual professional development efforts in helping practicing teachers understand the context of urban teaching. It also seems to argue against alternative certification programs, unless they selectively identify as their populations individuals who have participated in the lives of the urban community and schools over a considerable time period and who have been or will be given the chance to develop their reflective skills within the context of the teacher education or professional development program.

Revisiting the personal traits emphasized in this study, it is also apparent that implications exist for the selection of teachers or teacher candidates with the requisite personal characteristics or the ability to develop those characteristics within the context of a program that monitors their development. For these respondents, those characteristics included a humane, caring, positive, nonjudgmental attitude toward students coupled with personal strength and commitment to the task.

Finally, the implications of the findings reported in this study raise further questions concerning teachers' perceptions of the quality of urban schools. Since this study involved experienced urban educators, to what extent would replications of this study with other populations produce similar findings concerning the influence of selected pedagogical, contextual, and personological variables upon teachers' descriptions of success? Do former, unsuccessful urban teachers lack key personological traits necessary to survive and develop professionally in the context of urban schools? If so, to what extent might such traits be identifiable among preservice and beginning teachers? Do teachers who leave urban schools require additional assistance in understanding and working within the urban community? If so, how might we provide preservice and staff development efforts that produce a more thorough grounding in working successfully within the urban community? Answers to these and related questions may ultimately help to improve the quality of urban schools by focusing on critical determinants of success among urban teachers.

The findings of this study seem to provide both valuable insights for the creation of effective teacher education programs and a foundation on which further research can build. In the view of this sample of respondents, successful urban teachers understand that teaching is a complex undertaking that requires time. They know that conditions may be difficult, but they accept and enjoy the challenges of urban teaching, even as they wait for increased support for their efforts. They are individuals who care about themselves and their students. Perhaps above all, they are people who believe strongly in their ability to provide an effective learning environment that will make a difference in students' lives, no matter what the conditions of those lives may be, and who have the skills to make that belief a reality.

REFERENCES

Corcoran, T. B., Walker, L. J., and White, J. L. (1988). An imperiled generation: Saving urban schools. Princeton, NJ: The Carnegie Foundation for the Advancement of Teaching.

Corcoran, T. B., Walker, L. J., and White, J. L. (1988). *Working in urban schools*, Washington, D.C., Institute for Educational Leadership.

Dorman, A. (1990). Recruiting and retaining minority teachers. *Policy Briefs*, 8, North Central Regional Educational Laboratory.

Spradley, J. P. (1979). *The ethnographic interview*. New York: Holt, Rinehart & Winston.

AUTHORS' NOTE

The research reported here is the result of an ongoing collaborative effort of a consortium of urban teacher educators from metropolitan Cleveland, Detroit, and Milwaukee. Each of the authors listed is involved in implementating innovative teacher education programs for diverse learners in urban settings; the authors represent both genders and diverse multicultural groups. Each author has made significant contributions to the design, conduct, and interpretation of this study. Thanks are extended to graduate students Terri Johnson of Eastern Michigan University, Sandy Pettapiece of Wayne State University, and Fermin Burgos and Joan Whipp of the University of Wisconsin-Milwaukee for their excellent work in conducting interviews and/or coding participant responses. Finally, the authors wish to acknowledge the role of Dr. Michael Brown of Wayne State University for his participation in the initial work of the consortium and for the contributions to the design of the study he made during that time.

ENDNOTE

1. Initial interactions among members of the consortium were the result of shared interests in developing teacher education programs that increase the number of minority teachers through partnership efforts between universities, community colleges, and public school districts. In Cleveland, the partnership between Cuyahoga Community College and Kent State University is implemented through a program called *Preparing Minority Teachers for the 21st Century*. In Detroit, a collaborative relationship between Wayne County Community College, Eastern Michigan University, and Wayne State University is operationalized through the *Urban Teacher Program*. In Milwaukee, the connection between the Collaborative Urban Teacher Education Program at the Milwaukee Area Technical College and the School of Education's Center for Teacher Education at the University of Wisconsin-Milwaukee is part of a larger reform effort that includes all preservice programs and urban professional development schools. The consortium was founded when the authors met to describe these efforts at the Annual Meeting of the Association of Teacher Educators in New Orleans, 1991.

CHAPTER 2

Preparing Teachers for Diversity: A Study of Student Teachers in a Multicultural Program

G. WILLIAMSON MCDIARMID
JEREMY PRICE
Michigan State University

G. WILLIAMSON MCDIARMID is Associate Director of the National Center for Research on Teacher Learning and Associate Professor of Teacher Education at Michigan State University. In addition to research on learning to teach diverse learners, he is also investigating the knowledge and understandings prospective teachers develop in their arts and science courses.

JEREMY PRICE is a Research Associate at the National Center for Research on Teacher Learning at Michigan State University. His primary research interest involves the effects of social policy on the school experience of poor students and those of color.

The authors gratefully acknowledge the advice, support, and contributions of the planning committee of the ABCD project; Ellen Carter-Cooper and Deborah Clemmons, the project directors; Catherine Smith, Michigan DOE; and NCRTL research assistants Deborah Ongtooguk and Samgeun Kwon.

This research was supported in part by the National Center for Research on Teacher Learning (NCRTL), Michigan State University. The NCRTL is funded primarily by the Office of Education Research & Improvement, United States Department of Education (OERI/ED) with additional funding from the College of Education, Michigan State University (COE/ MSU). The opinions expressed in this paper are those of the author and do not necessarily reflect the position, policy, or endorsement of the OERI/ED or the COE/MSU.

ABSTRACT

Using data from pre- and postprogram questionnaires and interviews, the authors describe the views that a group of seventeen student teachers, drawn from five Michigan universities, hold of culturally diverse learners both before and after a three-day workshop intended to influence their views. The authors found that the multicultural presentations had little effect on students' beliefs about the capabilities of learners labeled "high" and "low" ability, about the use of stereotypes in making teaching decisions, or about providing genuinely equal opportunities to learn challenging and empowering subject matter. The authors suggest that teacher educators may need to rethink both the content and pedagogy of opportunities to learn about teaching socially and culturally diverse learners.

The stated purpose of the Accepting Behaviors for Cultural Diversity for Teachers (ABCD) project is:

> to provide teachers from the dominant white culture with the knowledge and skills to work with students of diverse cultural backgrounds and to view cultural diversity as a positive influence on learning. Secondly, the project will attempt to improve perception of expectations for students from culturally diverse backgrounds. (Office of Professional Development, 1988, p. 1)

To this end the project director convened a planning committee of teachers and district specialists, university teacher education faculty, Michigan Department of Education specialists, and representatives of organizations with a particular interest in multicultural education. The three-day workshop that this committee designed, which is described in detail elsewhere (Carter-Cooper, 1990), consisted of a series of presentations by various experts in areas such as racial prejudice, student self-esteem, classroom management, cooperative learning, learning styles, multicultural curricular materials, and specific cultural groups such as Asian Americans, Hispanic Americans, African Americans, and American Indians (the appendix lists the topics that constituted the training). The primary assumption underlying the training was that the student teachers lack certain information that is critical to working with culturally diverse students. In this regard, the content and format of the training is similar to multicultural courses that typify university-based teacher education programs and those offered by school districts (McDiarmid, in press-a).

EVALUATION DESIGN

The purpose of the evaluation was to find out what student teachers who participated in the ABCD training believe about learners, learning, teaching, subject matter, and the context in learning and teaching and how these fundamental beliefs were influenced by the program. Schwab (1960/78) and Kerr (1981), among others, argue that all teachers' actions are posited on what they know and believe about learners and learning, pedagogy and subject matter, and the social and political context. As systematic observation of program participants was beyond the project's limited resources, we designed an evaluation to reveal student-teachers' beliefs and the effects of a workshop designed to influence their knowledge and beliefs about diverse learners.

SAMPLE

The colleges and universities that agreed to recruit students for the program were responsible for selecting students, both for the experimental group and for the control group. Consequently, we cannot assume that these students were representative of those in the various preservice teacher education programs that participated in the project nor, of course, of teacher education students in general.

Some twenty-two students attended the first workshop. Of these, seventeen completed and returned the self-administered questionnaire. Thirteen of these seventeen completed the questionnaire after the program. The small number of students in the original sample and the small number who completed the questionnaire make interpretation problematic. Demographic characteristics of the sample are summarized in the appendix.

In reporting the results below, we have used data from a comparable group of preservice teacher education students collected as part of the Teacher Education and Learning to Teach (TELT) study conducted by researchers at the National Center for Research on Teacher Education between 1987 and 1991 (NCRTE, 1988). Students in this sample were enrolled in standard preservice teacher education programs and completed the self-administered questionnaire items during student teaching, near the end of their teacher education programs.

INSTRUMENTS

We used two instruments to collect data from participants in the ABCD program. We first used a questionnaire to collect students' views of teaching and learning. We took most of the items on the questionnaire from those used in the TELT study (Kennedy, McDiarmid, Ball, and Schmidt, 1992). Using items from the TELT questionnaire allowed us to compare students in the ABCD sample to the national sample of teacher education students in the TELT study.

In addition, the planning subcommittee on evaluation for the ABCD project developed seven additional items to tap student-teachers' beliefs about specific issues in multicultural teaching. We also conducted brief telephone interviews with the participating student teachers. During these interviews, we asked student teachers to respond to two teaching scenarios. These scenarios were taken from the interview instrument used in the TELT study, thus allowing us to compare students in the ABCD program with a national sample of students.

LIMITATIONS

The subcommittee's decision to pose questions about views of learners, learning, teaching, subject matter, and context without reference to ethnic differences was based on our knowledge of the social response bias that renders invalid most measures of attitudes toward racially and ethnically different others. When we did pose questions about poor students or those of color, we provided a context so that the respondent could agree or disagree with a "positive" or "neutral" stereotype (such as Native Americans are "shy"). We also provided, in our second interview scenario, a description of a classroom in which three of the students' ethnicity is identified. We wanted to see what role, if any, information on the students' ethnicity played in prospective teachers' thinking about teaching and learning. Although we tried to create measures that would allow us to reduce the social response bias, we recognize that the mere mention of ethnicity is likely to generate bias.

The decision to ask questions to reveal student-teachers' root beliefs produces instruments and an evaluation which are not highly sensitive to the effects of this specific program. The planning subcommittee charged with designing the evaluation believed, however, that the usefulness of an evaluation would lie in the information it could provide on how students would be likely to act in the classroom rather than in whether or not they master the information available through the program. Although arguments could be made for both types of evaluations, the subcommittee was persuaded that learning more about the beliefs that underlie student-teachers' activities would better serve the project than a more narrowly conceived assessment of participants' recall of the information presented. At the same time, the program could have influenced prospective teachers in positive and promising ways that our instruments failed to register.

RESULTS

STEREOTYPING

In the first interview scenario, we asked prospective teachers what they thought of an explanation proffered by colleagues for the physical marginalization of Native American students in their classroom:

> Imagine that you have have been hired midway through the school year to take over for a teacher who is going on maternity leave. During the first day, you notice a group of Native Americans sitting together at the back of the class, while white and Asian-American students are sitting in front. The Native American students don't volunteer to answer questions or to participate in discussions. Later, when you mention this to colleagues in the teachers' lounge, they tell you that the Native American students are naturally shy and that asking them questions embarrasses them so it's best not to call on them.

> What do you think of the teachers' explanation of the Native American students' behavior?

> How would you deal with the Native American students in this class?

In analyzing responses, we coded prospective teachers' reactions to the suggestion that the Native American students sat and behaved as they did because of a behavioral characteristic purported to derive from their membership in a particular ethnic group. If in their responses the prospective teachers agreed with or did not question the validity of the stereotype, "Native American students are naturally shy," we coded their responses as "accepts stereotype." If the teachers seemed unsure about whether or not the generalization was an adequate explanation for the students' behaviors, we coded the responses "unsure."

If the prospective teachers rejected the idea that stereotypes based on group membership are a valid basis for explaining students' behaviors or for making instructional decisions, we coded the responses as "rejects stereotype." Finally, some responses were simply not clear enough to code. In these, the teachers sometimes started with one position but, in explaining their responses, worked their way around to another. Others would seem to reject the stereotype but proceed to respond as if they accepted it as valid.

Before the program, 21 percent of the student teachers in the ABCD sample either accepted the characterization of Native American students as "shy" or weren't sure whether the characterization was accurate. Before the program, nearly 80 percent of the students rejected the characterization. Afterward, a small but not significant increase occurred in the percentage of responses that were so unclear, meandering, or conflicting that we couldn't determine the respondent's view of the stereotype. This may indicate that the program has stimulated students to think about the issue and that they are still trying to sort out their understandings.

The only student in the treatment sample who, before the program, accepted the stereotype responded as follows:

> Well, I would tend to think that their behavior is more appropriate for their background and it probably is . . . the way that they treat other people according to the Native American tradition. They tend to sort of stick together and not really volunteer, interact in a way that, say, Americans, Caucasians, do. (Siilik, 1)

This individual seems to have become more uncertain about her view of Native American students in the postprogram interview:

> Well, I mean it could be true but I am not really sure. I think there might be another reason why they wouldn't want to answer questions. I mean they might not want to call attention to themselves—not shyness necessarily—maybe a cultural trait or they somehow don't feel part of the group that they would learn in their culture, from their parents and other Native Americans—not to call attention to themselves as individuals. (Siilik, 2)

Although this student never explicitly rejects the generalization as a stereotype, this response in the second interview reveals her understanding that social behaviors considered appropriate in a pupil's primary group might conflict with the expectations embedded in the culture of classrooms (Jackson, 1968; Suina, 1985).

Several students in the sample seemed to sense that something was amiss with the characterization but weren't clear about what it was: "Well, I think it could be a valid reason based on her observations—not necessarily the correct one but it could be valid" (Beluga, 1). Unfortunately, we do not know what this student teacher meant by "valid." Others who also did not reject the characterization as a stereotype demonstrate skepticism about the generalization and feel they ought to do research to find out whether or not it is true:

> Well, what I would do is, since my knowledge of Native American students is limited, I assume at this point that that is a relatively accurate

statement, but I would want to research it further. I do believe that that's [the characterization of Native American students as shy] correct, however I would want to go and either discuss with some other people, in addition to those teachers, persons who are Native American and look in books and various other resources to find out more about the culture of those children and then from that point decide what I would like to do as far as having the students participate to their fullest in the class, which may not necessarily entail having them speak in a question-answer type situation but possibly do artwork or written type of work that could be shared with the class to maximize their talents and still make them a part of the classroom situation so that they aren't isolated . . . once I have researched the situation. (Ermize, 2)

Most students, both before and after the training, reject either the specific generalization about Native Americans or all stereotypes:

I tend to think they [the teachers] are being overly simplistic. There might be something to what they are saying; I am not really sure. I would disregard their explanation and I would run the classroom a little differently. I would think that they have some stereotypical responses that they developed that I would disregard. I wouldn't listen to what they were saying. (Goshawk, 1)

Oh, I think that's wrong . . . I don't think that there's any race or culture that's naturally shy. (Raven, 1)

Personally I guess I would think it's kind of a weak response. I wouldn't want to stereotype anybody in that way. I think everybody is different and I also think that with children, especially if they're elementary school children, they kind of become what you tell them they are. So if you insist that they are shy and shouldn't be answering questions, I think that's exactly what they do. (Grayling, 1)

Clearly, before any training at all, most student teachers in our sample recognize and reject stereotypes of ethnically different children.

In sum, we found that most student teachers reject generalizations even before the training. On this particular item, we found no statistically significant differences between students' responses before and after the training. At the same time, we did find that some of the student teachers seemed to become more uncertain about whether to reject the generalization based on ethnic group membership after the program.

UNDERSTANDING THE RELATIONSHIP BETWEEN ACADEMIC TASKS AND OPPORTUNITIES TO LEARN

A second scenario item was designed to elicit teacher trainees' understandings of the effects that different tasks have on students' attitudes, behaviors, and opportunities to learn. The item also was intended to tap program participants' awareness of teachers' responses to stereotypes of learners. In the scenario, the teacher has assigned different tasks to three students of color. The tasks present subject matter in distinctly different ways and have the potential for distinctly different learning consequences. For instance, while one student is practicing writing two letters, another is taping a story he will later play for the entire class. A few details about the children's family circumstances are added to see how respondents regard such information in making decisions about task assignments.

In analyzing responses to this item, we coded whether the prospective teachers addressed the differences in the tasks that the teacher had assigned to each of the three students. In addition, we also coded whether the prospective teachers addressed, in their responses, the consequences that such differences in learning tasks could have for learning. That is, did the prospective teachers note that Brian and James were given learning tasks—dictating a story compared to tracing letters—that lead to quite different knowledge and understanding?

Although about half of the students in the ABCD treatment group did at least discuss the academic tasks that the children had been assigned, none of them noted that tracing letters and dictating stories onto a tape to be played to an audience later afford children quite different understandings about written language and reading, not to mention about themselves as learners of both. The ABCD program did not seem to affect students' sensitivity to differences in academic tasks—insofar as this item measures such sensitivity. The following response is typical of those we got in the interviews:

> I don't think that she's showing any real racial discrimination at all. And it sounds like she's individualizing . . . . It sounds like she's matching the children's needs, their situations. James is the one with the problem. It sounds like she is giving him positive encouragement to a point. However, to single him out, to say things like that out loud too often, I think is wrong too. She's overdoing it. To mention once in a while that James is sitting quietly today and she really appreciates it, I think that's nice. But to overdo it will put a lot of shame on the child. And in terms

of Brian, he's in the self-contained learning center, he's taping the story which she's going to read to the whole class later. He's the competitive guy whose parents move around a lot. He's in all the different sporting activities. His father is a corporate executive. That's basically the facts . . . . I think [the teacher] is doing fine. I can't really see any problems as far as that goes. The only problem I do find is that they [James and Brian] don't get along, according to the mother. I would have to wonder why, you know, if that's encouraging the class or not. If a parent requests it, there's only so many things you can do. (Vole, 1)

The one element in the story on which many student teachers in our sample commented was the use of praise and reprimands:

I would probably try not to be as negative as, "Don't sit back in your chair." Because to just tell a child "don't" is not good. To use something more positive as in a "do rule." "Please sit up straight." Or, "Do sit up straight." Instead of "Don't lean back." (Vole, 1)

Indeed, half of the sample did not even mention the differences in the tasks that the children had been assigned—much less the differences in what children can learn from the tasks. Their attention was focused almost totally on the teacher's management of the children's behavior.

Student-teachers' responses didn't change significantly between the first administration of the interview and the second. To repeat, the small size of the sample makes registering meaningful change difficult at best.

STUDENT-TEACHER BELIEFS

School success and failure.   A key item on the questionnaire asked students to choose from among six factors the one they believe most responsible for success and failure in school. Three of the choices—home background, intellectual ability, and enthusiasm—are factors originating with the student and his family. The three remaining choices are teacher factors: attention to student uniqueness, effective teaching methods, and teacher enthusiasm or perseverance.

Before the training, 42 percent of the student teachers in the ABCD sample chose a student factor as the major source of school success. Nearly a quarter selected home background and 12 percent student enthusiasm or perseverance (see Table 2–1). Sixty percent of the students began the program believing that teacher factors were primarily responsible for student success. Twenty-four percent cited teachers' attention to student uniqueness

TABLE 2–1

Student-teachers' beliefs about the most frequent source of students' school success

Questionnaire administration	ABCD SAMPLE		TELT SAMPLE
	Pre-program (N = 17)	Post-program (N = 13)	Post-program (N = 149)
Student's home background	24%	15%	10%
Student's intellectual ability	6	8	5
Student's enthusiasm or perseverance	12	15	47
Subtotal: Student factors	[42]	[38]	[62]
Teacher's attention to the unique interests and abilities of students	24	23	13
Teacher's use of effective methods of teaching	24	15	17
Teacher's enthusiasm or perseverance	12	23	8
Subtotal: Teacher factors	[60]	[61]	[38]
TOTAL*	101%	100%	100%

TABLE 2–2

Student-teachers' beliefs about the most frequent source of students' school failure

Questionnaire administration	ABCD SAMPLE		TELT SAMPLE
	Pre-program (N = 17)	Post-program (N = 13)	Post-program (N = 149)
Student's home background	12%	15%	9%
Student's intellectual ability	0	0	1
Student's enthusiasm or perseverance	18	0	43
Subtotal: Student factors	[30]	[15]	[53]
Teacher's attention to the unique interests and abilities of students	29	46	12
Teacher's use of effective methods of teaching	29	15	23
Teacher's enthusiasm or perseverance	12	23	11
Subtotal: Teacher factors	[70]	[84]	[46]
TOTAL*	100%	99%	99%

*Totals less or more than 100 percent due to rounding.
Source: Teacher Education and Learning to Teach Study, National Center for Research on Teacher Education, 1990.

and an additional 24 percent chose the teacher's use of effective methods as the most frequent source of student success. After the ABCD program, the student teachers did not make significantly different choices: 38 percent believed that students themselves were primarily responsible for their success while 61 percent chose a teacher factor. By comparison, the student teachers in the TELT sample were much more likely to cite student factors than teacher factors.

As Table 2–2 shows, most student teachers in the ABCD sample attributed school failure primarily to teacher factors. Twenty-nine percent of the students cited the lack of teacher's attention to student uniqueness and 29 percent selected the teachers' failure to use effective methods. Thirty percent held students themselves responsible for their own failure in school.

As with the attribution of success, student-teachers' identification of the source of school failure did not change significantly after the training. Although not statistically significant, the proportion of students who cited the lack of attention to student uniqueness as the most frequent source of school failure increased to 46 percent. Proportionately, half as many students as before the training identified the source of school failure to be the teachers' failure to use effective methods. Overall, only 15 percent of the student teachers believed, after the training, that students are principally responsible for their own failure. This contrasts with the 53 percent of those in the TELT sample who cited student factors as the most frequent source of student failure.

Differences in types of tasks believed appropriate for "low" and "high" achievers. Research by Goodlad (1984) and Oakes (1985) has demonstrated that children placed in low-ability groups encounter opportunities to learn that differ in substance and quality from those that children placed in high-ability groups encounter. The questionnaire contained four items designed to tap student teachers' notions about tasks that they would consider appropriate for children who were labeled "low" and "high" achievers in mathematics and in writing. Asking the question in the context of two school subjects enabled us to examine the relationship between views of the subject and views of learners.

When we asked student teachers before the training which task they would emphasize most in teaching mathematics to "low achievers," 35 percent chose problem solving, while 24 percent chose making mathematics fun, and 18 percent selected helping students understand the theories behind the topics (Table 2–3). Asked the same question about "high achievers," 47 percent of the student teachers responded they would emphasize problem solving while 29 percent chose helping students understand the theories behind the topics. Only 12 percent of the student teachers said they would emphasize making mathematics fun with the "high achievers."

TABLE 2–3

Types of Mathematical Tasks that Student Teachers Believed Appropriate for Teaching High and Low Achievers

TOPICS IN MATHEMATICS	PERCENTAGE WHO BELIEVE TOPIC IS APPROPRIATE FOR . . .			
	High achievers		Low Achievers	
	Pre-program (N = 17)	Post-program (N = 13)	Pre-program (N = 17)	Post-program (N = 13)
Basic computational skills	0%	0%	12%	8%
Nontraditional topics, such as geometry and probability	12	23	0	0
Problem solving	47	62	35	46
Helping students understand the theories behind the topics	29	8	18	8
Making math class fun for students	12	8	24	39
Other	0	0	12	0
TOTALS*	100%	101%	101%	101%

TABLE 2–4

Types of Writing Tasks that Student Teachers Believed Appropriate for Teaching High and Low Achievers

TASKS IN WRITING	PERCENTAGE WHO BELIEVE TOPIC IS APPROPRIATE FOR . . .			
	High achievers		Low Achievers	
	Pre-program (N = 17)	Post-program (N = 13)	Pre-program (N = 17)	Post-program (N = 13)
Basic spelling and grammatical skills	0%	0%	12%	15%
Nontraditional types of writing, like sonnets and editorials	0	0	0	0
Developing and refining an argument in writing	36	54	18	0
Helping students understand the roles of audience and purpose in writing	24	31	35	39
Having fun through writing things like composing haiku	35	15	29	39
Other	6	0	6	8
TOTALS*	101%	101%	100%	101%

*Totals less or more than 100 percent due to rounding
Source: ABCD Project Evaluation, Michigan Department of Education and National Center for Research on Teacher Education, Michigan State University, 1989.

Although not statistically significant, differences appeared in student-teachers' posttraining responses. Making math fun was a slightly more popular choice for "low achievers" after the training. After the training, a greater proportion of student teachers said that they would emphasize problem solving with both "low" and "high" achievers. Unfortunately, because the questionnaire was self-administered, we don't know how respondents interpreted the phrase "problem solving." Our experience with this phrase in other research is that prospective teachers apply it to a range of activities—from computation to complex scenarios that require students to sift through a lot of information in figuring out a solution.

Asked before the program about appropriate topics in teaching writing to "low" achievers, 35 percent of the sample said they would emphasize helping students understand the roles of audience and purpose while 29 percent indicated that they would emphasize having fun through writing (Table 2–4). In responding to the same question about "high" achievers, 36 percent of the student teachers in the ABCD project said they would emphasize developing and refining an argument in writing while 35 percent said they would focus on having fun through writing. Nearly one in four would emphasize helping students understand the roles of audience and purpose.

Differences in student-teachers' responses after the training were not statistically significant, but the proportion of those who said they would emphasize having fun through writing with "low" achievers increased to 39 percent while a similar proportion indicated that they would work on audience and purpose. In working with "high" achievers, 54 percent of the sample said, after the training, they would emphasize developing and refining an argument in writing.

In sum, student teachers believe the academic tasks that are appropriate for "low" achievers differ from those that are appropriate for "high" achievers. In working with the former, making math fun is nearly as popular as problem solving, whereas in working with the "high" achievers problem solving is far and away the most popular choice. In writing, student teachers believe either that making writing fun or helping students understand audience and purpose is most appropriate with "low" achievers, whereas a majority think that they should emphasize developing and refining an argument when working with "high" achievers. The ABCD program appeared to have little influence on student-teachers' thinking about differential access to knowledge insofar as these items capture that thinking.

Source of ideas for teaching. We asked program participants about their past experience as students as a source of ideas about teaching and learning. Given the rapidly changing character of the pupil population, the increase in non-Anglo students, and the failure of many schools to serve non-Anglo students, we could question the value of the experiences many prospective teachers had in school as a guide to teaching in the classrooms of tomorrow. Yet, most student teachers in our sample agreed that they relied on their experience as students for a lot of their ideas about teaching and learning (Table 2–5). Ratings before and after the training weren't significantly different, nor was the mean of the ABCD sample significantly different from that of the NCRTE sample.

Views of ability grouping and tracking. Most student teachers in our sample agreed that teachers should avoid ability grouping, although they appeared not to feel strongly about their view (Table 2–5). The tenuousness of this belief is underlined by the fact that, after the program, student opinion shifted slightly, but not significantly, toward the use of grouping. On the issue of tracking in high school, most student teachers in our sample disagreed with the practice before the training and felt the same afterward. Compared with student teachers nationally, students in the ABCD sample appear slightly more skeptical about the value of tracking.

Expectations for "slow learners." Related to student-teachers' views of ability grouping is how they regard learners labeled as "slow." Although both before and after the program participants disagreed with the statement that teachers should focus on "minimum competency" in teaching "slow learners," the strength of their belief diminished slightly although not significantly after training (Table 2–5). Nearly a third of the sample disagreed strongly with "minimum competency" as a goal for "slow learners" before the training but only one student felt so strongly afterward. Student teachers in the national TELT sample were more likely to agree with the idea of "minimum competency" as the goal in teaching "slow learners" than were those in the ABCD program.

Standards for student performance. Before the program, a majority of our sample thought uniform standards should be applied to all pupils (Table 2–5). Most of these prospective teachers indicated that they felt strongly about the matter. After the training, even though the mean remained the same, a shift seemed to occur: Although fewer students disagreed with the idea of uniform standards, more students than before seemed unsure about how they felt and only one asserted that she felt strongly that standards should be the same for all students. Nationally, we found that *at the end of* students' preservice programs they were significantly less likely to agree that uniform standards for all pupils were a good idea (McDiarmid, in press-b).

TABLE 2-5

Means of ABCD and TELT Student-Teachers' Views of Teaching, Learning, and Learners (1 = Strongly Agree; 7 = Strongly Disagree)

	ABCD SAMPLE		TELT SAMPLE
	Pre-program (N = 17)	Post-program (N = 13)	Post-program (N = 143)
Ideas about teaching			
A lot of my ideas about teaching and learning come from my own experience as a student.	3.5	3.7	2.4
Tracking and grouping			
Teachers should avoid grouping students by ability or level of performance.	2.8	3.7	3.8
Required high school courses should have separate classes for low-achieving and high-achieving students.	5.0	5.0	3.8
Expectations			
When working with slow learners, teachers should focus nearly all their instruction on "minimum competency" objectives.	5.8	5.3	3.6
Standards			
Teachers should use the same standards in evaluating the work of all students in the class.	3.5	3.5	2.2
Individualizing			
It is impractical for teachers to tailor instruction to the unique interests and abilities of different students.	6.1	6.0	3.8
How students learn			
Students learn best if they have to figure things out for themselves instead of being told or shown.	3.8	3.1	2.9
Teacher's purposes			
The main job of teachers is to transmit the values of mainstream American culture.	5.3	5.2	2.6

The main job of the teacher is to encourage students to think and question the world around them.	1.9	1.5	2.0
The main job of the teacher is to teach subject matter.	3.5	3.4	3.4
Student ability			
There are some students who can simply never be good at writing.	5.6	5.0	4.8
Some people are naturally able to organize their thoughts for writing.	2.2	2.8	2.4
To be good at mathematics, you need to have a kind of "mathematical mind."	5.7	4.9	4.6
Teaching in English			
All students should be taught in English	3.2	4.3	3.3

Sources: TELT Study, National Center for Research on Teacher Education, 1990; Evaluation of ABCD Project, Michigan Department of Education, Office of Professional Development and NCRTE, 1990.

Individualization. For some educators, the answer to diversity is, ironically, individualization. That is, faced with learners who bring diverse interests, backgrounds, and capacities, many student teachers appear inclined to segregate students from one another during opportunities to learn. One could argue that individualizing instruction is problematic for a number of reasons, which we will explain at greater length in the discussion section. Like most student teachers in the TELT national sample who disagree with the statement that it is not practical to tailor instruction to each student, those in the ABCD sample overwhelmingly believe that such individualizing is practical (Table 2–5). This serves to underline what we found in students' response to Scenario #2 on the interview: an often uncritical endorsement of individualization as *the* way to deal with diversity (see Table 2–3).

How students learn. Both before and after the training, most students in our sample agreed that students learn best if they figure things out for themselves (Table 2–5). The reason this question was included was to find out how student teachers think about learning. Recent work in cognitive psychology suggests that, whatever students learn—whether it is what teachers want them to learn or not—they learn on their own (Resnick, 1983). That as many as 20 percent of the students in our sample disagreed with this statement is noteworthy. Student teachers in the TELT sample seemed inclined to agree with this statement.

Teachers' purpose.   We also asked students to respond to three parallel questions designed to assess their views of what teachers ought to be doing: transmitting mainstream values, encouraging students to think, or teaching subject matter. As shown in Table 2–5, most student teachers in the ABCD sample disagreed, before the program, with the statement that a teacher's primary job is "to transmit the values of mainstream American culture." We found no significant difference in student-teachers' beliefs after the program. On this item, student teachers in the ABCD program differed from those in the TELT national sample. The latter were inclined, at the end of their preservice programs, to agree with the statement.

An even larger proportion of student teachers appeared to agree, both before and after the ABCD program, that "the main job of the teacher is to encourage students to think and question the world around them." On the issue of whether the teacher's main job is to teach subject matter, we found less agreement. Although most student teachers agreed with this statement, a sizable proportion weren't sure or disagreed. The ABCD program did not appear to significantly influence student teachers' beliefs in this area.

The prospective teachers in our sample appear pretty sure that their main job is to encourage questioning and thinking, less sure that teaching subject matter is their main job, and doubtful that their main job is to transmit mainstream values.

Student ability.   Although "all students can learn" has become a mantra in U.S. education, evidence exists that prospective teachers continue to believe that the lack of innate ability or correct attitude, or a "disadvantaged" home environment, means that some pupils cannot, in fact, learn. Teachers who hold to such beliefs may use them to decide when to draw the line on their responsibility to see that children in their charge learn. We asked student teachers in the ABCD project three "agree–disagree" questions intended to probe their understandings of children's abilities in two specific subjects, mathematics and writing (Table 2–5). We included the learning of subject matter to provide some context for understanding their responses.

Most students disagreed even before the training with the idea that some students can never be good at writing. Most, however, also agreed with the statement, "Some students are naturally able to organize their thoughts for writing." The use of the word *naturally* was intended to get at their notions of innate ability—that is, whether they believed that ability to organize one's thoughts is something that is learned or is, somehow, genetically encoded.

At the same time, keep in mind that in everyday usage, *naturally* is sometimes also applied to what are clearly learned behaviors. After the program, an unmistakable although not statistically significant diminution occurred in the strength of participants' agreement. We included a similar statement about mathematics, although the notion of innate ability is explicit, not subtle: "To be good at mathematics, you need a kind of 'mathematical mind.'" Interestingly, no one before and only two students after the training agreed with this statement.

On all three of these statements, the means of the responses of those in the ABCD project were close to those in the TELT national sample.

Teaching in English.   We asked two questions designed to tap student-teachers' beliefs about the use of standard English in the classroom. The first, a Likert-scale item on the self-administered questionnaire, presented the flat statement: "All students should be taught in English" (Table 2–5). The second offered several different ways in which teachers might respond to the use of regional dialects in class. On both, students in our sample demonstrated considerable tolerance for the use of languages and dialects other than standard English.

On the Likert-scale item, the mean of student-teacher responses at the beginning of the program showed that many agreed with the statement that "all students should be taught in English." After the program, some of the students who had agreed with the statement appeared to become less sure about their conviction. Although the change wasn't statistically significant, nonetheless something, perhaps either the ABCD training or the experience of student teaching or both, appears to have caused some students to reconsider their position. The mean of the responses of student teachers in the national TELT sample at the end of their programs was roughly the same as that of the ABCD sample at the beginning of theirs.

When asked about the use of dialects in the classroom, students again appear fairly tolerant. Before the training, 69 percent of the student teachers in the ABCD sample agreed with the position that "dialects like Black English are fully legitimate languages and appropriate for classroom discussion and for expressive writing like poetry, but students must use standard English in writing expository prose and in formal speech." The more extreme positions of either excluding the use of dialects in the classroom or accepting them as fully appropriate for all purposes drew little support either before or after the training. Because we developed this item especially for this evaluation, we don't have national data with which to compare the responses of our sample. Comparing the students who went through the training with those in our control group who did not attend the training, we found no significant difference.

TREATING CULTURAL DIVERSITY IN THE CLASSROOM

We developed two items that are specific to this project and intended to get at issues that members of the evaluation subcommittee considered critical. The first presented six distinct positions on treating cultural diversity in the classroom. We structured the item so that students would have to choose the one position closest to their own. Most students (65 percent) embraced the idea that the best way to serve culturally different children is "to make sure that *all* students have the opportunity to understand the subject matter in ways that increase their capacity to figure things out for themselves." Twenty-four percent of the students before the training identified with the view that in working with diverse children they should "teach students that American society offers opportunities to everyone and that anyone who wants to improve his or her economic situation can do so if they work hard enough."

Students' views did not appear to change significantly after the training. Most (54 percent) still thought their responsibility was to make sure that children had equal opportunities to learn the subject matter. Although fewer student teachers identified their purpose as teaching "students that American society offers opportunities to everyone and that anyone who wants to improve his or her economic situation can do so if they work hard enough" and more agreed they would "honor and celebrate diversity by having students from different backgrounds share their foods, customs, language, and values with their classmates," these apparent changes could be due to chance.

The other item developed specifically for the program drew on a recent controversy in a Michigan community. Some parents in the community had pressured the school board go ahead with a play based on the Biblical Christmas story. We presented various positions on the issue, from no religious celebrations at all through equal treatment for all major religious groups to the explicit teaching of Christian values. Student-teachers' views were initially across the range, including quite a few (44 percent) that didn't fit in any of the categories we presented. Most students who wrote in their own preferences in the "other" category indicated that they would want to tie in the observation of various religious celebrations with academic work in such subjects as social studies.

Students' responses to this item seemed to show a clear effect of the program. Whereas only about 20 percent of the student teachers had agreed, before the training, with the statement that "if we celebrate Christian holidays, we also need to observe and celebrate, in a similar fashion, Jewish, Moslem, Buddhist, and so on, holidays," more than 60 percent did so afterward. We will discuss the implications of this below.

DISCUSSION

BELIEFS ABOUT LEARNERS: SOME ARE CREATED MORE EQUAL THAN OTHERS

The greatest paradox in looking at the results not only of the ABCD project but more broadly at teacher education is that students are exposed to increasing amounts of information about children who are culturally different from themselves, yet the proportion of those who subsequently recognize and reject stereotypes doesn't increase—and may even decrease. The source of this paradox may lie in how prospective teachers make sense out of the information they encounter. Although teacher educators intend that such information will lead prospective teachers to make decisions that increase the chances to learn for poor children and those of color, teacher-education students interpret the information to fit with their current understandings. The results, given the teacher educators' purpose, are often perverse:

> Well, I would tend to think that their behavior is more appropriate for their background and it probably is the way that they treat other people according to the Native American tradition. They tend to sort of stick together and not really volunteer, interact in a way that, say, Americans, Caucasians, do. (Siilik, 1)

As this quotation indicates, the presentation of information on particular groups may actually encourage prospective teachers to generalize and, eventually, to prejudge pupils in their classrooms. More commonly, teacher-education students, who are predominantly white, may become unsure about how to think about diverse children. On the one hand, they are taught to be suspicious of any generalization about a group of people; on the other, they encounter materials and presentations that, in fact, make generalizations about normative values, attitudes, and behaviors among different groups.

Most teacher-education students have not had the opportunity to explore their own beliefs about student differences and the role these play in teaching and learning. Rather, their preference seems to be not to confront the issue and to deal with differences by individualizing. The danger of this approach is that, as the data from this evaluation and the TELT study indicate, student teachers appear to pay little attention to the academic consequences of different opportunities to learn (McDiarmid, in press-a). Indeed, while exquisitely sensitive to the nuances of positive and negative praise and reinforcement, they appear almost oblivious to differences in academic tasks and the effects that different opportunities to learn can have on student understanding of the subject matter and views of themselves as learners (Table 2–2).

This was nowhere clearer than in the ABCD participants' responses to the questions on which tasks were appropriate for "high" and "low" achieving students (Tables 2–3 and 2–4). In both mathematics and writing, ABCD participants are much more likely to provide "high" achievers than "low" achievers with opportunities to learn high-level knowledge/problem solving in mathematics and developing an argument in writing. A significant proportion of student teachers in our study would emphasize making the subject matter "fun" with "low" achievers. We know that poor children and those of color are more likely to find themselves in "low-ability" groups or tracks. Consequently, as Oakes (1985) has argued on the basis of her data, these children are far less likely to have access to "high-status" knowledge than are middle-class, white children. Although well-coached in the "all children can learn" mantra, many student teachers believe—and begin teaching with the belief—that subject matter has to be "sugar-coated" for some children and that some topics—for instance, geometry and probability in elementary classrooms—are fine for "high" achievers but beyond "low" achievers.

SOME THOUGHTS ABOUT PROJECT GOALS

Many of the views that ABCD students held at the beginning of the program were consistent with the goals of the program: Most of them rejected stereotypes as a basis for making instructional decisions; most held teachers responsible for pupil learning; most were accepting of dialects as legitimate languages for the classroom; and most were committed to making sure that all children in a diverse classroom had a chance to understand the subject matter. At the same time, they held other beliefs and understandings that are arguably problematic in culturally diverse classrooms: They tended to think that "low" achievers needed to have subject matter sugar-coated to make it palatable while "high" achievers should engage challenging topics; they tended to view individualization uncritically as the way to accommodate diversity; and they tended to be preoccupied with management, verbal praise, and reinforcement at the expense of thoughtful consideration of the effects that various academic content and tasks have on meaningful learning and conceptions of self as learner.

These three views that emerge from our data could, in themselves, be objects of instruction. Rather than teaching specific skills or techniques, teacher educators could focus on the understandings that underlie teacher actions. As long as a teacher believes, for instance, that her elementary pupils who have previously performed below average on standardized tests cannot handle such topics as probability and statistics, she is unlikely to create opportunities for them to do so regardless of what skills or information about her students' cultural backgrounds she may have accumulated. Teachers who believe that the way to deal with diversity is to individualize learning tasks are unlikely to create opportunities for pupils to learn from one another, to experience making sense of a problem or issue with classmates, to develop an idea that knowledge is socially mediated. As Lampert (1990) has written about her own experience in teaching mathematics to elementary pupils:

> When students are able to reason about whether some operation or relationship makes sense in a familiar domain, they can be taught to make connections between what is familiar and the more abstract routines that pertain in the mathematical world of numbers and symbols. This connection makes it possible to shift the locus of authority in the classroom—*away from* the teacher as a judge and the textbook as a standard of judgement, and *toward* the teachers and students as inquirers who have the power to use mathematical tools to decide whether an answer or a procedure is reasonable. (p. 224)

Teachers who view their primary role as "the person in charge" and who believe the best measure of their effectiveness is how quiet their classrooms are and whether they cover the textbook are unlikely to create opportunities for pupils to develop a sense of their capacity to make sense out of the issues and problems they confront. Teachers who ignore the relationship between the meaningfulness of the knowledge to be learned and of the task to be done, on the one hand, and the attention pupils give to the task, on the other, are unlikely to develop tasks to challenge and engage pupils.

In an earlier study, I interviewed and observed teachers nominated as unusually effective by community members, colleagues, and administrators in rural, Native Alaskan villages. I found that, except for the Native teachers, before moving to the village these teachers knew little about the values and behaviors of the particular Native group they taught (McDiarmid, Kleinfeld, and Parrett, 1988). Once in the village, however, they put themselves in roles outside of school—as a player on a community basketball team, a participant in skin-sewing gatherings or weekly bingo nights, a member of a hunting or fishing group—in which they learned a great deal of specific information about the children they taught. These teachers also, of course, learned from the children themselves, creating opportunities—journals, discussions, chaperoning—for their students to tell them directly, firsthand about their understandings, concerns, interests, worries. Valuing *specific* information about their pupils and being inclined to find out what they needed to know seemed critical to these teachers' success.

In sum, a number of the perceptions that the project hoped to develop in participants may already have existed before the program—or, at least, the participants claimed to hold views that coincided with views the program promoted. The program presented students with a wealth of information— an approach widely used not merely in teacher education but in education generally. The lack of the right information—the "knowledge base"—may not, however, constitute an adequate explanation for teachers' failure to do a better job in helping poor children and those of color learn. Some teachers may have fundamental beliefs and assumptions—for instance, that some children can learn "high-class" knowledge and others cannot—that must be confronted and challenged. More information, particularly information that deals in generalizations about groups of learners, may be a weak device for challenging teachers' underlying views, views developed over a lifetime in a culture that spawned tracking and ability grouping to accommodate learner diversity.

SOME THOUGHTS ABOUT PEDAGOGY

That the ABCD project did not seem to have a major effect on student teachers' view of learners, learning, the context, and teachers' role in teaching culturally diverse students should not be surprising. When the NCRTE looked at the effects of five preservice teacher-education programs, we found that many of the beliefs prospective teachers brought with them remained untouched after two years of professional courses (McDiarmid, in press-b). Prospective teachers do not enter preservice programs as blank slates; they have served an apprenticeship of observation (Lortie, 1975) equal to 1740 working days—that is how long many have spent in classrooms watching teachers. As a contrast, prospective teachers spend, at most, the equivalent of 90 working days in teacher-education courses. A program such as the ABCD training constitutes about three working days.

Although not a measure of what is learned, the time prospective teachers spend watching others teach powerfully shapes their ideas of what their responsibilities are, what teaching and learning are like, and what classrooms should be like (Feiman-Nemser and Buchmann, 1986; Lortie, 1975; Jackson, 1968). The relative constancy in the practice of teaching can be explained, in part, by this long apprenticeship: Teachers teach by and large as they were taught themselves (Cohen, 1988; Cuban, 1984). This observation is critical when we realize that most prospective teachers attended schools in which the majority of children were white. Diversity was not as apparent to their teachers as it is likely to be in their own classrooms. Yet, students in this program, just like those completing other preservice programs, view their own experience as students as a useful and legitimate source of ideas for teaching (McDiarmid, 1990b).

Why aren't teacher-education programs more effective in changing students' beliefs and understandings? Although this question deserves much more attention than we can give it here, we would like to suggest that a major impediment is the pedagogy of teacher education. As part of the TELT study, we observed both teacher-education and liberal-arts courses and interviewed faculty. We have found some variety in the kinds of classes students attend, but the typical class is one familiar from other studies of college education that include observations of classes (Boyer, 1987) as well as from the experience of most of us who have attended college. Typically, students are presented with a mass of information in the form of research findings, generalizations, procedures, techniques, formulas, and so on—the substance of the field. Because discourse in the university classroom, like that in pre-collegiate classrooms, appears to be dominated by the instructor and the instructor's agenda, the opportunities for students to bring to the surface and express their initial understandings of a given subject are usually quite limited (McDiarmid, 1990a). The evidence is that many students learn what they need to pass their exams—but do not change their fundamental understandings and beliefs (Ball and McDiarmid, 1990; McDiarmid, 1990a).

Learning, as cognitive research over the past decade or so has been telling us, consists not in developing undeveloped faculties, stacking enough individual propositions on top of each other to build understanding, or filling in heretofore vacant mental lots:

> [People] do not simply acquire information passively until there is enough of it for "correct" rules and explanations to emerge. This tendency to construct ordered explanations and routines even in the absence of adequate information can account at least partly for another phenomenon . . . : robust beliefs that are resistant to change even when instruction (and thus better information) *does* come along. (Resnick, 1983, p. 26)

In learning, students act upon the information, ideas, and experiences they encounter within and through the structured and ordered understandings and knowledge they have from previous experiences and within and through specific social contexts. To assign meaning to experience, people rely on understandings built on previous experiences and on their social context.

If teacher education is to challenge and change prospective teachers' initial beliefs about learners, learning, subject matter, teaching, and the milieus, the content of courses and the approaches of instructors need to take account of prospective teachers' initial conceptions. The recent move to include more findings from research on teaching and more information on various cultural groups as a way of improving instruction and increasing the success of poor children and those of color seems unlikely, by itself, to produce the hoped-for results. Prospective teachers, like other learners, reconstruct the information and ideas they encounter to fit into their existing framework. Prospective teachers bring to preservice preparation definite ideas about learners, teaching, and learning. Unless they become aware of their own preconceptions and have the opportunity to examine them, they are likely to reconfigure whatever they experience to fit with their existing understandings.

Teacher-education programs—whether orchestrated by universities, school districts, or other agencies—need to attend to prospective teachers' understanding of learners, learning, subject matter, teaching, and the milieus and the interconnectedness of these. Prospective teachers need opportunities to examine their initial understandings as well their understandings of the ideas, information, and situations they encounter (for an example of such a foundations course designed to accomplish these ends, see Feiman-Nemser and Melnick, in press; McDiarmid, 1990b; for an example of a similarly designed mathematics methods course, see Ball, 1989). The content and pedagogy must be shaped, on the one hand, by the instructor's knowledge of the learners' initial beliefs and understandings and, on the other, by the instructor's knowledge of the critical ideas, information, and propositions as well as the structure and nature of knowledge in the field (Ball and McDiarmid, 1990; McDiarmid, Ball, and Anderson, 1989).

CONCLUSION

The ABCD project is the product of an unusual collaboration between practitioners—both classroom teachers and teacher educators—and specialists at Michigan DOE. During its first year, the planning committee designed a multicultural workshop for student teachers that was successfully implemented by the project personnel at Michigan DOE. The research presented here suggests the program did not change some of the fundamental beliefs student teachers hold about diverse learners, learning, and teaching. At the same time, the program could well have influenced student teachers in ways to which the instruments used were not sensitive. Moreover, we collected the post-program data a mere five months after the initial training. The beliefs and actions the program was designed to influence, many of which are complex and foundational, may not be amenable to change in the short term. Had we interviewed these same teachers a year or two after the program, the results might have been quite different.

REFERENCES

Ball, D. L. (1989, March). *Breaking with experience in learning to teach mathematics: The role of a preservice methods course.* Paper presented at the annual meeting of the American Educational Research Association, San Francisco.

Ball, D. L., and McDiarmid, G. W. (1990). The subject matter preparation of teachers. In W. R. Houston (Ed.), *Handbook on research on teacher education* (pp. 437–449). Oxford, England: Pergamon.

Boyer, E. (1987). *College: The undergraduate experience in America.* New York: Harper and Row.

Carter-Cooper, E. (1990). *The Accepting Behaviors for Cultural Diversity Project.* Lansing: Michigan Department of Education, Office of Professional Development.

Cohen, D. K. (1988). *Teaching practice: Plus ca change . . . .* Issue Paper 88–4. East Lansing: Michigan State University, National Center for Research on Teacher Education.

Cuban, L. (1984). *How teachers taught: Constancy and change in American classrooms, 1890–1980.* New York: Longman.

Feiman-Nemser, S. and Melnick, S. (in press). Changing beginning teachers' conceptions: A study of an introductory teacher education course. In S. Feiman-Nemser and H. Featherstone (Eds.), *Exploring teaching: Reinventing an introductory course.* New York: Teachers College.

Feiman-Nemser, S. and Buchmann, M. (1986). The pitfalls of experience. In J. D. Raths and L. D. Katz (Eds.), *Advances in research on teacher education, Vol. 2* (pp. 61–74). Norwood, N J: Ablex.

Goodlad, J. (1984). *A place called school: Prospects for the future.* New York: McGraw-Hill.

Jackson, P. (1968). *Life in classrooms.* New York: Holt, Rinehart and Winston.

Kennedy, M. M., McDiarmid, G. W., Ball, D. L., & Schmidt, W. *The Teacher Education and Learning to Teach Study: A guide to studying teacher education programs.* East Lansing: Michigan State University, National Center for Research on Teacher Education.

Kerr, D. H. (1981). The structure of quality in teaching. In J. Soltis (Ed.), *Philosophy and education* (80th yearbook of the National Society for the Study of Education, pp. 61–83). Chicago: University of Chicago Press.

Lampert, M. (1990). Choosing and using mathematical tools in classroom discourse. In J. Brophy (Ed.), *Advances in research on teaching, Vol. 1.* (pp. 223–264). Greenwich, CT: JAI.

Lortie, D. (1975). *Schoolteacher: A sociological study.* Chicago: University of Chicago.

McDiarmid, G. W. (1990a). The liberal arts: Will more result in better subject matter understanding? *Theory into Practice,* 29(1), 21–29.

McDiarmid, G. W. (1990b). Challenging prospective teachers' beliefs during an early field experience: A Quixotic undertaking? *Journal of Teacher Education 41*(3), 12–20.

McDiarmid, G. W. (in press-a). What to do about differences? A study of multicultural education for teacher trainees in the Los Angeles Unified School District. *Journal of Teacher Education.*

McDiarmid, G. W. (in press-b). Changes in beliefs about learners among participants in eleven teacher education programs. In Calderhead, J. (Ed.), *Research on teacher reflection.* London: Falmer.

McDiarmid, G. W., Kleinfeld, J. S., and Parrett, W. (1988). *The inventive mind.* Fairbanks, AK: University of Alaska, Center for Cross-Cultural Studies.

McDiarmid, G. W., Ball, D. L., and Anderson, C. A. (1989). Why staying one chapter ahead doesn't really work: Subject-specific pedagogy. In M. Reynolds (Ed.), *Knowledge base for the beginning teacher* (pp. 193– 205). Oxford, England: Pergamon.

NCRTE. (1988). *Teacher education and learning to teach: A research agenda.* Issue Paper 88–7. East Lansing: Michigan State University, National Center for Research on Teacher Education.

Oakes, J. (1985). *Keeping track.* New Haven: Yale University Press.

Office of Professional Development (1988). *Accepting behaviors for cultural diversity: A proposal to the Council of Chief State School Officers.* Lansing: Michigan Department of Education, Author.

Resnick, L. B. (1983). Toward a cognitive theory of instruction. In S. Paris, G. Olson, and H. Stevenson (Eds.) *Learning and motivation in the classroom* (pp. 5–38). Hillsdale, N J: Erlbaum.

Schwab, J. J. (1960/1978). Education and the structure of the disciplines. In I. Westbury and N. Wilkof (Eds.), *Science, curriculum, and liberal education: Selected essays* (pp. 229–272). Chicago: University of Chicago Press.

Suina, J. (1985) . . . And then I went to school. *New Mexico Journal of Reading,* 5(2).

APPENDIX

ABCD (Accepting Behaviors for Cultural Diversity) for Teachers: Topics Included in Three-Day Training

Day 1

Developing Cultural Comfort in the Classroom
People Perceive Differently
The Orange Experience
The Name Game
Learning Styles
Classroom Management in a Culturally Diverse Classroom

Day 2

Racism and its Impact on Self-Esteem and Instruction
Language and Discrimination

Day 3

Instructional Strategies for a Culturally Diverse Classroom
Theory into Action: What can be done at the personal, classroom, and building levels to enhance self-esteem through cultural awareness and instructional enrichment?

DESCRIPTION OF ABCD SAMPLE (N = 12)*

Ethnicity	
White	75%
Black	17
Hispanic	8
Sex	
Female	83%
Male	17
Geographical origin	
Small town or rural	50%
Cities or urban areas	50

Level of schooling student will teach	
Elementary	75%
Secondary	25

Subject student *most* enjoys teaching	
Language arts/reading	50%
History	17
Mathematics	8
Science	8
Social Science	8
Fine Arts	8

Subject student *least* enjoys teaching	
Science	33%
Fine Arts	17
Physical Education	17
Language arts/reading	17
Mathematics	8
Social Science	8

Where students plan to teach	
Small town or rural	50%
City/urban area	42

*We had complete demographic information on twelve of the seventeen student-teachers.

CHAPTER 3

Teaching in the Midst of Diversity: How Do We Prepare?

NANCY L. HADAWAY
University of Texas at Arlington

VIOLA FLOREZ
PATRICIA J. LARKE
DONNA WISEMAN
Texas A&M University

NANCY L. HADAWAY is an Associate Professor and Director of Field Experiences in the School of Education at the University of Texas at Arlington. Her research interests include multicultural and ESL/bilingual education as well as reading/writing across the curriculum.

VIOLA FLOREZ is Graduate Program Coordinator and an Associate Professor of Reading and ESL/bilingual education in the College of Education at Texas A&M University. Her research interests center around second-language literacy.

PATRICIA J. LARKE is an Associate Professor in the College of Education at Texas A&M University. She teaches courses in Educational Foundations and Multicultural Education. Her current research interests include multicultural teacher training.

DONNA WISEMAN is a Professor and Associate Dean in the College of Education at Texas A&M University. Her research interests include language and literacy and children's literature.

ABSTRACT

This paper summarizes a cluster of related research studies which were conducted to assess the nature and adequacy of the multicultural component in an existing teacher-education program. The first two studies address the level of cultural awareness among educators, both preservice and in-service, as well as the impact of classroom-based instruction in multicultural education. In addition, the third project discusses the development of innovative ways to adapt the university curriculum to prepare students more fully to meet the varying needs of the public school population. Implications for multicultural education programs at the school and university level are provided.

INTRODUCTION

The demographic trends for public schools reflect a powerful educational contrast. While teachers have been and continue to be predominantly non-minority, the student population is becoming increasingly minority (Hodgkinson, 1988; NEA, 1987, Quality Education for Minorities Project (QEMP), 1990). In consideration of this marked difference, educators are critically examining the efforts of university-based teacher preparation programs and their ability to realistically prepare future teachers to meet the needs of the vast range of students from differing social, cultural, economic, and linguistic backgrounds. Although multicultural programs may exist, they are often uneven in quality and are generally adjuncts to major programs or separate add-on courses to satisfy a mandate by the state or university (Grant, 1986). Whatever the origin of the program, however, multicultural education tends to be isolated and fragmented, resulting in an incomplete picture for teacher-education students. Since the research and the changing demographics in the United States continue to underline the need for future teacher educators to be more adequately prepared in dealing with students from diverse backgrounds, this paper explores one institution's efforts to assess the adequacy and impact of its multicultural component. Additionally, ways in which the university curriculum may be adapted to prepare students more fully to meet the varying needs of the public school population are examined.

STUDY 1: ASSESSING PRESERVICE TEACHERS' BACKGROUNDS

The "encapsulization" that comes from teachers' predominantly Anglo, middle-class, monolingual backgrounds may have serious ramifications in terms of teacher expectations and student achievement (Banks, 1992; Grant & Sleeter, 1989; Santos, 1986). Most notably, "Teachers are human beings who bring their cultural perspectives, values, hopes, and dreams to the classroom. They also bring their prejudices, stereotypes, and misconceptions. Teachers' values and perspectives mediate and interact with what they teach, and influence the way messages are communicated and perceived by their students" (Banks, 1986, pp. 16–17). Thus, educators must: (1) examine their own backgrounds and experiences to determine the values and attitudes they may bring into the classroom and then (2) move toward a realization that "their way" is not the only way (Adams, Pardo, & Schniedewind, 1992).

An information base is a step toward preparing teachers for diversity. Consequently, a first research effort was designed to explore preservice teachers' awareness of their own and others' backgrounds. The objectives were to determine whether preservice teachers lack relevant knowledge and background experience in multicultural settings, perceive a personal and/or professional need for multicultural training, and whether they would be willing to participate in such training (Hadaway & Florez, 1988).

As a means of gathering needed information on preservice teachers' level of preparation for a culturally pluralistic environment, a 14-item questionnaire was administered to 125 preservice teachers who were students in the teacher education program at a large state university. The sample included 68 students seeking secondary certification and 57 seeking elementary certification. Information was collected about specific coursework taken in the area of multicultural issues, individual attitudes toward and previous background experiences in a multicultural setting, the adequacy of their coursework/training, and anticipated future needs as they relate to teaching in a culturally pluralistic environment.

In regard to previous coursework in multicultural education, half of the students had received no specific coursework in multicultural education or perceived that they had not been exposed to multicultural information in their classes. Furthermore, the variety of answers from the remainder of the respondents demonstrated the fragmented nature of multicultural options available to teacher preparation students. Generally, students were left independently to choose courses from social science disciplines, languages, and education. Once enrolled in these courses, students were often expected to make the necessary connections to multiculturalism on their own.

Several of the questionnaire items attempted to elicit information from the respondents concerning their attitudes toward multicultural settings and to determine actual experiences they may have had in culturally pluralistic environments. Overall, students reported few personal experiences in culturally diverse settings. In addition, students noted that the multicultural efforts of the schools they had attended were, at best, fragmented. Perhaps most revealing were students' responses to a question asking what they enjoyed or did not like about a multicultural environment. Although one-third of the students made some positive statements about culturally pluralistic settings (that is, the variety and new perspectives, the chance to learn about one's own as well as another's culture), two-thirds of the students made only statements showing apprehension. These students apprehensively anticipated a difficult time dealing with the many differences, prejudice and discontent, racial friction and communication problems, lack of motivation, students' inadequate background, and more frequent discipline problems. In other words, students were working with some preconceived ideas that a culturally pluralistic setting was a problem environment where children came from lower socioeconomic backgrounds and were unmotivated and difficult to discipline.

Finally, the preservice teachers were asked if they were adequately prepared to teach in a culturally diverse environment. Ninety percent of the future teachers stated that they were ill-equipped to deal with diversity in the classroom. Additionally, they indicated a need for any type of relevant information to help them.

From the results of the survey, these preservice teachers fit the pattern of much of the research (Grant, 1986). Their previous experiences in culturally pluralistic settings are indeed limited. Only one-third had any relevant, long-term interaction with people of diverse social, cultural, or linguistic backgrounds. Moreover, their coursework appeared to be very fragmented, with no set sequence of multicultural courses or any consistent thread of integration of multicultural content discernible in the offerings. Students merely picked from a list of options which varied greatly in quality and quantity of information. However, one fact was clear. These future teachers were aware of the shortcomings of their backgrounds, and they realized they would be working in multicultural environments for which they were inadequately prepared. Thus, they were eager to obtain more training and skills.

STUDY 2: PREPARATION THROUGH COURSEWORK

"Teacher education programs in the United States have not changed as much as they should have in order to accommodate the rapid growth and development of our society and world" (Baker, 1977, p. 71). Historically, teacher preparation institutions have trained educators to work effectively with only one group: middle-class Anglo Americans. Thus, teachers are a product of an ethnocentric curriculum (Banks, 1987; Craft, 1981) which does not prepare them to deal with students who may come not only from different social, economic, linguistic, and cultural backgrounds but also from urban, rural, and even preindustrial cultures. Yet, one of the most essential missions of current teacher education programs is to help preservice as well as in-service teachers develop positive attitudes toward their own culture and the culture of others. "Such cultural consciousness helps [teachers] to value [their] culture without seeing it as normative, and to respect a variety of cultural experiences" (Adams, Pardo, & Schniedewind, 1992, p. 37).

Classroom-based instruction in multicultural issues has been a common method for laying some foundation of cultural awareness. Thus, this second research study examined the impact of multicultural coursework on the preparation of educators. The objectives were to: (1) ascertain the level of sensitivity and cultural awareness of preservice and in-service teachers and administrators upon entry into a multicultural course and (2) determine the impact of multicultural content and activities upon awareness and sensitivity. The Cultural Diversity Awareness Inventory (CDAI) (Henry, 1985), a 28-item self-report questionnaire with a Likert-type scale addressing general cultural awareness, the family, communication, assessment, and multicultural methods and materials, was utilized as the pre- and post-measure.

Three classes at a predominantly non-minority university were selected to participate in the survey: one undergraduate class of preservice elementary certification students (total pretest twenty-seven, posttest twenty-five) and two graduate classes of preservice administrators and in-service teachers/administrators (total pretest twenty-four, posttest nineteen). All participants were administered the CDAI as a pretest at the beginning of the semester and as a posttest at the end of the semester.

Three courses, Foundations of Education in a Multicultural Society, Strategies for Multicultural Teaching, and Educational Administration in Cross-Cultural Environments, served as treatment to raise the sensitivity levels and increase the cultural awareness information for participants. The course content included: (1) in-depth lectures about the historical, philosophical, and social foundations of the education of minority groups (that is, African Americans, Hispanics, Native Americans, and Asian Americans) and (2) cultural awareness activities (that is, researching the history, culture, values, and educational aspects—learning styles and effective teaching strategies—of minority students; role playing; self-disclosure exercises; and analysis of case studies).

Comparison of the results of the pre/posttests indicated the degree to which courses which had emphasized ethnic awareness positively changed the attitudes, beliefs, and values of educators, hopefully enabling them to work more effectively with minority students.

By using factor analysis with a varimax rotation involving 15 statements, four dimensions were formed: (1) sense of responsibility, (2) discomfort with a different culture, (3) accommodation of cultural differences, and (4) adaptation as the child's responsibility. Results of the posttest ($n = 44$) indicated that over two-thirds of the preservice and in-service teachers and administrators felt very strongly that it was the responsibility of educators to provide multicultural experiences for all students in their future or respective educational settings. Furthermore, participants' attitudes and beliefs about making the necessary accommodations for cultural differences increased significantly. Over half the 44 posttest respondents felt that it was not the student's responsibility to make needed adaptations to cultural adjustment in the school environment but rather that of the teacher and the administrator. And, two thirds of the participants indicated that they would institute physical environmental changes such as ethnic displays. However, posttest results continued to reflect much discomfort on the part of preservice and in-service teachers/administrators in working with children of different cultures and relating to minority parents.

Overall, a comparison of the pre/posttest responses demonstrated that multicultural education courses could raise the sensitivity levels and cultural awareness levels of educators through classroom instruction. Such understanding is important since educators who are not sensitive to the needs of minority students may not be aware of cultural conflicts that cause barriers in the learning processes of minority students (Gilbert and Gay, 1985; Gollnick & Chinn, 1986), and these barriers may result in minority students' underachievement. Effective teacher/school research has indicated that teachers/administrators who are successful with minority students possess high levels of sensitivity to the needs of those students (Brookover & Lezotte, 1977; Brookover et al., 1982). These teachers/administrators also possess the necessary cultural awareness knowledge to produce high-achieving minority students. Therefore, educators must be trained not to be threatened by individual differences but to build upon those differences to create a learning environment that is effective for all students, regardless of ethnic identity.

Yet, one course in multicultural education is not the solution. The philosophical concepts and processes of multicultural education must be integrated into the total teacher education program in order to prepare all educators to work effectively with the changing diverse population (Larke, 1990).

STUDY 3: PREPARATION THROUGH MULTICULTURAL INTERACTION

While multicultural coursework integrated into teacher education programs has potential benefits, as noted above, some educators question the actual long-range effects of classroom knowledge (Grant, 1986). In other words, "Is it really possible for colleges of education to influence pre- and in-service teachers to modify the attitudes, behaviors, perceptions, and beliefs of a lifetime in order to prepare those prospective teachers for successful cross cultural interaction in the public school arena?" (Santos, 1986, p. 20). These educators argue that what preservice teachers really need is actual hands-on experiences with cultural pluralism prior to their entry into the real classroom. This is another simplistic view which " . . . holds that if people from different cultural backgrounds interact, cultural understanding will automatically result" (Ozturk, 1992, p. 79). Thus, this final research effort focuses on a program innovation which combines cross-cultural interaction *and* cultural background knowledge for preservice teachers.

The Minority Mentorship Project at Texas A&M (Larke, Wiseman, and Bradley, 1990) was developed as a means of providing early hands-on field experience for elementary certification students. The project linked undergraduate students seeking elementary certification as long-term mentors (a three-year commitment lasting from the sophomore through senior years) with elementary minority students (mentees). The objectives of the project are to: (1) raise sensitivity levels of both participants (mentors and mentees) and (2) to develop instructional skills that are necessary for teachers to work effectively in a pluralistic, diverse society.

The Minority Mentorship Project began in the spring of 1987. Twenty-six elementary certification students were selected to participate in the mentorship program. After volunteers were solicited from undergraduate classes, they were interviewed and selected by a network of community leaders, teachers, and university personnel who volunteered their services for the project. All prospective mentors had completed thirty hours of university coursework, demonstrated a strong commitment to an education career, and possessed a strong desire to work with minority students.

Beginning in the fall of 1987, selected mentors enrolled in the first of six, one-hour seminars (one per semester) planned by a faculty member with expertise in multicultural education. This seminar was designed to broaden the pedagogical knowledge base, sharpen the teaching skills, and modify attitudes, values, and beliefs of elementary certification students who must learn to work effectively with minority students. In addition, the seminars provided supervisory support and guidance, open discussions regarding mentors' responsibilities and concern issues, guest speakers, and educational strategies to help the teacher preparation students meet the needs of the project.

On the other end of the project, the twenty-six minority elementary students (mentees) were nominated by their teachers. Guidelines for student selection included: (1) parental support and approval of the project; (2) willingness of the student to be involved in the project; (3) assessment of intellectual functioning and social/emotional development by teachers and other adults; and (4) self-evaluation by the student.

During the planned six semesters of the project, the mentor and mentee interacted in planned and informal activities. Over the course of the project, these activities included picnics, frequent phone contacts, letter correspondence, attendance at football and basketball games, visits to the college library, and special holiday dinners.

Overall, the basic focus of the program has been the regular tutoring sessions that were initiated during the second semester of the project. Mentors and mentees meet once a week at the mentees' schools and discuss school work or a common project selected by the pair. At this time, educational strategies are stressed and mentors and mentees become acquainted on a more personal basis.

The project has contributed to the decision processes of a few teacher preparation students. Three students have changed majors since beginning the project. One student related her decision directly to involvement in the project, stating that she had no idea what an obligation teaching was. It was the project activities that demonstrated the responsibility to her. Another student remained with the project even though she changed her career focus to journalism, stating that the experience in this project would be of benefit in any career.

Initial qualitative data collected through journals of the mentors show growth in acceptance and understanding of African-American and Hispanic children and their experiences in schools. The attitudes and feelings of both undergraduate students and elementary students have been affected by the interactions, which are guided by university personnel who are experts in multicultural education. Overall, feedback from the project indicates that preservice teachers are willing to learn about cultural differences and feel this learning is important to their careers as teachers.

CONCLUSIONS

From the results of the three research studies, it is apparent that these preservice teachers reflected the findings of other studies. Their previous background in culturally pluralistic settings was limited, and the coursework provided was fragmented. Rather than a multicultural program, they had been exposed to a series of hit-or-miss efforts from various directions. With such an incoherent framework, it would be difficult to prepare and sensitize anyone adequately to interact in the real classroom. However, these future teachers were aware of their limited experiential background and training, and they did want to obtain relevant information and participate in early field experiences with minority children.

The second study demonstrated that a course devoted to multicultural content could indeed raise the sensitivity levels and cultural awareness of educators. This finding reinforced the need to develop more-extensive and well-integrated programs.

Finally, the third research study highlighted the benefits of early hands-on experience in the field. Through mentorships, future teachers worked with minority children and observed firsthand the real-world classroom. Participation at this level helped teacher education students overcome personal barriers and stereotypes in working with the culturally diverse (such as minorities are underachievers, or unmotivated, or have academic problems) and emphasized the myriad of responsibilities involved in teaching.

IMPLICATIONS

University-based teacher education "can do much to help [future teachers] break the bonds of their culture-boundness, enabling them to become multicultural people" (Ozturk, 1992, p. 81). First, universities in collaboration with school district personnel, including in-service teachers *and* beginning teachers, can develop a coherent program of multicultural education. Who knows better the information and skills needed for the culturally pluralistic classroom than beginners who have only recently been confronted with schools' diversity and the gaps in their own background? And, because many school districts are just beginning to feel the impact of demographic shifts, surveys and questionnaires such as the ones used in these studies can be utilized by schools to highlight areas of multicultural staff development for experienced faculty as well.

Realistically, multicultural programs should begin with the schools, not the universities. As children enter the educational system, they should be constantly involved in learning about themselves and others and developing respect and tolerance for diversity. Schools need to move beyond celebrating diversity for a day or a week and truly integrate multicultural education across the curriculum. Well-trained beginning teachers can initiate this reform in the schools.

Finally, universities must create more opportunities for teacher education students to interact in multicultural settings and to try out information they have been provided. Early field experiences with some actual hands-on time is a necessity, although providing realistic experiences can be difficult given the geographic constraints of some universities. Reaching beyond geographic boundaries and linking universities and schools in different cities, states, regions, and countries is an option that can be explored further. Children in the schools could also benefit by such linkages because they need the chance to meet new people and expand their cultural horizons.

In conclusion, we are teaching in the midst of diversity. To be effective, we must move beyond our borders, both physical and emotional ones, and make a firm commitment to multicultural education. Only then will we be able to say that we have begun to prepare teachers and children to succeed in a culturally pluralistic world.

REFERENCES

Adams, B. S., Pardo, W. E., and Schniedewind, N. (1992). Changing the way things are done here. *Educational Leadership, 49,* 37–43.

Baker, G. C. (1977). Multicultural imperatives for curriculum development in teacher education. *Journal of Research and Development in Education, 11,* 70–83.

Banks, J. A. (1986). Multicultural education: Development, paradigms, and goals. In J. A. Banks and J. Lynch (Eds.). *Multicultural education in western societies* (pp. 2–28). New York: Praeger Publishers.

Banks, J. A. (1987). *Teaching strategies for ethnic studies* (4th ed.). Boston: Allyn and Bacon.

Banks, J. A. (1992). Multicultural education: For freedom's sake. *Educational Leadership, 49,* 32–36.

Brookover, W., et al. (1982). *Creating effective schools.* Holmes Beach, FL: Learning Publications.

Brookover, W., and Lezotte, L. (1977). *Changes in school characteristics coincident with changes in student achievement.* College of Urban Development of Michigan State University and Michigan Department of Education.

Craft, M. (Ed.). (1981) *Teaching in a multicultural society: The task for teacher education.* Sussex, England; The Falmer Press.

DeCosta, S. B. (1984). Not all children are Anglo and middle class: A practical beginning for the elementary teacher. *Theory into Practice, 23,* 154–155.

Gilbert, S., and Gay, G. (1985). Improving the success in school of poor Black children. *Phi Delta Kappan,* 133–137.

Gollnick, D. M., and Chinn, P. C. (1986). *Multicultural education in a pluralistic society.* Columbus, OH: Merrill.

Grant, C. A. (1986). Education that is multicultural—Isn't that what we mean? *Journal of Teacher Education, 29,* 45–48.

Grant, C. A. and Sleeter, C. E. (1989). *Turning on learning: Five approaches for multicultural teaching plans for race, class, gender, and disability.* Columbus, OH: Merrill.

Hadaway, N. L. and Florez, V. (1988). Diversity in the classroom: Are our teachers prepared? *Teacher Education and Practice, 4,* 25–30.

Henry, G. (185). *Cultural diversity awareness inventory.* Hampton, VA: Hampton University, Mainstreaming Outreach Project.

Hodgkinson, J. L. (1988). What's ahead for education. In K. Ryan and J. M. Cooper (Eds.), *Kaleidoscope: Readings in education* (5th ed.) (pp. 475–480). Boston: Houghton Mifflin.

Larke, P. J. (1990): Cultural Diversity Awareness Inventory: Assessing the sensitivity of preservice teachers. *Action in Teacher Education, 12,* 23–29.

Larke, P. J., Wiseman, D., and Bradley, C. (1990). The Minority Mentorship Project: Changing the attitudes of preservice teachers for diverse class-rooms. *Action in Teacher Education, 12,* 5–11.

Ozturk, M. (1992). Education for cross-cultural communication. *Educational Leadership, 49,* 79–81.

National Education Association. (1987). *NEA study of the status of public school teachers.* Washington, D. C.: NEA

Quality Education for Minorities Project. (1990). *Education that works: An action plan for the education of minorities.* Cambridge: Massachusetts Institute of Technology.

Santos, S. L. (1986). Promoting intercultural understanding through multi-cultural teacher training. *Action in Teacher Education, 8,* 19–25.

CHAPTER 4

The Micropolitical Context of Teachers' Work

GARY L. ANDERSON
University of New Mexico

JOSEPH J. BLASE
University of Georgia

GARY L. ANDERSON is Assistant Professor of Educational Administration at the University of New Mexico and Director of Latin American Programs in education. His current research interests include the politics of education, critical theory, the school principalship, Latin American education, and teacher, student, and community empowerment.

JOSEPH J. BLASE is Professor of Educational Leadership at the University of Georgia. His research is related to understanding the work lives of teachers. He has investigated teacher stress, relations between personal and professional lives of teachers, and teacher socialization. He has published widely on the micropolitics of teaching.

ABSTRACT

In this chapter the authors, drawing on several qualitative studies, describe the micropolitical context of teachers' work. Because of their different foci, the studies discussed here provide a unique opportunity to explore the micropolitics of teachers as they relate vertically upward to the school and district administration, downward to the students in their classrooms, and horizontally to their colleagues and the communities they serve. Strategies employed by teachers in their interactions with principals, colleagues, parents, and students are described. The chapter describes both the overt manifestations

of school micropolitics and the more subtle, symbolic realm of micropolitics in which power is exercised through various forms of silencing. The
chapter concludes with implications of micropolitical studies for teacher
education.

———————————————

During the last twenty years an impressive and diverse body of work on
teachers and teaching has been produced. In the years since Lortie's (1975)
classic sociological study of teachers, research on teaching has focused on
teacher thinking (Elbaz, 1983), the professional culture of teachers (Rosenholtz
and Kyle, 1984), the school as workplace (Little, 1982), the teacher as agent of
social reproduction (Anyon, 1980), teacher as researcher (Cochran-Smith and
Lytle, 1990), and teachers as leaders (Hart, 1990; Smylie & Brownlee-Conyers,
1991). This research has produced descriptions of teacher life and provided recommendations for improving teaching. Unlike previous research on teaching
which emphasized the teacher as a social actor in the classroom, this more
recent body of work places the teacher within broader organizational and social
contexts. These newer research perspectives, in contrast to viewing the teacher
as a passive implementer of curricula and instructional objectives in the classroom, reflect significantly greater diversity: They call for teacher empowerment in the form of a new understanding of teachers as semiautonomous
professionals in both the classroom and school contexts.

A recent development in teacher research has been to locate teachers
within a complex field of political forces. This research, in moving beyond
traditional and more limited notions of role conflict or teacher burnout, views
the workday life of teachers as an ongoing social construction that takes place
within a political force field, that is, a complex series of micropolitical transac-
tions between the teacher and such groups as students, administrators, colleagues, parents, and community groups. Although role conflict and burnout
may sometimes be the result of the constant management of this force field,
the explanatory power of the micropolitical perspective extends beyond this.
When the school and classroom are understood, at least in part, as a micropolitical construction, notions like cultural diversity, school failure, dropouts,
illiteracy, and innumeracy, as well as effective schools and teacher and student
empowerment can be approached with new eyes.

This chapter summarizes findings and presents data from three micropolitical studies that focused on school principals (Anderson, 1990, 1991), teachers
(Blase, 1987a, 1987b, 1988a, 1988b, 1991) and students (Anderson and Herr,
in press; Herr and Anderson, in press). Anderson described the political force
field of the principal and included data on teacher-principal interaction. Blase
focused on the political force field of teachers and included data on teacher

interactions with principals, students, parents, and other teachers. Anderson and Herr concentrated on the community and institutional forces (including teachers) impacting on the students' identity formation.

All three studies employed qualitative methods. Anderson's (1988, 1990, 1991) was an ethnographic study of two school principals and their schools, one in an affluent suburban school district and the other in an inner-city school. Over a two-year period (1985–87), sixty-six interviews were conducted with principals, teachers, students, and community members; twenty-eight meetings were observed; and over thirty documents were analyzed. The goal of the study was to obtain as many perceptions as possible of selected critical events in order to explicate the process of administrative meaning management.

Blase (1987a, 1987b, 1988a, 1988b, 1991) began with an interview-based case study (1983–86) in which teachers discussed what being "political" meant to them. Specific research questions examined (1) factors that contributed to political changes in teachers throughout their careers, and (2) meanings attached to the politics of interaction with principals, parents, students, and other faculty. As a follow-up to this study, open-ended questionnaires were distributed to full-time public school teachers in one southeastern, one northeastern, and one northwestern state. This part of the study examined the perspectives of 1,200 teachers on the everyday political strategies school principals used to influence them.

Data from the Anderson and Herr (in press) study were part of a larger oral history study whose purpose was to better understand the ways schools funnel student diversity and idiosyncracy into a narrow range of school-approved behavior. The researchers sought a phenomenological understanding of the micropolitics of students' lives in a variety of school settings. Data for this study were gathered from students in six schools stratified by social class—three located in the United States and three in Mexico.

Because of their different foci, the three studies discussed here provide a unique opportunity to explore the micropolitics of teachers as they relate vertically upward to the school and district administration, downward to the students in their classrooms, and horizontally to their colleagues and the communities they serve.

THE MICROPOLITICAL PERSPECTIVE

Traditionally, the study of the politics of education has been about conflict over vested interests, ideological commitments, and material resources. Studies of these conflicts have tended to focus on state and federal legislatures, school boards, unions, special-interest groups, and administrators. More recently, attention in education has turned to organizational politics or "micropolitics." To some, micropolitics refers to the less visible, behind the scenes negotiations of power; what Hoyle (1982) calls "the dark side of organizational life" in schools and school districts. (p. 87) In contrast, Blase (1991) has constructed a more inclusive definition of micropolitics that incorporates most of the factors discussed in the professional literature:

> *Micropolitics* refers to the use of formal and informal power by individuals and groups to achieve their goals in organizations. In large part, political actions result from perceived differences between individuals and groups, coupled with the motivation to use power to influence and/or protect. Although such actions are consciously motivated, any action, consciously or unconsciously motivated, may have political significance in a given situation. Both cooperation and conflictive actions and processes are part of the realm of micropolitics. Moreover, macro- and micropolitical factors frequently interact. (p. 11)

In addition, Anderson (1991), writing from a critical theory perspective, views micropolitics as a political struggle over the definition of the school and its social purposes. For the schools' clients, micropolitics may also form a context for their own identity formation. In this view, micropolitics is a form of meaning management or what Anderson calls "cognitive politics," in which the management of organizational and social meaning is at stake, and often takes place unobtrusively and out of the awareness of social actors.

THE POLITICAL FORCE FIELD OF THE TEACHER

TEACHER-ADMINISTRATOR POLITICS

One common theme across the studies mentioned above relates to teachers' sense of vulnerability and how this affects the development of a conservative—that is, reactive—everyday political work perspective. According to Blase (1988b), such conservatism relies on the use of reactive political strategies by teachers that grow out of a strong need for self-protection. Underlying this conservatism is the recognition by teachers that they work in a "fishbowl," that their actions are incessantly scrutinized by others, and that disagreements with others frequently produce conflict. Although most teachers tend to develop a conservative political orientation, this process is more evident with those who work with "closed" principals than with "open" principals.

Closed principals exhibit such characteristics as authoritarianism, inaccessibility, inflexibility, and conflict avoidance. With such principals, teachers typically acquiesce to their demands and those of parents, conform to the formal policies and informal norms of the school, and ingratiate themselves by saying what is expected despite their true thinking.

Open principals are viewed as nonmanipulative, participatory, collegial, informal, accessible, and supportive. With these principals, Blase (1988a) found that diplomacy is the political strategy of choice for teachers. Diplomacy is more proactive than acquiesence, conformity, and ingratiation and is used with both open principals and "reasonable" parents. Diplomatic tactics include tactfulness, politeness, friendliness, positiveness, and empathy for others. Diplomacy also reflects an attempt at honest communication with principals as the following teacher comments illustrate:

> You always approach him with concrete ideas yet leave room for his interpretation and input too.

> Sometimes I tell him what I think we should do and let him respond . . . but usually I ask questions, "What do you think of this idea?" . . . let him respond or choose.

Often, however, teachers reported using more indirect and subtle approaches:

> When he came by, I showed him the poor equipment . . . but I didn't say anything else, not yet.

> I'll use informal social contact to hint about my concerns.

TEACHER-PARENT POLITICS

Although the school principal is a key figure in the teacher's political force field, Blase (1987a) argues that no less important is the influence of their students' parents. Teachers' political orientation toward parents is seen to vary in relation to whether parents are considered supportive (for example, "They listen and want to help") or unsupportive (for example, "Many are unreasonable . . . irrational). The overall pattern he observed in the data indicates that teachers' everyday political orientation tends to be diplomatic: It is conservative, cautious, and pragmatic. This orientation is developed to protect the teacher from parental criticism and to create opportunities to influence parents on substantive issues. Sources of potential conflict with parents are the teaching of values, student discipline, student performance, extracurricular involvement, and the teachers' personal lives. As one teacher put it:

College does absolutely nothing to prepare you for the kind of public figure you are going to end up being. The community has a stereotype of teachers . . . they must act within certain boundaries of behavior . . . . Politically, you have to define the way you come across to people within the constraints of their stereotypes . . . . Let's say I was an atheist, this is something I could not go around and advertise.

Teachers develop defensive strategies with parents. For example, at conferences teachers are careful about what they tell parents about their child. Cases are built on the basis of fact ("You're careful about not judging . . . . You don't state suspicions that he's on drugs or something"). The facts are presented to parents in an oblique and often low-key manner:

Knowing the kinds of things that people react to, I wouldn't say your kid's lazy and never does anything. I'd say, well, I'm having a problem motivating him . . . to do his homework; I'm owning the problem.

In meetings with parents, teachers control their emotions ("You can't be frank with most parents"); they strive to present an image of an objective, nonjudgmental professional.

INTRAFACULTY POLITICS

Besides the micropolitics of teacher-parent interactions, there is also the micropolitics that exists among teachers. According to Blase's (1987b) work, intrafaculty politics are characterized by teachers as positive and negative. Positive collegial relations are associated with the strategy of diplomacy described above. The overriding consequence of interpersonal diplomacy is the development of a sociocultural context consistent with norms of reciprocation (Gouldner, 1966). In other words, this form of politics is consistent with the norms of equitable exchange and mutual benefit. Diplomacy in this sense means knowing when to "bite your tongue" and not lose your temper. Teachers conform to norms of conventional politeness, which help reduce the possible deleterious effects generated by negative feelings and differences in values and goals among teachers. Politeness norms are seen as enhancing rapport among teachers and appear to increase the stability, predictability, and longevity of working relationships among them ("There are so many problems that crop up. We can really make life miserable for each other.")

Another positive aspect of politics centers on intrafaculty support (Blase, 1987b). Support involves sharing materials, helping colleagues by covering classes and study halls, recognizing colleagues for their successes and accomplishments, empathizing with fellow teachers, offering advice, and "blowing off steam" with each other.

Negative aspects of intrafaculty politics are associated with self-serving purposes and behavior of teachers defined as "offensive" by others. Examples of such behavior include ingratiation, confrontation, and passive-aggressive political action. Blase's (1987b) data suggest that actions of this type disrupt the school and reduce intrafaculty cohesion. Lower levels of trust, support, friendliness, and morale, as well as increases in conflict and alienation, are linked to negative political actions.

Although teachers view such actions as having adverse consequences, they believe that these actions are, at times, important for protection and influence purposes. Specifically, negative political actions among teachers were promoted by:

- **ingratiation:** "Sucking up to the committee chairman."
- **flaunting:** "She makes sure everybody knows what she's done."
- **spying:** "There are ways of providing information to the administration . . ."
- **criticalness:** "Teachers who put you down to look good."
- **aggressiveness:** "They're belligerent and overbearing."
- **lack of involvement:** "There is little concern . . . the paycheck is their goal."
- **self-centeredness:** "He will talk about himself . . . no interest in anyone else."
- **nonsupportiveness:** "Some teachers aren't willing to help . . ."
- **incompetence:** "Can't control the kids, or teach for that matter."
- **aloofness:** "You only associate with certain colleagues . . ."

The following quote illustrates that intrafaculty politics sometimes overlaps teacher-administrator politics and can be used for purposes of influence.

> I have identified two teachers to whom my principal listens. I try to influence him through them by expressing my opinions in their presence. I don't ask them openly to intercede, but rather attempt to get them to take a particular stance themselves in the hopes they will relate to the principal an opinion approximately my own. (A Secondary School Teacher)

TEACHER-STUDENT POLITICS

With regard to students, Blase (1991) also found that teachers construct a political orientation for purposes of influence and protection. Influence considerations are grounded in such factors as the student's idiosyncratic nature and the responsibility of convincing students of the importance of academic work. A protectionist stance is created largely because of teachers' sense of vulnerability to criticism from students and their parents. Nonsupportive administrators, information distortion, and a general lack of adequate authority on the teachers' part contribute to this aspect of their political orientation. Influence and protectionist considerations evolve from problems related to instruction, discipline, and extracurricular activities, as well as personal factors.

THE MICROPOLITICS OF SILENCE AND LEGITIMATION

Every teacher knows that some topics of discussion are "off limits," at least in public forums. During interviews with teachers, Anderson (1991) found that there were often occasions when teachers would ask that the tape recorder be turned off or that a comment be held in confidence. In many schools there is an eerie silence around certain issues. Fine (1991) has documented ways that school policies and practices often silence student and teacher voices so as to smooth over social and economic contradictions. For example, in the high school she studied, she found a structural fear of *naming*.

> Naming involves those practices that facilitate critical conversation about social and economic arrangements, particularly about inequitable distributions of power and resources by which poor and minority students and their kin suffer disproportionately. The practices of administration, the relationships between school and community, and the forms of pedagogy and curriculum applied were all scarred by the fear of naming, provoking the move to silence (Fine, 1991, p. 34)

McNell (1988) has also documented the ways teachers censure themselves in response to this fear of naming. This silencing of teachers derives not only from power relations within the school and community, but also from their role-related need to legitimize the institution of schooling as a fair and meritocratic enterprise despite daily evidence to the contrary. In addition to the set of teacher political strategies described above are the subtle and powerful forms of unobtrusive ideological control (Tompkins and Cheney, 1985)—what Anderson (1991) calls "cognitive politics"—that are exerted on teachers. Cognitive politics has to do with issues such as what can and cannot be named in a school, the use of euphemistic language (students in magnet schools are "de-selected," not expelled), and how teacher culture is "managed" within a school or school district.

For instance, in an affluent, largely white, suburban school district studied by Anderson (1991), the superintendent cultivates a harmonious philosophy and hires administrators and teachers who personify it. Staffs in this district are referred to as "teams" or "families"; arguments are considered "conversations" or "interactions"; problems are defined as "challenges" or "growth experiences." Optimism, workaholism, and harmonious relations are rewarded. Teachers and administrators also use the vocabulary of psychological typing. For example, the district's teachers and administration were largely "amiables" or "expressives." Being an accepted member of this school district means learning to use the vocabulary of harmony and consensus.

Anderson (1991) suggested that the administrative agenda is to construct a reality in which conflicts of interest are largely absent and in which the status quo (a white, affluent suburb located a twenty-minutes' drive from the squalor of an all-black inner-city neighborhood) is seen as nonproblematic. Within the district and the society at large, most principals and teachers are aware that such a harmonious reality is an illusion. A major part of the teacher and administrator's job, however, is to manage the legitimacy of a harmonious and nonproblematic definition of the district's social reality and the language out of which it is constructed. Teachers who are too outspoken are not fired; rather they are dealt with through cognitive politics: They are labeled as "negative" and marginalized from the centers of power until they learn the culture and either conform or leave on their own.

Anderson (1991) also learned that cognitive politics occurs between teachers and students. Students construct their identities, in part, within the context of school and classroom micropolitics. Drawing on the work of the Russian philosopher of language, Mikhail Bakhtin, Quantz and O'Connor (1988) suggest how voices are silenced within the micropolitics of schools and classrooms:

> In trying to understand human behavior, we must be cognizant that some voices are legitimated by the community and, therefore, vocalized, while others are nonlegitimated and, therefore, unspoken . . . . Thus, as the multiple voices within the individual and within the community struggle to control the direction of the acceptable dialogue, ideological expressions may be reinforced, reinterpreted, or rejected . . . (pp. 98–99)

As students and teachers silence those inner voices that are not legitimated by the educational institution, diversity of thought becomes less common and conformity to the school's socially organized ideology is achieved. Anderson and Herr (in press) have found that teachers often fail to legitimate discourse relating to issues of diversity and inequality based on race, class, gender, or sexual orientation, except when such issues are dealt with abstractly, that is, not related to the students' own lives in their own schools and classrooms. When students find that they are invisible and that their voices are not legitimated in school, their voices often go underground and become manifested in student subcultures and in student acting-out behavior.

The following quote from "Victor," a Hispanic student in an advanced Spanish class, is typical of the micropolitics of voice. In this case the central issue is ethnicity (Herr and Anderson, in press).

> . . . . And having a Hispanic teacher . . . I really don't get along with Señora Hernandez—she's a good person, don't get me wrong; she's a really good person, but I kind of felt uncomfortable with her . . . . What I do is, I switch. I go to school, I'm school (Anglo). Then I switch. I go home with the neighborhood kids and I, then I switch to Hispanic and then I'll turn around to being an Anglo . . . . It's like Dr. Jekyll and Mr. Hyde. I kind of didn't like being put in that situation because who was I, Dr. Jekyll or Mr. Hyde, you know? And I had to be Victor (in Señora Hernandez' class), and that's kind of hard for me to do, being Victor, just being the person I was. (A Hispanic student in a largely Anglo private school explaining why he is a "discipline problem" in Ms. Hernandez' class).

Victor's Hispanic teacher is a reminder to him of his ethnic dilemma. Because dialogue about being Hispanic in an Anglo school is not legitimated, Victor's private dilemma is acted out in anti-social ways.

SUMMARY AND IMPLICATIONS FOR TEACHER EDUCATION

Micropolitics is about power—who has it, who wants it and for what purpose, and how it is used to achieve individual and group goals. The studies described in this chapter emphasize that teachers are at the center of a complex political force field; politics forms the very context in which they work. This political force field may be subtle, as in the case of unobtrusive forms of control, or it may be overt and strategic, as when teachers actively calculate the outcomes of political activity. It may involve defensiveness or resistance to authoritarian and hierarchical forms of power, or it may result in coalitions in which power becomes "power with" and is characterized by mutuality and synergy (Dunlap and Goldman, 1991)

Although politics is pervasive in schools, few teachers enter their first year of teaching prepared to deal with the deeply political nature of their jobs. It is often a source of great disappointment to new teachers to discover that the actions and decisions of administrators and teachers may have more to do with conflict and bargaining over vested interests than with the needs of children. Like many of the subjective aspects of school life, the politics of the workplace is generally considered unworthy of systematic treatment in teacher preparation programs.

We strongly believe that prospective teachers must be prepared for the micropolitics of schools and classrooms, not by instilling a cynical or Machiavellian approach to the workplace, but by providing them with a political lens through which to better understand and act in the school setting. If teachers are to be advocates for children, they must be able to promote decisions and policies that will be beneficial for all children. This advocacy role, whether it takes place in the classroom, the school, the union, the district, or society at large, requires a reflective stance toward the political realities of education.

Providing teachers with such a perspective means broadening the focus of teacher preparation from the classroom to organizational and social issues that ultimately impact their teaching. Schon (1987) and others have called for replacing approaches to practitioner preparation based on "technical rationality" with approaches based on "reflective practice." A reflective approach requires a broadening of what teacher educators define as their knowledge base. An emphasis which includes political aspects of organizational life moves us away from a science of teaching and closer to teaching as a social practice. We believe that if new teachers are prepared to view themselves as political actors, it is less likely that they will accommodate to and eventually accept the status quo or, at the other extreme, give in to despair and cynicism.

A political lens on school life is particularly relevant to issues of diversity. Just as Victor discovered the ethnic politics of being a student, teachers discover that in every school there is a politics of gender, race, class, and sexual preference. The micropolitical literature on teacher diversity is extremely sparse. Accounts are needed of what it is like to be a lesbian or gay teacher, a middle-class teacher in a poor school, a middle-class teacher in an affluent private school, an Anglo teacher in a school attended by Hispanics. The possibilities are endless, and each set of micropolitics impacts the quality of the relationships teachers build with each other and their various constituencies. Since the quality of these relationships indirectly influences student development, we believe it is our responsibility to understand them better and to help new teachers thrive in the diverse school settings they will encounter.

REFERENCES

Anderson, G. L. (1988, April). *The management of meaning and the achievement of organizational legitimacy: A critical ethnography of school administrators*. Paper presented at the Annual Meeting of the American Educational Research Association, Boston.

Anderson, G. L. (1990). Toward a critical constructivist approach to school administration: Invisibility, legitimation, and the study of non-events. *Educational Administration Quarterly*, 26(1), 38–59.

Anderson, G. L. (1991). Cognitive politics of principals and teachers: Ideological control in an elementary school. In J. Blase (Ed.) *The politics of life in schools: Power, conflict, and cooperation* (pp. 120–138) Newbury Park: Sage.

Anderson, G. L. and Herr, K. (in press). The micropolitics of student voice: Moving from diversity of bodies to diversity of voices. In C. Marshall and P. Zodhiates (Eds.) *New politics of race and gender: The 1992 yearbook of the politics of education association*. New York Falmer.

Anyon, J. (1980). Social class and the hidden curriculum of work. *Journal of Education*, 161, 67–72.

Blase, J. (1987a). The politics of teaching: The teacher-parent relationship and the dynamics of diplomacy. *Journal of Teacher Education*, 38(2), 53–60.

Blase, J. (1987b). Political interactions among teachers: Sociocultural context in the schools. *Urban Education*, 22(3), 286–309.

Blase, J. (1988a). The teachers' political orientation vis-a-vis the principal: The micropolitics of the school. In J. Hannaway and R. Crownon (Eds.), *The politics of reforming school administration: The 1988 yearbook of the politics of education association* (pp. 113–126) New York: Falmer.

Blase, J. (1988b). The everyday political perspective of teachers: Vulnerability and conservatism. *International Journal of Qualitative Studies in Education*, 1(2), 125–142.

Blase, J. (1991). Everyday political perspectives of teachers toward students: The dynamics of diplomacy. In J. Blase (Ed.) *The politics of life in schools: Power, conflict, and cooperation* (pp. 185–206) Newbury Park: Sage.

Cochran-Smith, M. and Lytle, S. (1990). Research on teaching and teacher research: The issues that divide. *Educational Researcher*, 19(2), 2–11.

Dunlap, D. and Goldman, P. (1991). Rethinking power in schools. *Educational Administration Quarterly*, 27, 5–29.

Elbaz, F. (1983). *Teacher thinking: A study of practical knowledge*. London: Croom Helm.

Fine, M. (1991). *Framing dropouts: Notes on the politics of an urban public high school*. New York: SUNY Press.

Gouldner, A. (1966). The norm of reciprocity: A preliminary statement. In B. J. Biddle and E. J. Thomas (Eds.) *Role theory concepts and research*. New York: Wiley.

Hart, A. (1990). Impacts of the school social unit on teacher authority. *Educational Administration Quarterly*, 27(3), 503–532.

Herr, K. and Anderson, G. (in press). Oral history for student empowerment: Capturing student's inner voices. *International Journal of Qualitative Studies in Education*.

Hoyle, E. (1986). *The Politics of School Management*. London: Hodder and Stroughton.

Little, J. W. (1982). Norms of collegiality and experimentation: Workplace conditions of school success. *American Educational Research Journal*, 19(3), 325–340.

Lortie, D. (1975). *Schoolteacher*. Chicago: University of Chicago Press.

McNeil, L. M. (1988). *Contradictions of control: School structure and school knowledge*. New York: Routledge.

Quantz, R. and O'Connor, T. (1988). Writing critical ethnography: Dialogue, multivoicedness, and carnival in cultural texts. *Educational Theory*, 38, 95–109.

Rosenholtz, S. J. and Kyle, S. (Winter 1984) Teacher isolation: Barrier to professionalism. *American Educator*, 10–15.

Schon, D. (1987). *Educating the reflective practitioner*. San Francisco: Jossey-Bass.

Smylie, M.A. and Brownlee-Conyers, J. (1991, April). *Teacher leaders and their principals: Exploring new relationships from a micropolitical perspective*. The annual meeting of the American Educational Research Association, Chicago.

Tompkins, P. K. and Cheney, G. (1985). Communication and unobtrusive control in contemporary organizations. In R. D. McPhee and P. K. Tompkins (Eds.) *Organizational communication: Traditional themes and new directions* (pp. 179–210) Beverly Hills: Sage.

Contexts: Implications and Reflections

Martin Haberman

APPLICATIONS

In "Reflections of Urban Education: A Tale of Three Cities," Suzanne Pasch, Marvin Pasch, Robbie Johnson, Steven Ilmer, JoAnn Snyder, Ella Stapleton, Awila Hamilton, and Paul Mooradian describe the factors that experienced urban teachers identify as critical to teaching success. It is noteworthy that the data in their report are similar for all three cities. Part of the explanation might be that African Americans are the dominant minority in all three sites. My feeling is that their results would hold up across the country since the dominant factor is poverty and the issues that arise from underfunded schooling for children in poverty.

These writers organize their data by themes and subthemes. The pattern thus revealed indicates that practicing urban teachers regard teaching skills, personal traits, an ability to deal with learner needs, and society/home/community/culture as the four most frequent explanations of urban teachers' success.

The components of the first theme, teaching skills, are clearly learned skills. Some maintain these skills can be taught in undergraduate preservice programs. Others maintain they are learned only by actually teaching. But all (reasonable people) would agree there is a critically important body of such skills which can and must be learned to function as an effective teacher.

The other dominant themes seem to me to be much more reflective of the teacher as a person and as an individual committed to a particular ideology. Personal traits (empathetic, open-minded, positive, dedicated, patient, loving, flexible, and self-confident) are much more likely to be developed in places other than university classes. Indeed, the obvious implication, for me, is that if these traits are truly crucial, then selection is far more important than training. It is clearly easier to recruit and select people who begin with such predispositions than to struggle trying to change candidates who lack these attributes or manifest their opposites, that is, egocentric, close-minded, negative, uncommitted, nervous, uncaring, inflexible, and fearful.

The theme of "learner needs and characteristics" also does not seem ideally suited to university study and coursework. This theme does not seem to reflect either learning the skills of teaching or reflecting the personal predispositions of effective teachers. It seems to refer to a system of beliefs—a series of commitments. Believing that all children can learn, being committed to knowing children—particularly urban children—and enjoying, caring, and respecting them, seems to transcend teacher training. Again, the issue might be raised that if this theme actually does represent an ideology and not simply knowing concepts regarding ethnic diversity or the content of federal equity statutes, then selection of future teachers might be more important than training.

Similarly, the fourth most frequent theme relates to society/home/community/culture. The need to know the community refers to more than cognition about the neighborhood. It refers to *wanting* to know, valuing and respecting the knowledge sufficiently to use it in teaching children. Teachers cannot and do not connect new knowledge to children's backgrounds unless they value those backgrounds. We can all think of ways future teachers might learn about Black writers or how to speak some Spanish. How do we teach teachers to see value in these subjects and to seek ways of making meaningful connections between the curriculum and the children's cultures? Teachers' *comfort* with diversity—not their cognitive knowledge about diversity—is the essence of this theme. The single most dominant theme I have observed among white, middle-class preservice students regarding ethnic diversity is fear, such as, "Will I be able to control the class?" To achieve this theme, "Comfort with Diversity," more is required than is common now in current forms of preservice teacher education.

In sum, when we examine and think about the four dominant themes, only the first (pedagogy or teaching skills) is clearly a set of learned behaviors. The other three themes predominantly reflect the personality, ideology, and commitments of the teachers. Indeed, I would argue that even in the area of pedagogy, the great emphasis on discipline, communication, and multiple strategies reflects the ongoing struggle of majority teachers to come to terms with themselves as they try to teach children in poverty. "A Tale of Three Cities" is a genuine contribution to the literature!

McDiarmid and Price in "Preparing Teachers for Diversity: A Study of Student Teachers in a Multicultural Program" evaluate the impact of a three-day workshop on student teachers' beliefs about learners labeled "high" and "low" ability, the use of stereotypes, and providing equal opportunities for learning challenging subject matter. Not surprisingly, the lifelong beliefs of students are not readily changed by workshops or courses or even direct experiences. McDiarmid and Price point to the dynamic that confounds most of those engaged in this effort. "The greatest paradox . . . is that students are exposed to increasing amounts of information about children who are culturally different from themselves yet the proportion of those who subsequently recognize and reject stereotypes does not increase—*and may even decrease*." (Italics have been added.)

Following the same fruitless path to a grander dead end, we have offered seven weeks of direct experiences and had field-experience students work with minority children in poverty in urban summer schools. There was no positive change in their perceptions of children, parents, schools, or neighborhoods (Haberman and Post, 1992). We concluded that not enough time had been spent with preservice students on an individual and group basis, debriefing them regarding their interpretations of their observations. My conclusion is that *people perceive what they believe* and that without constant (daily) debriefing they merely use their direct experiences to reinforce what they already believe. Christine Sleeter has done pioneering work on this dynamic. She has studied how white teachers construct race (Sleeter, 1992a) and how they resist racial awareness (Sleeter, 1992b). Essentially, Sleeter's data indicate that teachers "fit" new experiences into the constructs they already hold. Rather than be shaped or changed by new ideas, they merely place new experiences and knowledge into the system they already have. Sleeter's work is worthy of careful analysis since it represents a more extensive, personalized, year-long effort to affect teachers' perceptions.

McDiarmid and Price remain committed to improving preservice teacher education and recommend that teacher education program elements be reconsidered, that there be an increase in discourse, and that more data be collected. My reaction here is similar to the one generated by the Pasch et al. data. It might be that selection is a more fruitful means of changing future teachers' perceptions than the search for more powerful program elements.

The contribution of N. L. Hadaway, V. Florez, P. J. Larke, and D. Wiseman, "Teaching in the Midst of Diversity—How Do We Prepare?" jumps into the middle of this controversy, that is, fragmented and limited change among students. There is a note of realism sounded as the writers call for multicultural program elements to begin in public schools, not universities. The authors present some evidence that early hands-on experience in the field will help preservice students overcome stereotypes and personal barriers to working in culturally diverse situations. It is reassuring to read about the success of this effort. It is important not only to cite it but to bear it in mind since it is clearly counter to the bulk of the evidence, which argues for the difficulty (impossibility?) of changing deep-seated perceptions. The Hadaway et al. study recommends that preservice teachers work on this issue with in-service teachers. Again, this is a positive, hopeful note which should be kept in mind and replicated. This will have to be done carefully since most urban teachers hold negative views of children, which they are most willing to share with neophytes. Estimates of the percentage of urban teachers who blame the victim, the victim's family or lack thereof, and the victim's neighborhood run as high as 90 percent in several of the major urban school districts. Simply placing neophytes with experienced teachers may not be any more salutary than simply providing more direct experiences for them to *selectively* perceive. Once the issue of choosing and carefully selecting only the best in-service mentors and coaches is raised, the problem of numbers rears its ugly head. Would schools of education be willing to limit their enrollments to the number of in-service coaches who are genuine models of multicultural teaching and who seek to secure equity for all? The numbers might drop dramatically.

G. L. Anderson and J. J. Blase in "The Micropolitical Context of Teachers' Work" set the context in which all of this change (and nonchange) will occur. They delimit some of the power relationships in which teachers will find themselves. They outline the press of the school bureaucracy as well as the political forces which control the school setting—local and federal. Their call for including this vital form of knowledge in the base of teacher preparation is clear and most appropriate. (John Dewey advocated the formation of teachers' unions in 1918 for many of the same reasons. He also advised that future teachers participate in out-of-class and out-of-school activities as an integral part of their teacher preparation.) The Anderson and Blase piece raises the same fundamental question as the three preceding studies. How can future teachers' perceptions, ideology, and commitments be changed and expanded? More courses? More direct experiences? In either case, who would be the teacher and what would be the curriculum? And from my point of view, perhaps selecting people predisposed to accept and function in a broader teacher role to begin with is a more fruitful way to proceed than to admit individuals who are fearful or apolitical and then seek ways of changing them.

These four studies are a useful contribution to the literature. They provide a basis for considering the context in which preparing teachers for children in poverty must occur. While they do not cover the range of issues, they do not pretend to do so. I believe the basic issue is poverty and the discrepancy between the cultures of most teachers and children. Bridging this gap is the challenge faced by traditional teacher education as well as by new forms of teacher education. My expectation is that the problem will worsen as the number of children in poverty grows and the need for more effective, culturally diverse urban teachers continues to increase. The likelihood of a child born this year being on welfare sometime between birth and age eighteen is one in three for whites and four out of five for blacks. The number of education faculty who have had three or more years of experience actually teaching in urban schools continues to be less than 1 percent. *Can education faculty teach what they don't know?* The source of the craft portion of the knowledge base for successful urban teachers is other successful teachers.

Following are some of the principles which guide the day-to-day teaching of effective urban teachers. The question of how to prepare (or to simply select) culturally aware, sensitive individuals to operate on these principles is still to be resolved.

STARS' PRINCIPLES OF LEARNING

1. The children can always learn more. What it comes down to is the teacher's effort and energy.
2. The notion that a teacher can predict how much a child can learn of a particular subject matter is dangerous nonsense.
3. Providing children the opportunity for fresh, novel, stimulating experiences is an extremely powerful incentive to learn.
4. Children will throw themselves wholeheartedly into projects when they have truly participated in selecting and planning the enterprise.
5. Children try hardest when they are fairly certain of success but not absolutely positive.
6. Children learn most from teachers who believe that effort, rather than ability, predicts achievement.
7. Responding to external rewards will take children only so far. The rewards which lead to lifelong learning are those one gives oneself.
8. Nonjudgmental coaching elicits learning; constant criticism stamps it out.
9. Children learn most when their honest questions are connected with the great ideas (key concepts) of particular subject matters.
10. Threats and punishments, constant teacher direction, or repeated failure lead children to demonstrate (a) apathy, (b) defiance, (c) hostility toward others, and (d) self-depreciation.

These principles of learning do not add up to a theory. Some can be supported by research, others are supported by the cumulated craft wisdom of star teachers. What these principles represent are a set of guidelines to which stars conform their teaching behaviors. More than anything else, these principles represent a set of beliefs that have come to characterize the constituency I refer to as star teachers. This ideology serves as both the guide to their behavior *and* at the same time reveals stars' assumptions about the nature of the learner, the nature of learning in school, and the nature of teaching.

REFERENCES

M. Haberman and Linda Post (1992). Does direct experience change education students' perceptions of low-income minority children? *The Midwestern Educational Researcher*, Spring, 1992.

C. E. Sleeter (1992a). "How white teachers construct race" in C. McCarthy and W. Crichlow (eds.). *Race, Identity and Representation*, New York: Routledge.

C. E. Sleeter (1992b). Resisting racial awareness: How teachers understand the social order from their racial, gender, and social class locations. *Educational Foundations*. (In press)

DIVISION II

Diverse Processes in Studying Teaching

Processes: Overview and Framework

LESLIE HULING-AUSTIN
Southwest Texas State University

AND

W. ROBERT HOUSTON
University of Houston

LESLIE HULING-AUSTIN is Professor of Secondary Education at Southwest Texas State University, where she also directs the LBJ Institute for the Improvement of Teaching and Learning. Her primary research interests include teacher induction and mentoring, the change process in teacher education, and the recruitment and retention of minority teachers.

W. ROBERT HOUSTON is Professor and Associate Dean for Academic Affairs, College of Education, University of Houston. He has authored or co-authored 38 books, and has worked with schools, state departments, and universities in 42 states and 17 foreign countries. He was president of Association of Teacher Educators in 1985-86 and was editor of the *Handbook of Research on Teacher Education*, which was published by Macmillan in 1990.

INTRODUCTION

The processes of instruction and analysis are intractably intertwined. Not only do effective professionals engage in instructional processes, but they derive practice from analysis and reflection. As the educational enterprise has become more complex, reflection and research methodology have become more complex, sophisticated, relevant, and central to improved instruction.

CHANGE AND COMPLEXITY

Educational systems of twenty-five years ago are no longer appropriate. They are based on assumptions, cultures, and technologies that are no longer relevant. The simple life and dedicated, though often ineffective, teaching were the hallmarks of a past era.

Diversity in students is matched by diversity of curricula, diversity of instructional methods, diversity of educational goals, and diversity in ways to evaluate the quality of schooling and the achievements of students. Yet with increased complexity and diversity, educators have often resisted implementing the changes needed to remain relevant. The present is comfortable in its tangibility, so much so that it often is invisible to those involved. Only in retrospect or the mirrored vision of an external source is it revealed.

In a period of rapidly accelerating change, the future becomes increasingly unpredictable. The two conflicting goals of stability and change have dominated the history of human thought. Parmenides and Heraclitus, predecessors of the Greek philosopher Socrates, were prototypes of these divergent approaches to reality. For Parmenides, *stability* was the one reality, continuous and changeless; change in the form of creation was inherently contradictory and illusory. For Heraclitus, the striving of opposites and consequent *change* was the only reality and stability was illusory, expressed in the quotation, "One cannot step twice in the same river."

Society has changed rapidly in the past twenty-five years, and so too has technology. International competition has increased rapidly, nations have splintered (for example, the Soviet Union) while others have sought strength in unity (for example, the European Common Market). Events of half a world away are not only instantly visible on American television, but impact our stock market, political systems, and social mores.

These cultural frameworks influence instruction and analysis. They provide the often invisible canvas upon which teachers ply their profession. To analyze effectively the processes used by veterans and prospective teachers requires multiple measures, improved instruments, and broadened perspective of the process and its outcomes. Figure PII–1 illustrates this complexity.

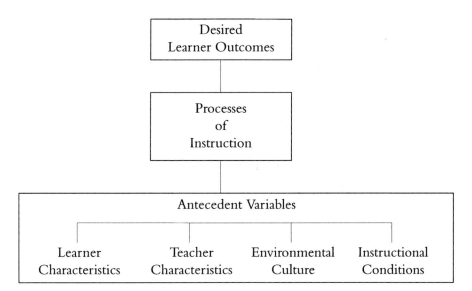

FIGURE PII-1
Complexity of Instructional Variables

The *processes of instruction* are designed to promote the desired outcome variables and, in the complex interaction of multiple variables and multiple indicators, become even more complicated.

Antecedent variables, according to Yarger and Smith (1990) are "conditions and variables that affect teacher education, that, while not directly related to process, influence, guide, and even direct that process" (p. 27). For descriptive purposes, we have identified four classes of antecedent variables: learner characteristics, teacher characteristics, environmental culture, and instructional conditions.

The diversity that is America is often reflected in the *characteristics of learners*. Students vary widely in their intellectual achievements; size, stature, and dexterity; motivation and interest; and experiences. So too do *teachers* differ. Not only do they vary in their personal characteristics, but also in their professional characteristics (knowledge base, skills, and compatibility with the community culture) that lend themselves to differing instructional processes.

The *environmental culture* of the school and community influences the processes in the classroom. Culture and ethnicity influence the thoughts and values of students and teachers, the experiences considered relevant by parents and community. Legislative context and the autonomy of the school or university from external influences, accreditation, and other nonlocal sources are important conditions that affect instruction. Whether a state mandates a particular test, its content, and whether the results are made public are strong conditions that affect school processes.

Instructional factors include the extensiveness of resources such as videotape players, computers, instructional supplies, and materials. Also included are their availability and accessibility. Computers located in the classroom are more readily integrated into instruction than those that are in a laboratory and accessible only at certain scheduled periods, or that must be reserved in advance. But instructional conditions are broader than instructional resources. They include the climate in the school, interactions with the principal and other teachers, extent of collegiality and experimentation, attitudes toward taking risks and changing processes, emphasis on diversity in teaching or demonstration of standard instructional processes, extent to which excellence is rewarded and recognized, and the positive or negative valance of the school culture.

BROADENED CONCEPTUALIZATION OF DIVERSITY OF PROCESSES

Figure PII–1 illustrates the interactive nature of antecedent factors and desired learner outcomes with the processes of instruction. Shifting the emphasis in one area changes the others. But considering the effectiveness of processes in teacher education requires the consideration of several other factors. In mapping the domains to be considered in such analyses, eight areas should be considered.

1. *Purpose* (for example, for research, program evaluation, individual teacher self-analysis, teacher assistance by a peer or mentor, or assessment to maintain employment status). The purpose of the analysis and the primary user of its results influence the processes, as is shown in Figure PII–2.

Primary User	Primary Use
Teachers	Improve own practice
Administrators	Evaluate teacher practice
Teacher Educators	Improve preservice and inservice education; assess trainee practice
Decision Makers	Policy at local, state, and national levels
General Public	School appraisal

FIGURE PII–2
Purpose of Evaluation Depends upon User

2. *Content* (for example, knowledge of content or instruction; skills of teaching; performance in teaching; outcome variables such as student achievement, dropout rates, or attendance.)
3. *Source and Subjects* (for example, who collected data from whom).
4. *Setting* (for example, solitary activity, small group, schoolwide activity).
5. *Scope and Duration* (single episode or longitudinal study; specific skill or subject area, or a general examination of instruction).
6. *Construct* (for example, real or simulated).
7. *Process* (structured or unstructured; quantitative or qualitative).
8. *Procedures* (for example, test, videotaped episode, written vignette).

These eight areas will be used in the Critique/Analysis to analyze the four studies included in this section and to demonstrate various aspects of the diversity represented in these particular research efforts.

MULTIPLE ANALYSES NEEDED

The conditions of instruction are interactive, not independent. Some teachers are more effective with some types of learners, or in certain community settings, or when certain instructional conditions are involved. Each condition individually or in concert with others impacts the processes of learning. To consider only one condition in assessing the processes of instruction severely limits the ability to understand and evaluate instruction.

Some assessments involve only one condition or a combination of them. Such studies are necessary to identify the constructs involved in the process. The more powerful studies, however, take into consideration as many of the relevant factors as possible.

Whether this is accomplished by ethnography, qualitative studies, or quantitative studies; whether through psychological or sociological methodology; or by studies of limited incidents or long-term exploration, is irrelevant. All are needed, but when combinations of methodology are used, the process becomes more powerful.

Within the classroom, the teacher is not the only element controlling the environment. Not only antecedent variables, but contexts of instruction affect processes. In elementary classrooms, for example, the instructional processes are different in skills centers where teachers diagnose students' reading achievement and determine instruction on results; in role-play centers where house or work orientations are developed through free play; in discussion circles; in decision-making sessions; or on field trips to community attractions. All four antecedent variables are part of each instructional process, but influence the process in different ways and with different emphases. Context makes a difference.

Individual methods of inquiry all have their limitations—limitations in perspective and in the accuracy of information. Drawing on multiple sources of evidence is assumed to be more representative of the teacher's performance than a single source of information. "Among the data sources commonly used are classroom observations, informal visits by administrators, portfolios, interviews with teachers, peer evaluations, teacher tests, principal ratings, pupil evaluations of teacher performance, and evidence of student growth" (Andrews & Barnes, 1990, p. 575).

The amount of time and effort involved in multiple methods of assessment is a major consideration. Portfolios can quickly become paperwork nightmares. Several systems have simplified portfolios (Barnes, 1987; Georgia Department of Education, 1985) and interviewing processes (Furtwengler, 1987).

Single instruments can stifle professional judgment as well as enhance it. Cohn (1992, p. 127) describes a teacher in Dade County Public Schools who was evaluated by the Teacher Assessment and Development System (TADS), an observational system with 81 specific criteria or performance indicators. "The idea of being assessed separately on so many specific items during a single class period seemed problematic to a number of teachers" (1992, p. 127). Teachers were expected to exhibit each indicator during the observation period, and not to do so led to substandard ratings. Neither did the instrument allow for events over which the teacher had little control (for example, a student who fell asleep in class), or permit professional judgment based on evidence known to the teacher but not to the observer (that is, in this case, given the circumstances, it might have been better to let the student sleep). "Once a teacher started a lesson within this evaluation framework, he was expected to follow through even though he might not think it was working as planned or he might see a more promising direction to pursue" (Cohn, 1992, p. 127).

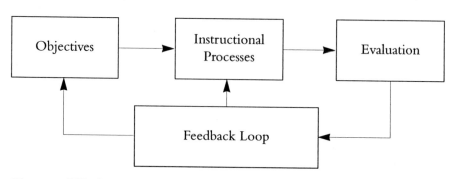

Figure PII-3
Classical Evaluation Paradigm

WHEN EVALUATION IS INSTRUCTION

The classical paradigm in education is found in Figure PII–3.

Evaluation follows instruction, with a feedback loop for correction; the process is basically linear. This need not be the case. Evaluation and instruction can be intertwined in such a way that they are one and the same. The use of classroom vignettes is one method of instruction that also assesses prospective teachers' understanding of the factors involved, and the potential solutions to problem situations. Concurrent self-analysis by a teacher during the act of teaching is another example—a sort of self-monitoring process that directs the teacher to continue current actions or to shift to other strategies.

FOUR RESEARCH REPORTS

In four studies included in this section of the *Yearbook*, authors have used varying methods to examine and analyze instruction that illustrate some of the variance described in the introduction. Johnson describes a self-analysis in which she uses videotaped lessons to make specific, instructor-identified improvements in instruction (that is, reduce teacher talk, reduce literal questions, increase figurative questions, and eliminate interruptions). Reiman and Parramore, on the other hand, based their study on Kolberg's stages of moral reasoning. For thirteen prospective teachers, years of field experience and on-site tutoring, self-analysis, and reflection led to improvement in moral reasoning.

Kagan and Tippins used classroom case studies to assess the developmental changes of novice teachers. These written descriptions included all the information needed to clarify the situation. Differences were found between elementary and secondary student teachers and between in-service and preservice teachers. Rowley and Hart extended the use of case studies by adding two media-based steps to the written vignettes and small group interaction. A videotaped episode between a mentor teacher and beginning teacher and a videotape of the analysis of the case by four veteran teachers further broadened teachers' knowledge of the situation and of potential processes.

These four case studies further extend our understanding of the processes of teacher education that have potential for improving practice.

CHAPTER 5

Classroom Cases as Gauges of Professional Growth

DONA M. KAGAN
George Mason University

AND

DEBORAH J. TIPPINS
University of Georgia

DONA KAGAN is a Professor at George Mason University, where she helps coordinate an innovative, site-based master's program located at the university's Prince William Institute. The program revolves around the concept of teacher research and prepares teachers to work in collaborative school-based teams.

DEBORAH J. TIPPINS is an Assistant Professor at the University of Georgia where she has a dual appointment in the Department of Science Education and the Department of Elementary Education. Her research interests include teacher belief, teacher education, and the contextualized nature of teaching and learning.

ABSTRACT

Twelve elementary and secondary student teachers wrote classroom cases at the beginning, middle, and end of their field experiences. The cases were analyzed for signs that the teachers' perceptions of pupils and classrooms had changed during the course of student teaching. Self-evaluations and supervisors' evaluations of growth were also obtained. The secondary teachers, whose cases focused on discipline, appeared to equate teaching with controlling a class. By the time they had completed student teaching, these novices had not moved far from their initial perspectives, continuing to see their pupils in terms of two dimensions only:

academic achievement and the potential for disruptive behavior. Cases written by the elementary student teachers told a different story. They suggested that learning to teach at the elementary level meant learning to understand pupils' dysfunctional behaviors and the multifaceted nature of children. Learning to teach also meant realizing that there are many things teachers cannot fix.

This is the third study documenting our investigation of classroom cases written by teachers. Because the complete theoretical and empirical foundation for this inquiry is described in the reports of our prior investigations (Kagan, 1991; Kagan & Tippins, 1991), only a brief summary is presented below.

ASSUMPTIONS AND BACKGROUND

Like other researchers of teachers' narratives (for example, Connelly & Clandinin, 1988; Munby, 1987), we initially regarded classroom cases as narrative literature. We based this approach on three assumptions: (a) the narrative mode represents a way of perceiving and organizing reality (Bruner, 1986; Polkinghorne, 1988); (b) thus, one can assume that the content and structure of a narrative may reflect its author's cognition; and (c) the classroom cases written by teachers, as examples of the narrative mode, may implicitly express the teachers' perceptions and pedagogical beliefs.

In an earlier study, we compared classroom cases written by pre- and in-service teachers. The teachers were free to focus on any kind of instructional or disciplinary problem, true or fictitious, and could define and order narrative components (setting, problem, resolution, and so on) in any ways they chose (Kagan & Tippins, 1991).

We discovered that three themes differentiated the classroom cases written by the two groups of teachers: the internal conflicts catalyzed within a teacher by a classroom problem; the long-term evolutionary nature of problems; and their ethical overtones. Seventy-eight percent of the cases written by in-service teachers manifested one or more of these themes, compared to 16 percent of the cases written by the preservice teachers (Kagan & Tippins, 1991).

Our analysis of these themes suggested that experienced teachers perceived classroom problems as commonplace events that catalyze internal conflicts within a teacher; that problems grow and evolve over time; and that solutions are rarely neat. In contrast, the cases written by the preservice teachers indicated that they defined classroom problems as events that disrupt routines but do not impinge upon a teacher's internal life (Kagan & Tippins, 1991).

We wondered whether classroom cases, written at intervals during student teaching, could be used to assess developmental changes in the novices' perceptions of pupils and classrooms. This study was designed to explore that issue.

METHOD

PARTICIPANTS

Twelve student teachers participated in this study. Five were elementary teachers enrolled in an undergraduate teacher-education program at the University of Georgia. Each taught in a suburban elementary school (in kindergarten, grades, 1, 3, and 4, respectively) for ten weeks, one academic quarter. The second author served as their university supervisor.

Seven of the student teachers were at the secondary level, enrolled in a teacher-education program at the University of Alabama: five as undergraduates, two as fifth-year master's students. Each completed sixteen weeks (one academic semester) of student teaching. The two graduate student teachers kept a single assignment throughout the semester, each working with an experienced English teacher at the same suburban high school. The other five secondary teachers had double majors and were required to complete a "split assignment." This meant that they spent half the semester working with a secondary English teacher, the other half with a secondary history teacher. The first author supervised the secondary student teachers.

The teacher-education programs at both universities are similar. Each entails an initial block of foundational coursework, several clinical experiences lasting from two to four weeks, and one quarter or one semester of student teaching. Student teachers are observed and evaluated four to six times by their university supervisors. As supervisors, we share a constructivist approach to classroom teaching and tend to provide similar kinds of feedback to our student teachers. Prior to this study, none of the student teachers had read or written classroom cases as part of their university coursework.

PROCEDURE

Each elementary student teacher wrote six classroom cases: two at the beginning, two at the middle, and two at the end of the student teaching experience. Since most of the secondary teachers completed split assignments, they were required to write only three cases at the same intervals.

All of the teachers were told that each case should describe a real or fictitious classroom problem in sufficient detail to understand the situation. Any or all of the following narrative components could be included: descriptions of characters and setting, the problem, dialogue, solution, consequences, moral.

The teachers were also provided with three sample cases written by pre- or in-service teachers. Although writing the cases was required as part of student teaching, the cases were not graded. They were not returned or discussed with any of the student teachers, and to the best of our knowledge the student teachers did not share them among themselves.

We also asked each student teacher to evaluate his or her professional growth at the end of the student teaching experience by responding in writing to the following:

> Look back to the first weeks of student teaching and evaluate any changes that have occurred in your beliefs or practices. How have your lessons and attitudes changed?

The teachers' responses to these questions are referred to throughout as "self-evaluations of growth."

As supervisors, we each wrote evaluations of our own student teachers at the end of the quarter/semester. We used gross criteria, mentally comparing each novice's growth to that of other student teachers we had known. We wrote a brief paragraph for each teacher in which we categorized growth as little, moderate, or great and explained the nature of the growth. These paragraphs are referred to throughout as "supervisors' evaluations of growth."

DATA ANALYSIS

We each analyzed the cases independently by first reading through all fifty-one, then rereading and taking notes in different but complementary ways.

The first author took holistic notes, commenting on the focus, tone, and affect of each case. The second author completed a chart with headings inspired by our prior study: nature of the problem (disciplinary, instructional, motivational, and so on); nature of the solution (quick and neat or prolonged and messy); how the problem affected the student teacher; how the pupil-teacher relationship was depicted (in terms of control, counseling, and so on).

We then exchanged notes and independently prepared lists of findings. For every finding we each provided supportive evidence in the form of quotations taken from the cases or the evaluations of growth. These lists of findings were ultimately merged and used to write the subsequent sections of this article. Pseudonyms are used throughout.

RESULTS

THE SECONDARY STUDENT TEACHERS

The secondary student teachers wrote a total of twenty-one cases, fourteen (67 percent) of which dealt with problems of discipline or class control. Ten of these fourteen cases had simple, happy solutions; only three ended uncertainly. The remaining seven cases dealt with the following kinds of problems: 3 = motivational, 2 = instructional, 2 = general classroom policy. All but one of these cases had simple solutions.

Of the total twenty-one cases, only two expressed the student teachers' affective responses to the classroom problems under discussion. One of these affective cases told of a student teacher's failure to remind her pupils of an upcoming deadline for an assignment. Although many pupils forgot to hand it in, the student teacher upheld the deadline: "I didn't let the students know, but it bothered me for several days. Maybe I had been unfair. I still agonize about my decision."

The other affective case described a student teacher's attempts to break up a fight in the hall outside his classroom. The incident caused him to speculate: "This problem had a safe ending, but I hope this type of situation never occurs again. I suppose that is only a dream, but as a teacher I seem to have built my life around a dream." It is significant to note that both affective cases were written at the end of the student teaching semester.

Three of the seven cases written at the beginning of the semester were highly melodramatic. For example, one was a story about a high school athlete who the student teacher discovered was using drugs. The teacher helps the student find a "cure," and years later the student returns to express his gratitude. He also goes on to play professional football.

None of the secondary teachers' cases that were written at the beginning or middle of the semester conveyed a sense of longevity, the feeling that the problem under discussion was abiding or evolutionary. Thus, in sum, the first two sets of cases did not manifest the three themes we found to be characteristic of experienced teachers (Kagan & Tippins, 1991).

However, the cases that were written by the secondary teachers at the *end* of the semester were qualitatively different. Five of these seven cases were either unresolved, reflected the teacher's doubts, or described a highly complex teacher-pupil interaction. In these later cases, one could see the emerging realization that classroom problems are complex, distressing, and often insoluble. This can be illustrated with an excerpt taken from one of these cases:

Since I am quite young and look even younger, I have found it increasingly difficult to keep order in the classroom. The students are seventeen and eighteen years old and tend to regard me more as an equal than an authority figure. Students continue to talk after the bell has rung, while I am giving instructions, and during the last five minutes of class. This is not a problem when my cooperating teacher is in the room. It bothers me that the students do not see me as a real teacher with real power. I have been able to solve this problem in certain situations but not in others. I continue to try different ways to quiet them, but I realize there is no one, simple solution.

We are particularly interested in relationships between the cases and the evaluations of the novices' growth, both the self-evaluations and the supervisors' evaluations. Each of the twenty-one cases was consistent with its author's self-evaluation but not necessarily with the supervisor's. Two illustrations follow:

Three of the student teachers felt they had grown most in "learning to discipline pupils." Each of these teachers wrote cases about disciplinary problems that were neatly resolved, in effect expressing their self-perceived mastery of class control.

Bill evaluated his growth in terms of "learning to know and motivate pupils on an individual basis." Two of the three cases he wrote concerned pupils whose membership in gangs undermined their academic potential and Bill's attempts to motivate them.

The Elementary Student Teachers

The five elementary teachers wrote a total of thirty cases, which dealt with the following kinds of classroom problems: 10 (33 percent) = disciplinary, 3 = instructional, 1 = general class policy, 1 = politics (concerning a teacher's aide who could not follow directions). Of the ten disciplinary cases, seven had neat solutions, while only three remained unresolved. The remaining fifteen (50 percent) were multifaceted studies of individual pupils who posed profound instructional or disciplinary problems. We came to call these fascinating cases "clinical studies," for reasons explained below.

The theme of each clinical study was the unique personality of a child and how it affected academic behaviors, peer interaction, and family interdynamics. The complexity of these portraits stood in sharp contrast to the cases written by the secondary student teachers, who saw their pupils in terms of only two characteristics (academic achievement and the potential for disruptive behavior).

At closer range, the clinical studies fell into four subgroups: 11 contained explicit psychologizing (for example, "Mary was used to being the class scapegoat. When other children made fun of her, she snapped back and sought to hurt them. She had come to be the instigator of cruelty in an effort to lash back in despair."); 11 remained unresolved; 2 had neat, happy resolutions, and 3 included descriptions of the teachers' affective responses (for example, "Caroline needs stability in every possible way . . . . I show her support in any way I can . . . . I will miss her when I have to go, and I wish her well."). As this tabulation suggests, these cases were essentially exercises in clinical diagnoses: student teachers' attempts to understand the origins of pupils' dysfunctional behaviors.

The student teacher's attempt(s) at intervention played an important part in each clinical study. Most of the clinical studies had no real ending, for the problems were too profound to ever be truly solved. One did not feel that the teachers "psychologized" in an attempt to impose professional distance, as Connell (1985) suggested in his study of Australian teachers. Instead, the student teachers tended to display their honest emotional responses to the pupils they described.

We began to appreciate the significance of the clinical studies when we examined their chronology: five (30 percent) were written at the beginning, three (20 percent) at the middle, and seven (50 percent) at the end of the student teaching experience. Thus, they appeared to reflect a maturing perspective of pupils and classrooms.

We also looked closely at the student teachers who wrote clinical studies. Ellie wrote six (the largest number); Amy, Diane, and Melissa wrote four, three, and two, respectively. Each of these student teachers was described by her university supervisor as achieving a great amount of growth during the quarter.

Ellie was described as learning "to use positive reinforcement rather than punishment." In her self-evaluation, Ellie said she learned "how to overcome hostility with love." Amy was described as learning "to establish a positive classroom climate and to be a diagnostician." Amy evaluated her own growth in terms of "learning to respond flexibly to individual pupils." Diane was described as gaining "self-confidence and management skills."

Thus, the generation of clinical studies was associated not only with the final phase of student teaching, but also with reports of professional growth. Growth was manifested through the studies themselves in two ways: by a chronological shift from simplistic disciplinary cases to complex clinical studies; and by a shift from resolved to unresolved clinical studies. Melissa, whose growth was described in terms of "learning to relate to pupils individually," is an example of the first pattern. Excerpts from two of her cases appear in Table 5–1; the first was taken from a disciplinary case written at the beginning of the quarter, the second from a clinical study written at the end of the quarter.

TABLE 5-1

Comparison of a Disciplinary Case Written at the Beginning of Student Teaching and a Clinical Study Written at the End (Melissa, grade 3)

EXCERPT FROM THE DISCIPLINARY CASE

The students had just gotten started on their math test, when my cooperating teacher asked me to keep an eye on them . . . . The test is going smoothly, when students begin to raise their hands with questions.

"I'm sorry, I can't help you answer the problems, because this is a test," I say.

From the back of the room where I am sitting, I begin to hear a gurgling noise from Anthony. The class begins to giggle and turn around to see where the noise is coming from. I quietly walk over to Anthony's desk and ask him to stop . . . He stops.

I manage to get the class settled and back on task. In about five minutes, Anthony begins to erase something on his paper, and discovers that his eraser makes the squeakiest noise he's ever heard. The class begins laughing . . .

"Anthony, move your desk away from the group," I order.

"No," he tells me.

After recovering from the shock that this boy flat out disobeyed me, I walk to his desk and say firmly, "Yes!"

"I'm taking a test," he tells me . . .

Not wanting to give in, I pull his chair. He then kneels on the floor and continues to write.

"Let's go," I say . . . pulling his desk. He moves out of the way and decides he better go.

. . . Anthony completed his test with no further interruptions to the class.

EXCERPT FROM THE CLINICAL STUDY

Mark is an unusually sensitive third-grader. The slightest thing can bring tears to his eyes. If he misses a problem or does not get an A . . . I can see him become visibly upset . . . . [He] appears to have average ability, but works very hard . . . I think of him as an overachiever.

I have talked with Mark and tried to help him see that getting a problem wrong or not getting an A is not the end of the world. This has not appeared to help the problem . . . . I worry that he is putting too much pressure on himself and is getting too much pressure from his parents.

I have talked to his parents at conferences. They have high expectations for Mark and do not feel there is any problem . . . . They will be of no help . . . .

Other than continuing to reassure Mark that it's all right to get a B sometimes, I have not been able to come up with other ways of solving this problem.

TABLE 5-2
Comparison of an Easily Resolved Clinical Study Written at the Beginning of Student Teaching and an Unresolved Clinical Study Written at the End (Ellie, grade 4)

EXCERPT FROM THE RESOLVED CLINICAL STUDY

David's problem was that he was extremely bright and quick. He attended the gifted program once a day for an hour, but the remainder of his days were spent in boredom. He finished his work quickly and accurately, then spent his time drawing. David was not being challenged to work up to his potential.

The teacher had to cover topics in a very explicit, slow manner so that the average children could keep up and catch on. For David, these lessons seemed to drag on and on. He was amazed at how stupid the other kids were . . . .

The teacher saw David slip away daily into his art. She had to create a way to challenge him. After discussing the problem with other teachers, she decided to use David as a tutor and peer teacher in the room. Sometimes when he completed his work early, she would let him walk around the room helping other students. Other times, she would allow him to go to the library to research a topic for presentation later to the class.

David thoroughly enjoyed his new responsibilities as class tutor and teacher. He did not hold his intelligence over the other boys and girls. He now had a purpose, a way to explore and express himself. The teacher was also pleased with the arrangement, as it freed her to help other students and freed her mind of worry about David.

EXCERPT FROM THE UNRESOLVED CLINICAL STUDY

Michael was a very defiant and cruel child. He would hurt the other children by hitting them or calling them names. He was forever muttering some obscenity or insult under his breath. He rarely did his required work in school, nor did he care about it. He lied about his personal life, trying to appear normal. What could the teacher do?

First she tried a calm, loving approach, thinking that what Michael really needed was a good dose of care. Michael's response to her outreach was to fill her with lies. He told her his father was a policeman . . . . [She discovered] his father and brother were both in jail. He was a terror to his neighborhood, and his mother had no idea what to do with him.

The teacher was angered and saddened by the news. Michael was trying to create an imaginary life for himself, so he would appear acceptable . . . . He was trying to bolster his own self-confidence by putting others down. He was criticizing their families so the other students would not have a chance to make fun of his. He had built a great wall of hate around himself for defense . . .

Now that she had some insight into Michael's motivation and behavior, she was still at a loss for a remedy. She began to give him more classroom jobs to perform, so he would feel an integral part of the class. She made efforts to call on him, so he could contribute . . . She tried to really listen to his comments, and discovered a fairly intelligent boy struggling to be heard and noticed for the gifts he had, which were so overshadowed by his bad behavior.

The other students were asked to help Michael relate in a more positive manner. She also staffed him into a behavior disorder program for one hour a day.

With time and care Michael began to call other students' names less often, and he began to do his work more regularly. He still lied, whenever he needed to. Mostly, he knew that his teacher cared for him and would not let him get away with his old tricks. She would be there for him when he needed her.

Ellie, whose growth was described above, is an illustration of the second pattern of growth. Although she wrote only clinical studies, the ones she produced at the beginning of the quarter had relatively neat solutions; the ones she wrote at the end remained problematic. Excerpts from two of Ellie's clinical studies appear in Table 5–2. In the second excerpt, note her attempts to psychologize the problem and her description of her own affective response to Michael.

The clinical studies resembled the cases written by experienced teachers in our earlier study (Kagan & Tippins, 1991) in that each focused intensively on one pupil, presented a complex perspective, and described protracted intervention efforts. One clinical case written at the end of the quarter had ethical overtones. It concerned a child who was regularly pulled out of class to receive special help in a resource room. As a result, he fell behind in his regular class work and was frustrated. The teacher wondered: "How can teachers claim to have a child's best interests at heart, when the help they provide only serves to compound his problems?"

DISCUSSION

The classroom cases written by the twelve student teachers did express professional growth, but not in terms of precise calibration. That is, we did not identify discrete signs that correspond to particular degrees of growth. Instead, the cases were most meaningful when viewed in chronological series and, as such, might serve to enrich or validate a supervisor's impressions.

Interestingly, the cases written by the secondary student teachers reflected only self-evaluations of growth, while the cases written by the elementary teachers reflected both self- and supervisor's evaluation of growth. Perhaps this was because growth among the secondary teachers appeared to be relatively simple compared to the profound shift in perception manifested by the elementary teachers. Where the secondary novices came to realize that disciplinary problems are often complex, their elementary counterparts came to a new understanding of children's dysfunctional behaviors—an appreciation for the depth and breadth of factors that can affect a child's social and academic behaviors in the classroom.

A similar pessimistic shift in attitudes was reported in Hoy & Woolfolk's (1990) study of preservice teachers. After completing student teaching, the preservice teachers in that study were more concerned with maintaining order and were less confident they could overcome the influences of environment and family.

Perhaps the greatest value of the classroom cases lay in what they implied about the differences between the perspectives and experiences of the elementary and secondary novices. The secondary teachers appeared to equate teaching with class control, an observation that is consistent with empirical literature on the concern of preservice and beginning teachers (see Borko & Livingston, 1989; Bullough, 1987; Ryan, 1986). By the time they had completed student teaching, these novices had not moved far from their initial perspectives.

It seemed as if the secondary student teachers moved through the semester wearing blinders that severely limited perceptual change. This may have been a function of the overwhelming scope of their assignments: having to interact with four to five different classes of twenty-five pupils apiece. One can logically assume that this created a relatively depersonalized classroom experience. Five of the secondary student teachers completed split assignments, which only exacerbated the situation. Each had to interact with as many as 250 pupils during the semester and had to win the respect of two different sets of adolescent classes. It is no wonder these novices became obsessed with the issue of class control.

The cases written by the elementary student teachers told a different story. They suggested that learning to teach meant coming to understand the complex interaction between family and school life and the multifaceted nature of children. As the novices began their student teaching, they viewed pupils' dysfunctional behaviors as mere disciplinary problems. By the end of the quarter, they saw the dysfunctional behavior as an inherent part of a child's personal history. Stories about discrete classroom-control problems gave way to thick, complex studies of unique children.

For the elementary teachers, learning to teach also meant accepting the immutable nature of some problems. Thus, the clinical studies documented the emergence of a richer, more mature, but significantly darker vision of classroom teaching.

IMPLICATIONS AND SUGGESTIONS

Although the reading and writing of classroom cases have become popular topics of discussion in the literature of teacher education, cases are generally regarded as instructional tools: vehicles for encouraging self-reflection (see Merseth, 1991). We have used cases differently: as heuristic artifacts—narratives that may reflect their authors' cognitions and perceptions. Thus, we make no distinction between true or fictitious cases, but focus only on what a case implies about teaching and classrooms. We do not suggest that the latter approach is superior to the former, only that it is no less valuable. If cases are as powerful as current literature suggests, it seems only reasonable to assume that there are multiple lenses through which one could view them.

The cases written by the twelve student teachers suggest that novices preparing to teach at the secondary level may need special assistance in coming to see pupils as complex individuals with characteristics beyond those of academic performance and the tendency to disrupt class routine. Asking student teachers to complete "research" assignments that require them to investigate and analyze extracurricular aspects of their pupils' lives may be useful in this regard. One might also question the wisdom of "split assignments," which may prevent novice teachers from getting to know pupils well and may overemphasize the importance of discipline and class control.

REFERENCES

Borko, H., & Livingston, C. (1989). Cognition and improvisation: Differences in mathematics instruction by expert and novice teachers. *American Educational Research Journal, 26,* 473–498.

Bruner, J. (1986). *Actual minds, possible worlds.* Cambridge, MA: Harvard University Press.

Bullough, R. (1987). Planning and the first year of teaching. *Journal of Education for Teaching, 13,* 231–250.

Connell, R. W. (1985). *Teachers' work.* Sydney, Australia: Beorge Allen & Unwin.

Connelly, F. M., & Clandinin, D. J. (1988). *Teachers as curriculum planners: Narratives of experience.* New York: Teachers College Press.

Hoy, W. K., & Woolfolk, A. E. (1990). Socialization of student teachers. *American Educational Research Journal, 27,* 279–300.

Kagan, D. M. (1991). Narrative semiotics and teachers' beliefs regarding the relevance of formal learning theory to classroom practice. *Journal of Education for Teaching, 17,* 245–262.

Kagan, D. M., & Tippins, D. J. (1991). How teachers' classroom cases reflect their pedagogical beliefs. *Journal of Teacher Education, 42,* (4), 281–291.

Merseth, K. K. (1991). *The case for cases.* Washington, DC: American Association for Higher Education and the American Association of Colleges for Teacher Education.

Munby, H. (1987). Metaphor and teachers' knowledge. *Research in the teaching of English, 21,* 377–397.

Polkinghorne, D. E. (1988). *Narrative knowing and the human sciences.* Albany, NY: State University of New York Press.

Ryan, K. (1986). *The induction of new teachers.* Bloomington, IN: Phi Delta Kappa Educational Foundation.

CHAPTER 6

Promoting Preservice Teacher Development through Extended Field Experience

ALAN J. REIMAN
BARBARA M. PARRAMORE
North Carolina State University

ALAN J. REIMAN is a Clinical Assistant Professor who works jointly in the Departments of Curriculum and Instruction and Psychology at North Carolina State University and in the Wake County Public School System. He currently is at work on an eight-year study of preservice teacher education and teacher induction.

BARBARA M. PARRAMORE is a Professor in the College of Education and Psychology at North Carolina State University, and first head of the Department of Curriculum and Instruction, 1975–1985, where she directed the department's development and accreditation of its undergraduate and graduate programs. She is currently participating in a longitudinal study of preservice and in-service experiences of an initial group of North Carolina teaching fellows.

ABSTRACT

Results are given of an investigation of the effects of an extended field experience on students in preservice teacher education in which they served as tutors with concomitant guided reflection designed to foster psychological maturity. Students participating in the intervention had two additional semesters of coursework and field experience (tutoring). Effects of the extended program were measured for indicators of change in students' justice reasoning, conceptual level, and ego development. It appears that carefully structured field experiences with concomitant guided reflection should be explored further as a valuable part of preservice teacher education.

The purpose of this study was to investigate the effects on preservice teachers of extended preservice field experience with concomitant guided reflection on selected indicators of psychological maturity. The research questions emerged from a review of studies of teacher characteristics, preservice teacher education, and recent work with cognitive-developmental psychology. The findings are from an ongoing longitudinal study of a nontraditional group of undergraduate teacher-education students at North Carolina State University called the teaching fellows.

THE PROBLEM

Studies of teacher characteristics conducted in the late 1950s and early 1960s by Getzels & Jackson (1963) were largely unproductive in identifying relationships between teacher behaviors and student learning. However, during the 1960s and 1970s, researchers began providing evidence of actual links between teaching processes and pupil outcomes (Brophy, 1979; Dunkin & Biddle, 1974; Flanders, 1970) as well as demonstrating the effectiveness of teachers' careful use of time, use of feedback, use of questioning, and monitoring of student learning. These teacher behaviors have been related consistently to student achievement (Rosenshine, 1987; Walberg, 1986). But how effective are preservice programs of teacher preparation in presenting such research findings and introducing theory in ways accessible to the preservice teacher?

Joyce & Clift (1984), in their comprehensive review of preservice teacher education, indict nearly all elements of preservice teacher education. As a result of their inquiry, their proposals for reform in preservice teacher education call for more "careful coordination" of training elements, a balance of theory and skill transfer, and careful on-site supervision (pp. 10–11). Berliner (1985), after a review of national trends in teacher education, has made a strong case for carefully structured field and laboratory experiences for preservice students with concomitant self-analysis, reflection, and instructor feedback. The challenge to teacher educators, however, is how to structure undergraduate teacher education so that it is meaningful for the preservice teacher. This problem has been explored in developmental psychology.

Developmental educators (for example, Sprinthall & Thies-Sprinthall, 1983) have argued that how students function and process experience in teacher education settings is strongly influenced by their psychological maturity (cognitive structures). They assert that those student teachers who are more conceptually complex, more autonomous, and more ethical will radiate a more responsive and flexible teaching style in their work with students. This work rests on a considerable body of research findings (Blasi, 1980; Lee & Snarey, 1988; Loevinger, 1976; Loxley & Whitley, 1986; Miller, 1981; Rest, 1986).

Our research question emerged from this corpus of research and theory, the purpose being to investigate the effects of extended preservice field experience (primarily a new role of classroom tutor) with concomitant guided reflection on selected indicators of psychological maturity for preservice student teachers. The student characteristics that were selected for study consisted of the following cognitive measures: justice reasoning, conceptual level, and ego development.

METHOD

Sample. Subjects were undergraduate students at North Carolina State University enrolled in various teacher-education curricula. All were scholarship recipients in a nontraditional program called the teaching fellows.

Pretest-Posttest Design. The intervention design followed a pretest-posttest format and used an experimental group (N = 13) which received the intervention and a comparison group (N = 13). The experimental group received a year (two semesters of university coursework) that featured structured field experiences and on-site tutoring with concomitant self-analysis and instructor-facilitated reflection through formal and informal conferences and intensive journal writing with instructor feedback.

Both groups were composed of students who chose to enroll in a teacher education program at the university. The participants in the experimental group volunteered to participate in the additional field experiences during their sophomore or junior year. Coursework included a middle schools' course with a field experience and a tutoring course that placed students in the public schools as tutors.

The comparison group was paired with the experimental group based on pretest scores on the Defining Issues Test developed by James Rest (1986). This test and two other measures were administered during the first month of the participants' freshman year. The same three measures were administered during the final month of the participants' senior year, just prior to graduation. Independent *t*-tests were performed.

INTERVENTION

The intervention included two additional semesters of coursework and field experience (tutoring) with concomitant guided reflection. The overall purpose of the intervention was to increase dimensions of students' justice reasoning, conceptual complexity, and ego development. The directional hypotheses posited that encouraging continuous guided reflection as the students undertook the significant and complex new helping role of tutor would foster psychological growth.

To ensure that all participants in the experimental group were involved in continuous reflection, careful written feedback was given on coursework and journals submitted by the students while serving as tutors. This instructor feedback acknowledged feelings, offered praise and encouragement, clarified student ideas, and prompted deeper analysis of the tutoring experiences through questioning. Instructor feedback and student reflection were initiated weekly during the tutoring experiences.

The intervention applied five conditions that a larger body of research has reported as promoting psychological growth of learners (Sprinthall & Thies-Sprinthall, 1983). Among these are: participating in a significant new experience; being guided in reflection on that experience; having a balance between experience and reflection; experiencing support as well as challenge throughout; and encountering continuity of the experience.

MEASURES

Justice reasoning. Justice reasoning was measured by the Defining Issues Test or DIT (Rest, 1986). The DIT is a recognition test that assesses how persons analyze six social-moral dilemmas and judge appropriate courses of action. The test is based on Kohlberg's six-stage theory of moral reasoning. The DIT uses a multiple-choice rating and ranking procedure. Scoring involves calculating a principled-thinking score (P score), that indicates the relative importance attributed to principled moral considerations in making decisions. A shorter three-dilemma version (used for this study) may also be given when an overlapping assessment design has been initiated. The P score for the three-dilemma assessment correlates at 0.93 with the rank P score for all six dilemmas.

Conceptual level. The Paragraph Completion Method test (PCM) was used to measure conceptual level (CL) of respondents' cognitive complexity and interpersonal maturity. This semiprojective test consists of six open-ended topic stems; three assess how the individual thinks about conflict and uncertainty; the other three stems assess how the individual thinks about rule structure and authority. Scoring is determined by calculating the mean of the three highest responses. Protocols were scored by an external consultant. Interrater reliability ranges from 0.80 to 0.95. The most comprehensive review of content and predictive validity was conducted by Miller (1981). Well over two hundred studies have been conducted using the PCM.

Ego development. Ego development was measured with the Constantinople test (1967, 1969). It assesses phases four through six of Erikson's theory of developing ego maturity. The instrument consists of thirty single words or phrases. Subjects indicate which items are most characteristic of themselves by marking their self-perceptions on 7-point scales. An identity-diffusion and an identity-resolution index are computed by calculating the mean of the responses to the thirty items.

STRENGTHS, LIMITATIONS, AND SPECIAL CIRCUMSTANCES

The major strength of the study was its quasi-experimental design. Campbell & Stanley (1963) identified potential threats to internal validity as being minimal when a pretest-posttest design is used on both the experimental and the comparison group. Nonetheless, there are several potential limitations to the design of this study.

The strength of the pretest-posttest design rests on the premise of randomization. This study relied upon volunteers for the experimental group; both groups applied to participate in the teaching fellows program. Although the use of volunteers is a potential confounding variable, the use of volunteers in the natural setting has been identified by Gage (1985) as the norm, and means only that the investigator needs to limit generalizations to volunteer groups. Accepting this qualification, the study maintained internal validity.

Threats to external validity must also be addressed. A potential concern is the question of an interaction between testing and the intervention. These two conditions of time and selection reduce this threat to external validity. The posttest was administered four years after the pretest, thereby reducing the potential interaction. The possible interaction between selection and the intervention raised another legitimate threat. Both the experimental group and the comparison group consisted of volunteers who had relatively high levels of motivation and commitment to the teaching fellows program. Referring again to Gage (1985), this is not a threat as long as findings are generalized to volunteer groups.

The potential for a reactive effect was also possible. Posttests were initiated during the final month prior to the participants' graduation. It is possible that they could have been less motivated during the assessment. This could lead to a Type II error.

Regarding special circumstances, the students in the study were nontraditional. They had been attracted to participate in the teaching fellows program through a unique scholarship program provided by the state Legislature. The program requires a high school senior to make a teaching career decision prior to entrance into his or her college or university of choice. Upon completion of a teacher-education curriculum, a teaching fellow must teach a minimum of four years. In return, the state provides a scholarship of $5,000 for each student for four years. The students selected were often among the top 10 percent of their high school classes and posted Scholastic Aptitude Test scores 30 percent higher than the state average.

RESULTS AND DISCUSSION

Independent t-tests were performed to determine the statistical significance of gain scores on the three measures. A one-tailed test of significance was used with an alpha of 0.05 set as an indication of significance.

There was a statistically significant pretest-posttest gain score on the Defining Issues Tests for the experimental group when compared with a matched group. The results are reported in Table 6–1 and show that there was a significant difference. The t value was 2.520, which was significant at 0.01 level of confidence. This finding appears consistent with an emerging body of research (Rest, 1986) that shows justice reasoning gains when subjects are placed in role-taking experiences with concomitant guided reflection.

TABLE 6–1

Change in mean gain of the Defining Issues Test scores for experimental and comparison groups

Group	PRETEST	POSTTEST	MEAN GAIN	S.D.	T VALUE*
Experimental N = 13	38.53	56.94	18.47	14.48	2.520
Comparison N = 13	40.49	46.40	5.97	16.19	

* (df = 24, significance = p <.01, one-tailed)

TABLE 6-2

Change in the mean gain of the Paragraph Completion Method scores for the experimental and comparison groups

Group	PRETEST	POSTTEST	MEAN GAIN	S.D.	T VALUE★
Experimental N = 13	1.64	1.94	0.30	0.49	NS
Comparsion N = 13	1.60	2.00	0.40	0.382	

★(df = 24, no significance, one tailed)

A second question explored whether there would be a statistically significant pretest-posttest gain score on the Paragraph Completion Method test for the experimental group when compared to the comparison group. The mean gain scores for both the experimental and the comparison groups are given in Table 6–2. There was no significant difference. Both groups had gain scores that were nontrivial.

Table 6–3 shows the pretest-posttest gain score on the Constantinople test for the experimental group when compared to the comparison group. There was no significant difference. Both groups had gain scores that are comparable to trends found by Constantinople (1969) for undergraduate students.

The three empirical estimates of psychological growth indicate that the additional tutoring experiences may have stimulated some developmental change, although the results were not consistent. On estimates of justice reasoning, the student tutors achieved scores that were statistically different from

TABLE 6-3

Change in mean gain of the Constantinople scores for the experimental and comparison groups

Group	PRETEST	POSTTEST	MEAN GAIN	S.D.	T VALUE★
Experimental N = 13	29.77	29.85	0.08	0.49	NS
Comparsion N = 13	27.54	27.87	0.33	0.33	

★(df = 24, no significance, one tailed)

those of their peers in the traditional course sequence. On the other hand, in terms of conceptual growth and ego growth, there were nontrivial gains for both the experimental group and the comparison group. As presently designed, the tutoring experiences may not have provided sufficient cognitive challenge or been of appropriate length to foster growth of the experimental group that was statistically different from the comparison group.

The significant difference between the experimental and comparison groups on the Defining Issues Test warrants further discussion. According to Kohlberg (1969), the types of social experiences that are particularly conducive to development of moral reasoning are "role-taking" experiences. Role-taking experiences are those experiences that enable the person to take another's point of view. Greater role-taking opportunities with guided reflection over time lead the individual to develop more elaborate ways of coordinating human interests, and thus a more complex conception of justice (Rest, 1986). The Defining Issues Test is built, partially, on the concept of role taking. For this reason it may be more sensitive to role-taking interventions. The field experiences and tutoring experiences that were made available to the experimental group were sustained role-taking experiences that potentially contributed to the large gain scores of the experimental group.

In this study, the effects of role-taking experiences were measured on three cognitive measures: the Defining Issues Test, the Paragraph Completion Method test, and the Constantinople test. Both groups showed sizable gains on the Paragraph Completion Method test. Based on the results of the study, it appears that carefully structured field experiences with concomitant guided reflection should be explored further as a valuable part of preservice teacher education.

IMPLICATIONS

Results of recent studies suggest that simply placing students in a practicum does not automatically offer prospective teachers valuable experiences (Goodman, 1986). Rather, they may promote a utilitarian perspective through trial-and-error approaches (Ross, 1987), drive a classroom management mentality (Lortie, 1975), constrain the novice's ability to choose appropriate teaching behaviors (Sanders & McCutcheon, 1986), and rarely prompt novices to translate theory into practice in any purposeful way (Buchmann, 1984). This study, drawing on cognitive-developmental theory as a framework, has shown that by carefully selecting a slightly more complex helping role (tutoring) with guided reflection, the preservice teacher moves toward more complex levels in ethical reasoning. Carefully designed field experience can make a difference in desired ways.

The litany of problems in preservice education (for example, episodic, contradictory, isolated, and discontinuous experiences) warrants more careful attention to those theories and constructs that hold promise as guiding frameworks for the practice of teacher education. Few in professional education would disagree with teacher preparation goals such as the fostering of conceptual competence and ethical sensitivity. In fact, Goodlad & Sirotnik (1990) recently suggested that teaching is fundamentally a moral enterprise. Yet, having a vision of more ethical practice without guiding theory is, at best, misguided.

Joyce & Clift (1984) underscored one of the long-standing problems in preservice teacher education: the lack of directing conceptual constructs and research for the educator of preservice teachers. Indeed, Lanier and Little characterized teacher education as one of "consistent chaos in the course work" (Lanier & Little, 1986, p. 546). We suggest that cognitive-developmental theory linked to preservice education has advantages as an applied theory.

Every since John Dewey (1933, 1938), at least, educators have grappled with the problem of how to learn from experience. For teacher educators, this problem has, for lack of theory, wandered between the cosmic and the trivial as educators have experimented with the current vogue. Certainly, the present avant-garde in teacher education is to focus on developing reflective practitioners (Feiman, 1979; Goodman, 1985; Ross, 1987; Schon, 1987; Zeichner & Liston, 1987).

The study reported here adds to a larger body of literature on cognitive-developmental theory and research findings that has explored how growth may be promoted for prospective teachers through field experiences. The findings are encouraging. Clearly, there is no quick or inexpensive fix. Preservice teacher development demands significant commitments of time and energy and carefully designed opportunities for learning.

REFERENCES

Berliner, D. C. (1985). Laboratory settings and the study of teacher education. *Journal of Teacher Education, 16*(6), 2–8.

Blasi, A. (1980). Briding moral cognition and moral action: A critical review of the literature. *Psychological Bulletin, 88,* 1–45.

Brophy, J. E. (1979). Teacher behavior and its effects. *Journal of Educational Psychology, 71*(6), 733–750.

Buchmann, M. (1984). The use of research knowledge in teacher education and teaching. *American Journal of Education, 92*(4), 421–439.

Campbell, D. T., & Stanley, J. C. (1963). *Experimental and Quasi-experimental designs for research,* Houghton Mifflin Company.

Constantinople, A. (1969). An Eriksonian measure of personality development in college students. *Developmental Psychology, 1*(4), 357–372.

Constantinople, A. (1967). Perceived instrumentality of the college as a measure of attitude toward college. *Journal of Personality and Social Psychology, 5*,
196–201.

Dewey, J. (1933). *How we think: A restatement of the relation of reflective thinking
to the educative process.* Chicago: Henry Regnery.

Dewey, J. (1938). *Experiences and education.* New York: Macmillan.

Dunkin, J. J., & Biddle, B. J. (1974). *The study of teaching.* New York: Holt,
Rinehart, and Winston.

Feiman, S. (1979). Technique and inquiry in teacher education: A curricular
case study. *Curriculum Inquiry, 9*(1), 63–79.

Flanders, N. A. (1970). *Analyzing teacher behavior.* Reading, Mass.: Addison-
Wesley.

Gage, N. L. (1985). *Hard gains in the soft sciences: The case of pedagogy.* Bloomington, IN: Phi Delta Kappa.

Getzels, J. W., & Jackson, P. W. (1963). The teacher's personality and characteristics. N. L. Gage (Ed.), *Handbook of research on teaching,* Chicago: Rand
McNally.

Goodlad, J., & Sirotnik, K. (1990). *The moral dimensions of teaching.* San Francisco, CA: Jossey-Bass.

Goodman, J. (1985). What students learn from early field experiences. *Journal of Teacher Education, 25*(6), 42–48.

Goodman, J. (1986). University education courses and the professional
preparation of teachers. *Teaching and Teacher Education, 12*(2), 102–109.

Joyce, B., & Clift, R. (1984). The Phoenix agenda: Essential reform in
teacher education. *Educational Researcher, 13*(4), 5–18.

Kohlberg, L. (1969). Stage and sequence: The cognitive-developmental
approach to socialization. In D. Goslin (Ed.), *Handbook of socialization theory and research,* Chicago, IL: Rand McNally.

Lanier, J., & Little, J. (1986). Research in teacher education. In M. C. Wittrock (Ed.), *Handbook of Research on Teaching.* 527–569. New York:
Macmillan.

Lee, L., & Snarey, J. (1988). The relationship between ego and moral devel-
opment: A theoretical review and empirical analysis. In D. Lapsley and C.
Power (Eds.), *Self, ego, and identity: Integrative approaches,* 151–178. New
York: Springer Verlag.

Loevinger, J. (1976). *Ego development: Conceptions and theories.* San Francisco:
Jossey-Bass.

Lortie, D. (1975). *Schoolteacher.* Chicago: University of Chicago Press.

Loxley, J., & Whiteley, J. (1986). *Character development in college students: Vol. II. The curriculum and longitudinal results.* Schenectady, NY: Character Research Press.

Miller, A. (1981). Conceptual matching models and interactional research in education. *Review of Educational Research, 52*(1).

Rest, J. R. (1986a). *The defining issues test.* (The Center for the Study of Ethical Development, Burton Hall, University of Minnesota, Minneapolis, MN 55455).

Rest, J. R. (1986b). *Moral development: Advances in research and theory.* New York: Praeger.

Rosenshine, B. (1987). Explicit teaching and teacher training. *Journal of Teacher Education, 38*(3), 34–36.

Ross, D. D. (1987). *Reflective teaching: Meaning and implications for preservice teacher educators.* Paper presented at the reflective inquiry conference. Houston, TX.

Ross, E. W. (1987). Teacher perspective development: A study of preservice social studies teachers. *Theory and Research in Social Education, 15*(4), 225–243.

Sanders, D., & McCutcheon, G. (1986). The development of practical theories of teaching. *Journal of Curriculum and Teaching, 2*(1), 50–67.

Schon, D. A.(1987). *Educating the reflective practitioner.* San Francisco: Jossey-Bass.

Sprinthall, N. A., & Thies-Sprinthall, L. (1983). The teacher as an adult learner: A cognitive-developmental view. In G. A. Griffin, (Ed.), *Staff development: Eighty-Second Yearbook of the National Society for the Study of Education,* pp. 13–35. Chicago: University of Chicago Press.

Walberg, H. (1986). Synthesis of research on teaching. In M. C. Witrock (Ed.), *Handbook of Research on Teaching.* New York: Macmillan.

Zeichner, K. M., & Liston, D. P. (1987). Teaching student teachers to reflect. *Harvard Educational Review, 57*(1), 23–48.

CHAPTER 7

Catching and Releasing Expert Teacher Thought: The Effects of Using Videotaped Representations of Expert Teacher Knowledge to Promote Preservice Teacher Thinking

JAMES B. ROWLEY
PATRICIA M. HART
University of Dayton

JAMES B. ROWLEY is an Assistant Professor in the Department of Teacher Education at the University of Dayton, where he teaches courses in the secondary education program. Dr. Rowley's current research interests are focused on the study of new instructional methods for the professional development of classroom teachers, which are based on collaborative relationships between teacher educators and school-based practitioners.

PATRICIA M. HART is an Assistant Professor in the Department of Teacher Education at the University of Dayton, where she teaches courses in the elementary education program. Dr. Hart's current research interests lie in the areas of whole language and multicultural education and in the application of multimedia technology to teacher preparation.

ABSTRACT

Veteran classroom teachers possess a wealth of expert knowledge that can be of value in the professional preparation of K–12 classroom teachers. Recent research on teacher thinking is beginning to make clear the diverse ways in which experienced teachers interpret, process, and respond to classroom stimuli. While such studies help teacher educators understand expert/novice thinking, they make few suggestions on how such knowledge can be used to enhance preservice or entry-year teacher preparation. This paper describes the results of using a media-based, instructional methodology designed to bring the expert thinking of veteran classroom teachers into the preservice teacher-education classroom. In this study, expert teacher thinking is the focus of clinical experiences aimed at helping beginning teachers develop the strategic knowledge instrumental to professional practice.

BACKGROUND AND OBJECTIVES

One important challenge facing schools, colleges, and departments of education seeking to redesign programs for the professional development of classroom teachers is the challenge of finding effective ways to involve expert, school-based practitioners in the preparation of preservice education students. The purpose of this paper is to report data generated by a study of a media-based instructional methodology designed to bring the expert thinking of veteran classroom teachers into the preservice teacher-education classroom, where it can become the focus of clinical experiences aimed at helping prospective teachers develop the strategic *knowledge* (Shulman, 1986) instrumental to professional practice.

While the debate over whether the research on teacher thinking can contribute to the improvement of teacher preparation continues (Floden et al., 1990; Clark and Peterson, 1986; Bromme and Brophy, 1986), this study represents an attempt to respond to Shulman's (1986) observation that one reason teacher thinking research has had minimal impact on teacher education is because it has, at least to date, tended to produce chiefly *propositional knowledge*. While such knowledge is important because it supports a conception of teaching as a highly complex and personal process requiring far more than technical expertise, it has contributed little to improved teacher preparation. Recent studies, for example, comparing expert and novice teachers have done much to advance the proposition that expert teachers have highly developed metacognitive skills and information-rich schema that inform and influence their application of content and pedagogical knowledge (Sabers, Cushing, and Berliner, 1991; Berliner, 1986; Clark and Peterson, 1986). The pressing challenge currently facing teacher educators, however, is the task of designing and delivering professional development programs and activities that are not only respectful of such knowledge, but which hold the promise of helping beginning teachers understand, value, and acquire such knowledge in the most expeditious ways possible.

To date, the development of written teaching cases has constituted teacher education's most popular response to Schulman's 1985 plea for the creation of instructional methods that can help developing teachers acquire strategic understanding and develop extended capacities toward professional judgment and decision making. While there is emerging empirical evidence to document the effect of written case methodology on preservice teacher thinking (Tillman, 1992; Kleinfeld, 1991; Welty, Silverman, and Lyon, 1991; Wilson, 1989), important progress is being made on other fronts, such as the articulation of what a case literature for teaching should look like (Broudy, 1990; Barnes, 1987); experimentation with alternate strategies for the classroom utilization of cases (Meserth, 1991; Sykes, 1989); and the participation of classroom teachers in case preparation (Shulman, 1991; Carter, 1988). Again, the preponderance of such work has concentrated on one form of case methodology: the written case, which is typically processed by undergraduate students under the guidance of a professor of education. While such an approach holds promise, it is a promise constrained, in the view of these writers, by its lack of opportunity for prospective teachers to hear, see, discuss, analyze, and reflect on the views of expert practitioners toward the case in question. The teacher education methodology described herein represents an approach to reality-based, problem-focused teacher education that is enriched and extended by integrating the knowledge of expert classroom teachers.

PROCEDURES FOR CATCHING AND RELEASING TEACHER THOUGHT

As the title of this paper implies, this project employed an angling metaphor as its conceptual frame. Specifically, the researchers were intent upon catching expert teacher thought in as pure a state as possible for the purpose of later releasing it to be caught again by preservice teachers as well as by mentor teachers preparing for practice in entry-year support programs. Given this goal, the eight most commonly reported problems of beginning teachers (Veenman, 1984) were selected as the foci of a series of eight instructional cases, each containing a written vignette, artifact, videotaped mentor/protege role play, and videotaped veteran teacher discussion.

Each case in the series begins with a written vignette that describes a beginning teacher's confrontation with a specific professional problem demanding a strategic response. In an effort to make the *bait* as realistic as possible, the problems portrayed were based on interviews with first-year teachers. This paper, for example, reports data from the study of a case entitled "Karen's Challenge," which involves student discipline at the elementary level. In approximately 700 words, readers are introduced to a first-year teacher named Karen who, despite trying a variety of approaches, is at a loss in handling the deteriorating classroom behavior of two third-grade boys. It is mid-December, and Karen is finally resigned to the fact that she needs to seek the help of her mentor, despite concerns about appearing to be unable to handle her own professional problems. As is the case in "Karen's Challenge," each vignette concludes open-endedly with the beginning teacher deciding to approach his or her mentor for guidance.

Accompanying each vignette is an additional *lure*, which takes the form of an artifact providing additional insight on the problem being explored. In "Karen's Challenge," for example, a statement of personal philosophy on student discipline excerpted from her undergraduate portfolio serves as the artifact.

Each case also includes a ten to twelve minute video role play of a beginning teacher in conference with a mentor teacher about the problem described in the written scenario. In order to produce each role-play video, the researchers invited three practicing mentor/protege teams to participate. To promote spontaneity of responses, teams were not provided details on the case until they arrived at the video production studio. Five minutes prior to taping, the beginning and mentor teachers were given the written scenario and the artifact to read in isolation and were instructed, once tape was rolling, to engage in a spontaneous conference on the problem. The role plays were taped in a television studio with multiple cameras and a simple set designed to simulate a school or classroom setting.

Once all three role plays were recorded, the videotapes were reviewed and one *keeper* selected. Selection criteria included the naturalness of the role players, the genuineness of their interpersonal interactions, and the depth and breadth of ideas explored. The next step in the production process involved inviting a panel of four veteran teachers to view the keeper role-play and to be taped themselves engaging in a focused group discussion of the problem under consideration. Veteran teachers were selected based on their meeting one or more of the following expert criteria: having been formally recognized for outstanding performance by their school, school district, or some external agent; having been chosen to serve as a mentor teacher, or having been recommended by colleagues or by teacher educators as outstanding practitioners.

RESEARCH PURPOSES & DESIGN

The primary purpose of this study was to assess the effect of the use of a videotaped role play and videotaped expert teacher discussion on the thinking of preservice teachers. Specifically, the researchers sought to determine how being exposed, via video, to the expert knowledge of veteran teachers might influence a preservice teacher's analysis of a specific professional problem requiring a strategic response. Insights into such possible influences were acquired by employing qualitative data analysis techniques to analyze written responses to a series of five questions posed by the researchers.

In an effort to pursue the above research objective, two sections of a first-year education course offered at a private midwestern university were selected as the comparison groups. Both sections of "Introduction to the Profession of Teaching" met twice weekly during the fall semester of the 1991/92 school year. Comparative data on sex, age, and type of teaching certification being sought confirmed that the students enrolled in the two sections were quite similar in their demographic composition. The videotape group (Group V) consisted of eighteen female and four male students with a mean age of 21.6. There were twelve Group V members (Vs) majoring in secondary education, nine Vs preparing for elementary school teaching, and one student who was undecided. Comparatively, the traditional group (Group T) was composed of twenty-one female and three male students with a mean age of 21.2. There were eight Group T members (Ts) majoring in secondary education and 14 preparing for elementary school teaching. Additionally, one T was concentrating in special education and one was undecided.

The comparative treatments were administered midway through the fifteen-week semester and were completed in one 90-minute class period. Group V was exposed to the videotaped role play and the videotaped focus group discussion supporting "Karen's Challenge." Group T examined "Karen's Challenge" using small group and whole class discussion techniques.

On the days the treatments were administered, the groups received identical introductions to the activities; they were told that the guest instructors were developing new teaching materials for education classes and that their respective classes had been selected to help field test those materials. Immediately following the introduction, the groups were given the written vignette "Karen's Challenge" and were instructed to take five minutes to read and think about the vignette. No discussion between class members was permitted during this time. At the end of five minutes, students were given a sheet of paper containing the following two questions: **Question 1**: What do you think is the central issue in Karen's Challenge? And, **Question 2**: what do you think is the key to resolving the issue you identified above?

Students were given five minutes to respond to the two questions designed to collect additional data for comparing the two groups prior to the alternate treatments being administered.

Next, Group V members were informed that they would view a ten-minute role play of a conference between Karen and her mentor, Sherrie. The group was also told that the role players were in fact a real first-year teacher and her actual mentor. Comparatively, Group T was asked to "count off" and to quickly form small groups by like numbers. Each of the five small groups was then instructed to select two members to participate in a ten-minute role play of a conference between Karen and her mentor. Students playing Karen were encouraged to identify with Karen's thoughts and feelings while the mentor role players were asked to help Karen resolve her problem. The remaining students in each group were asked to serve as observers. After ten minutes, time was called and students returned to their regular classroom seats. After the videotaped role play was viewed and the student role play/discussions completed, the researchers passed out a second paper containing a single question. The comparative versions of **Question 3** were: Group V: After viewing the role play of "Karen's Challenge," do you have any new insights or perspectives on the problem? If so, please describe. Group T: After role playing and discussing "Karen's Challenge," do you have any new insights or perspectives on the problem? If so, please describe.

After five minutes, time was called and responses to Question 2 collected. Next, Group V members were informed that they would next watch a thirteen-minute video in which four veteran elementary teachers were discussing the videotaped role play that they had just viewed. The VCR was activated and students saw the four teachers viewing the closing seconds of the role play and then discussing "Karen's Challenge." Comparatively, students in Group T were asked to form a seminar circle. One of the researchers then assumed the role of group facilitator and invited students to share their thoughts about how "Karen's Challenge" might be met. The researcher maintained the role of facilitator and purposefully avoided sharing his own views on the problem. After thirteen minutes, the discussion was brought to a close and students were instructed to return to their regular seats. At the conclusion of the videotaped discussion in Group V, and at the end of the seminar discussion in Group T, students in both groups were handed a third sheet of paper containing the following two questions that were identical for both groups: **Question 4**: In your opinion, what should Karen's goal(s) be in this case? **Question 5**: Please recommend at least three specific actions that you think Karen should take to achieve her goal(s). Once again, time was carefully monitored and after five minutes students were instructed to stop writing and turn in their papers.

DATA ANALYSIS

A three-step, qualitative methodology was employed to analyze the data generated by the comparison groups' responses to the five questions posed by the researchers. In Step I, the researchers conducted independent analyses of the written responses for the purpose of identifying and naming categories that could be used to order the data. In an effort to promote greater diversity of interpretations, the analyses were conducted prior to the researchers discussing the data and each researcher developed his or her own coding systems.

In Step II, the researchers met to compare their coded data sets, negotiate categorical schemes for each of the five questions, and determine frequencies of response within each category for both groups V and T. An important part of Step II involved the researchers in the process of comparing coding systems by examining specific subjects' responses as exemplars of a particular code. In Step III, the researchers compared the frequency data generated in Step II and searched for qualitative and quantitative commonalities and differences in the responses of the two groups.

RESULTS AND DISCUSSION

Findings from the analysis of subjects' written responses to the five questions are reported in the order they were asked.

Question 1:   What do you think the central issue is in the story "Karen's Challenge"?

Three categories emerged from the analysis of responses to Question 1. They were: *Student Discipline, Karen's Self-Conceptions,* and *Lack of Collaboration/Communication.*

There were sixteen Group V responses (73 percent) and twenty Group T responses (83 percent), that suggested the key issue in "Karen's Challenge" was maintaining student discipline. Several subjects in both groups, for example, referred specifically to Karen's inability to control two male students, "Jeron and David," while others wrote that Karen had "no effective discipline plan" or that she had simply "lost control." There were nine Group V (41 percent) and seven Group T responses (29 percent), that focused on a variety of issues related to Karen's professional conceptions of self. "Karen has apparently lost confidence in her ability as a teacher" wrote one Group V student while a Group T student observed that "Karen is feeling like a failure, her self-esteem seems to have been affected." Regarding the final category, eight students in the V Group (36 percent) and three in the T Group (13 percent) felt that the key issue in the vignette was Karen's failure to share her problem with other professionals. Exemplary of this sentiment were responses such as, "Karen should have been more willing to share her problem with her mentor" and "I think if she would have sought out some support earlier in the year the problem could have been nipped in the bud."

Question 2:   What do you think is the key to resolving the issue(s) you described above?

The majority of responses to this question were categorized as dealing with *professional collaboration*. There were fifteen Vs (68 percent) and fifteen Ts (63 percent) who suggested that Karen should consult with another professional in an effort to solve her problem. While the majority of such recommendations in both groups were for Karen to speak with her mentor, a few respondents suggested other professionals. For example, two Vs and one T thought contacting the principal was a good idea, whereas three Vs and five Ts referred to seeking advice from other teachers in general. One student in each group recommended that Karen share her problem with the school's guidance counselor.

The second most popular category of response dealt with Karen's need to develop *Discipline Policies and Procedures*. Here, ten Vs (45 percent) and twelve Ts (50 percent) referred to the need for Karen to clearly communicate and consistently enforce classroom rules. Such suggestions from both groups were stated in the form of general principles to adhere to rather than specific practices to employ. Question 2 responses occurring with considerable less frequency included three Vs (14 percent) and four Ts (17 percent) suggestions that a parent conference was needed and three Vs (14 percent) and three Ts (13 percent) reference to Karen's need to be more reflective about the problem.

After comparing Group V and Group T responses to Questions 1 and 2, the researchers concluded that, in addition to sharing comparable demographic profiles, the students in the two groups tended to share highly similar interpretations of "Karen's Challenge" and highly similar thoughts as to what was necessary to meet that challenge.

Question 3:   After viewing the role play of (Group V) or after role playing and discussing Karen's Challenge (Group T), do you have any new insights or perspectives on the problem? If so, please describe them.

Following the alternate interventions, students in Groups V and T were given five minutes to respond in writing to Question 3. Analysis of responses revealed that 11 Vs (50 percent) and eight Ts (33 percent) shared the insight that *Having a Mentor Is Important.* In addition, five Vs (23 percent) and seven Ts (29 percent) acknowledged how important a *Student's Home Life* is when trying to resolve a discipline problem. Beyond sharing these two insights, the two groups had little in common in responding to Question 3. Table 7–1 summarizes the categories and frequencies of response for both groups to Question 3.

Some interesting differences between the responses of the two groups are evidenced in Table 7–1. First, Group V learned through the videotaped role play that Karen had in fact tried a wide variety of approaches to resolving her problem, including separating the troublesome students, contacting the parents, and, in the case of one child, inviting the mother to spend time in her classroom observing her son's behavior. In fact, Group V students learned that part of Karen's loss of self-confidence was because so many of her ideas failed to solve the problem. They also heard Sherrie, Karen's mentor, suggest involving the school counselor to see if there were additional contributing factors. This led to a brief discussion of how important it is to concentrate on the causes of student misbehavior rather than only on the symptoms. Sherrie also reminded Karen how rewards rather than punishments tend to be more effective in influencing behavioral change in elementary students. Finally, the two teachers seemed to agree that David was the instigator and perhaps the key to resolving the problem. As Table 7–1 reports, a number of students included one or more of these observations in their responses. It is also interesting to note that six Group V students commented that they knew more about the problem after seeing the video role play.

After role playing or observing their classmates' role play, and after discussing the problem in small and large group settings, Group T students had noticeably different responses to Question 3. The ten Ts who recommended Karen should try different discipline tactics included four suggestions for "physically separating the problem boys," three suggestions that Karen use "assertive discipline" techniques, two suggestions for "denial of privileges," and one suggestion that she employ "mild desists." Karen's need to regain control was a major concern of the T Group and numerous responses indicated that involving the principal or having a one-to-one talk with the boys for the purpose of letting them know "who is the boss," or "who is in charge" could possibly be of importance in this situation. A handful of other Ts reported that Karen needed to find a way to channel the boys' energies. "Maybe Jeron or David could be used as delivery boys when something has to go to the office" was the suggestion made by one student while another recommended that "they could be kept busy helping the teacher with a variety of classroom tasks such as cleaning the board." Finally, three Ts apparently

TABLE 7-1

Response Frequencies (f) and Percentages (%) for Groups V and T for Question 3

GROUP V (N = 22)			GROUP T (N = 24)		
Response Categories	*f*	%	**Response Categories**	*f*	%
Mentors are important	11	50.0	Mentors are important	8	33.0
Home life is important	5	22.8	Home life is important	7	29.1
Karen has tried many tactics	9	40.9	Karen should try other tactics	10	41.2
Karen should involve the counselor	7	31.8	Karen needs to regain control	10	41.2
Reward rather than punish	6	27.2	Principal should be involved	7	29.1
Focus on causes versus symptoms	6	27.2	Let boys know who is the boss	7	29.1
David is the instigator	4	18.1	Karen's self-confidence is key	3	12.5

Note. Question 3: After viewing the role play of (Group V) or after role playing and discussing (Group T) "Karen's Challenge," do you have any new insights or perspectives on the problem? If so, please describe them.

had gained appreciation for how Karen's lack of self-confidence was contributing to her problem. "If Karen doesn't prove to herself that she can solve this problem it could affect her future as a teacher" was how one student responded.

Question 4: In your opinion, what should Karen's goal(s) be in this case?

Six response categories were identified as a result of the analysis of responses to Question 4 that was administered after Group V had viewed the veteran teacher discussion and after Group T had participated in a whole-class seminar discussion of "Karen's Challenge."

As Table 7–2 makes clear, the V and T groups were quite similar in identifying what they believed Karen's goals should be in this case. One interesting difference was the reference of five Vs to the importance of trying to find the cause of Jeron's and David's deviant behavior.

Question 5: Please recommend at least three specific actions that you think Karen should take to achieve her goals.

Some of the most interesting differences between the Groups V and T emerged in the responses to Question 5 that was designed to elicit strategic responses to "Karen's Challenge."

TABLE 7-2

Response Frequencies (f) and Percentages (%) for Groups V and T for Question 4

Response Categories	GROUP V (N = 22)		GROUP T (N = 24)	
	f	%	f	%
Regain control of the class	10	45.4	11	45.8
Better behavior from Jeron and David	9	40.9	8	33.0
Get to the root of Jeron and David's problem	5	22.7	0	0
Create a more open relationship with the mentor	3	13.6	8	33.0
Regain her self-confidence	4	18.1	3	12.5
Make sure learning occurs in her classroom	3	13.6	3	12.5

Note. Question 4: In your opinion, what should Karen's goal(s) be in this case?

First, it was interesting to note that 12 Vs and 8 Ts recommended that Karen should arrange a one-to-one conference with each of the problem boys. Of particular interest, however, were the different motives that were expressed for holding such a meeting. All twelve of the Vs, for example, stated that the purpose of the conference would be to help determine the causes of the child's behavior. The veteran teacher discussion viewed by Group V included several references to the desirability of finding some time to meet with the boys alone to better understand their needs and possible motives. Specific suggestions included "inviting them to lunch" or "asking them to stay in from recess to help on a special project." Comparatively, all eight of the Ts felt that Karen should use the conference as a way of "asserting her authority" and "letting the boys know that she was in control, not them!"

Echoing the sentiment of Sherrie, the role-play mentor, the veteran teacher group acknowledged how employing rewards or privileges work best, "especially with that age group." In making their strategic recommendations, eighteen Vs (81 percent) made specific reference to employing rewards or privileges rather than punishments or denial of privileges in attempting to promote change in Jeron's and David's behavior. No member of the T Group made such a suggestion. This trend was also true regarding recommendations for the use of behavior contracts, another idea enthusiastically endorsed by the veteran discussion group. There were ten Vs (44 percent) compared to zero Ts suggesting that Karen employ such an approach. As Table 7–3 makes clear, such differences in response for Groups V and T held true for references to other specific strategies such as "time out," "documenting the boys' disruptive behaviors," and "involving the guidance counselor."

The most popular response of the T Group to Question 5 was to clarify classroom rules and to make sure that students understood the consequences of breaking them. There were seventeen Ts (71 percent) compared to only

TABLE 7–3

Response Frequencies (f) and Percentages (%) for Groups V and T for Question 5

Response Categories	Group V (N = 22)		Group T (N = 24)	
	f	%	*f*	%
Individual conferences with the boys to gain insight on possible causes of behavior	12	54.4	1	4.2
Meet privately with the boys to assert herself as being in control	0	0	8	33.3
Reward the boys' good behavior with positive reinforcement including special privileges	18	81.2	0	0
Employ behavior contracts with Jeron and David	10	44.4	0	0
Employ "Time Out"	5	22.7	0	0
Document the boys' behavior using "kid watching journals"	5	22.7	1	4.2
Contact the guidance counselor for additional information on Jeron and David	5	22.7	0	0
Refer Jeron and David to the principal	1	4.5	6	25.0
Clearly communicate rules and consequences	2	9.0	17	70.8
Admit her past mistakes to the students and start over	0	0	4	16.6
Work with her mentor more openly	2	9.0	15	62.5

Note. Question 5: Please recommend at least three specific actions that you think Karen should take to achieve her goals.

two Vs (9 percent) who made such a recommendation. Also of interest was the fact that eight Ts (33 percent) suggested that Karen needed to be more assertive and regain control of her classroom. No member of the V group made such a suggestion. Additionally, six Ts (25 percent) recommended that Karen should refer the boys to the principal, a position shared by only one member of the V Group. Finally, well over half of the Ts (63 percent) expressed the belief that Karen needed to work more closely with her mentor, a perspective referred to by only two Vs (9 percent).

CONCLUSIONS

Before reporting the preliminary conclusions of this study, it should be noted that the manner in which the videotaped segments were employed with Group V is not representative of how the researchers envision such devices being used in the actual teaching of a case such as "Karen's Challenge." Their use in this study was purposely structured to obtain written representations of preservice teacher thinking. One obvious purpose of the video segments will be to stimulate fuller and richer discourse between students and instructors, discourse that in this study was purposely constrained in the interest of science. Additionally, the researchers recognize that many differences in the responses of the V and T Groups are clearly attributable to the fact that the V Group developed different perceptions of "Karen's Challenge" as a result of viewing the role play that introduced new dimensions to the problem. Nonetheless, the following observations seem noteworthy.

Conclusion A: Results of this study suggest that using videotaped representations of expert teacher thinking may serve to help beginning teachers move beyond propositional knowledge such as "Don't smile until Christmas" and begin to reflect on and employ knowledge of greater strategic value in dealing with professional problems such as student discipline. Specifically, this investigation suggests that one potential value of the instructional methodology studied is that it may provide beginning teachers with a broader menu of strategic responses to specific problems typically experienced by entry-year teachers. Responses to Question 5, for example, made clear that the preservice teachers exposed to the videotaped protocols (Group V) suggested the use of more specific, strategic responses to "Karen's Challenge" than did members of Group T.

Conclusion B: Results of this study also suggest that being exposed, via video, to expert teacher thinking may encourage beginning teachers to value more highly the need to resolve one's own teaching dilemmas through autonomous action or peer collaboration as opposed to referring problems to a superordinate. The expert teachers portrayed in the videotapes supporting "Karen's Challenge" were models of self-efficacious professionals committed to resolving their own classroom problems. Although they did make references to the need to "refer to the office" in some cases, it was a practice not strongly emphasized. When compared with Group T subjects, the preservice teachers in Group V evidenced a more positive disposition toward attempting to resolve the problem without employing the school principal.

Conclusion C: Preservice teachers in Group V demonstrated a more clinical attitude toward professional problem solving when compared to their peers in Group T. The fact that Group V teachers were clearly affected by the veteran teachers' emphasis on dealing with "causes as opposed to symptoms" suggests that hearing and seeing veteran teachers model such a positive disposition toward clinical approaches to problem solving may influence beginning teacher thinking.

Conclusion D: Finally, the preservice teachers in Group V evidenced an ability to retain and apply the knowledge of veteran classroom teachers to a specific professional problem posed in a laboratory setting, suggesting that the instructional methodology employed in this study may have significant value as a vehicle for integrating expert teacher knowledge into the preservice teacher education curriculum.

IMPLICATIONS FOR BEGINNING TEACHERS AND SCHOOLS

The instructional methodology described and reported herein represents an effort to bring university-based teacher educators and experienced classroom practioners together in a shared effort to improve preservice teacher education. Importantly, it constitutes an approach to case-based instruction that integrates the practice-focused, expert knowledge of veteran classroom teachers with the research and theory-based knowledge valued by teacher educators.

In an ideal situation and setting, teacher educators would have ready access to expert classroom teachers who, at the most timely instructional moment, could be brought into the teacher education classroom to share their informed and experienced perspective on the various issues and questions being raised by the case literature being studied. Even more ideally, several expert teachers with relevant experience would engage in collegial discourse, examining the case from the multiple perspectives provided by their diverse experiences. Although such a scene could be played out in the kind of professional-development schools proposed by the Holmes Group and others, a host of political and logistical constraints make it unlikely to occur in most educational settings in the foreseeable future.

Encouragingly, as this study has demonstrated, modern media and technology are capable of removing such constraints and making such a potentially powerful learning experience possible.

REFERENCES

Barnes, H. L. (1987). Intentions, problems, and dilemmas: Assessing teacher knowledge through a case method system. (Issue Paper 87–3). East Lansing, MI. The National Center for Research on Teacher Education.

Berliner, D. C. (1986). In pursuit of the expert pedagogue. *Educational Researcher, 15,*(7), 5–13.

Bromme, R., & Brophy, J. (1986). Teacher's cognitive activities. In B. Christiansen, G. Howson, and M. Otte, (Eds.), *Perspectives on mathematics education*, (pp. 99–140). Norwood, NJ: Ablex.

Broudy, H. S. Case studies-why and how. *Teachers College Record*, Spring, 449–459.

Carter, K. (1988). Using cases to frame mentor-notive conversations about teaching. *Theory into Practice, 27,* 214–222.

Clark, C. M., & Peterson, P. L. (1986). Teacher's thought processes. In M. C. Wittrock, (Ed.), *Handbook of research on teaching*, (3d edition, pp. 255–296). New York: Macmillan, 1986.

Floden, R. E., Klinzing, H. G., Lampert, M., & Clark, C. (1990). Two views of the role of research on teacher thinking. (Issue Paper 90–4), East Lansing, MI, the National Center for Research on Teacher Education.

Kleinfield, J. (1991, April). Changes in problem solving abilities of students taught through case methods. Paper presented at the meeting of the American Educational Research Association, Chicago, IL.

Meserth, K. K. (1991). The early history of case-based instruction: Insights for teacher education today. *Journal of Teacher Education, 42,* 243–249.

Sabers, D. S., Cushing, K. S., & Berliner, D.C. (1991) Differences among teachers in a task characterized by simultaneity, multidimensionality, and immediacy. *American Educational Research Journal, 28*(1), 63–88.

Shulman, J. H. (1991). Revealing the mysteries of teacher-written cases: Opening the black box. *Journal of Teacher Education, 42,* 250–262.

Shulman, L. S. (1986) Those who understand knowledge growth in teaching. *Educational Researcher, 15*(2), 4–14.

Sykes, G. (1989). Learning to teach with cases. *Colloquy, 2*(2), 7–13.

Tillman, B. (1992). *A study of the use of case methods in preservice teacher education.* Unpublished doctoral dissertation, Ohio State University, Columbus.

Veenman, S. (1984). Perceived problems of beginning teachers. *Review of Educational Research, 54*(2), 143–178.

Welty, W. M., Silverman, R., & Lyon, S. (1991, April). Student outcomes from teaching with cases. Paper presented at the meeting of the American Educational Research Association. Chicago, IL.

Wilson, S. M. (1989). A case concerning content: Using case studies to teach subject matter. (Craft Paper 89–1). East Lansing, MI, the National Center for Research on Teacher Education.

CHAPTER 8

On Becoming A Responsive Teacher: A Self-Observational Process Analysis

LYNN NATIONS JOHNSON
Western Michigan University

LYNN NATIONS JOHNSON is an Assistant Professor at Western Michigan University in the Department of Education and Professional Development where she teaches in the elementary education program. Her current research focuses on the development of responsive dialogue in teachers and on multiculturalism in education.

ABSTRACT

The present study is a process analysis of one teacher who sought to learn how best to assist the performance of her students during class dialogue sessions. The class dialogues were videotaped, the tapes were transcribed, and the transcriptions along with the videotapes were analyzed for patterns in behavior and perspective which benefited and those which inhibited responsive dialogue. A journal and field notes were used as additional sources of data. The final analysis documented specific behavioral changes as well as changes in perspective which promoted coherent dialogue, and hence the critical thinking of her students as they engaged in the dialogue process. First, the teacher experienced a fundamental change in her perspective of her role. In addition to seeing herself as solely a disseminator of knowledge, the teacher came to view herself as an orchestrator of student learning and a critical participant in the development of her students' abilities to think critically. In addition, several behavioral changes took place. Teacher talk time was effectively reduced to approximately 50 percent of class dialogue time; literal and figurative questions were presented to the class in a more-balanced, carefully sequenced fashion as she refined her question-asking technique; teacher and student interruptions were eliminated; and the teacher learned conceptually to connect statements and topical episodes within each dialogue as she sought to assist effectively the cognitive performance of her students.

As transmitters of language skills, belief systems, and categories of judgment, among other kinds of knowledge, parents have enjoyed far more success than others, including classroom teachers (Goodlad, 1984; Greenfield, 1984; Hoetker & Ahlbrand, 1969; Snow, 1979). Ironically, many teachers who are parents themselves shed some of their most effective teaching methods when they enter the school, and only don them again when they return home (Tharp & Gallimore, 1988). What are these characteristics of parental teaching which have been neglected in the classroom? And how would a teacher adapt these strategies in the school setting? The first aim of this paper is to examine the differences between these two styles of teaching and their results. Additionally, the author will describe and analyze her own efforts to enhance her responsiveness to students, a key factor in the effectiveness of parental teaching.

HOW PARENTS TEACH

Parents look for instructional direction in the questions and answers from their children. Generally speaking, the method of teaching used by parents is naturally responsive (Greenfield, 1984; Snow, 1979; Zukow, 1983). When a child needs to learn a particular skill or concept, the parent identifies the child's level of performance and understanding, then seeks to build a foundation gradually, based on the child's questions and answers. Though two parents may perceive a child's level of understanding and needs differently, both are guided by that perception in their response to him or her. The teaching style is called "natural" because parents who have been observed teach this way in the course of their everyday living. The style is not contrived, nor is it limited to one race, culture, or socioeconomic group. Moreover, the effectiveness of this teaching style is reflected as it is used to pass language and other cultural traits from one generation to the next. Most people have gained the basic language skills that allow them to succeed within their native cultures through naturally responsive teaching or dialogue between parent and child. This style serves as the primary pedagogical model for most people through their most formative years.

HOW CLASSROOM TEACHERS TEACH

The picture for classroom teaching is very different from natural parental teaching. Despite the importance of a responsive domestic model in their pre-adult years, there is no indication that teachers in the United States employ a responsive teaching style in their classrooms (Hoetker & Ahlbrand, 1969; Goodlad, 1984). Studies of professional teacher behavior and cognition have revealed a tendency toward routinization of thought and instruction as well as the avoidance of critical analyses of teaching routines. Teachers spend more time in recitation, a teacher-dominated method of instruction allowing minimal student responses, than in any other teaching activity (Hoetker & Ahlbrand, 1969; Goodlad, 1984). Teachers take their instructional cues for recitation from worksheets, textbooks, and other materials, and prefer those tasks which will occupy students the longest time (Shavelson & Stern, 1981).

STAGE ONE OF THE RESEARCH: PREPARATION FOR DIALOGUE

The differences between the conditions of classroom and parental teaching account for many of the differences in outcome. In particular the teacher's setting is formal, whereas the parent's is typically informal; and where the parent typically teaches one child at a time, the teacher usually teaches from 1 to 35 children. Additionally, the parent attends to the child's skill and intellect for instructional direction, whereas the teacher attends to the curriculum officially adopted by the state. For the parent, curriculum is not critical; for the teacher it is central. Furthermore, time is variable for the parent; for the teacher it is fixed. The parent may have the option of morning, afternoon, evening, or weekend teaching. The parent has seven days a week with a broad choice of hours. The teacher realistically has four to five hours of actual instruction time on each of five days a week, while the remaining one to two hours of the school day are occupied by transition periods, recesses, and lunches.

Given these differences between the instructional conditions of parents and professional teachers, I considered how to adopt methods of parental teaching in my own seventh-grade classroom. Using methods of self-observation, I analyzed my own efforts to develop a naturally responsive style of teaching, which is labeled dialogue in the current study.

The theoretical foundation for dialogue research is based on the work of Vygotsky (1978). Vygotsky viewed cognition as thinking. It exists and operates on at least two interactive levels: the technical-biological or practical level, for example, memory and perception; and the abstract level, such as imagination and conceptualization. Cognition is not predetermined, but is shaped through social interaction and individual initiation within the environment. First the individual experiences through his or her interaction with others; as the experience affects the individual and is internalized, the person's thought processes are added to and/or changed. With this theory of learning guiding my work, I began to pursue a course which would foster my own cognitive growth as well as that of my students. I studied videotapes of successful responsive teachers from the Kamehameha Early Education Project (KEEP) in Hawaii and other teachers employing dialogue in a project conducted by Schneider, Hyland, & Gallimore (Hyland, 1984; Schneider, Hyland, & Gallimore, 1989; Tharp & Gallimore, 1988).

The literature focusing on classroom dialogue (Adler, 1983; Cazden, 1986; Goodlad, 1984; Hoetker & Ahlbrand, 1969) points to the need to reduce the amount of time the teacher talks during periods of instruction (teacher talk time), for other changes in classroom dialogue to proceed effectively. Keeping this in mind, as well as the visual images of responsive teachers from the KEEP project, I attempted to conduct classroom dialogue (Tharp & Gallimore, 1988).

STAGE TWO OF THE RESEARCH: LEARNING TO CONDUCT DIALOGUE

In December 1985, the attempt to conduct dialogue began. A baseline for dialogue skill was determined through analysis of a video- and audiotape of the first session. Each subsequent attempt at dialogue was video- and audiotaped. At the completion of each taped period of instruction I recorded my immediate thoughts in a journal—thoughts regarding my perceived degree of success in conducting dialogue, particular problems that surfaced, choices made, and the rationales for those choices. Later in the day, and many times thereafter, I reviewed the tape and recorded my self-observations as field notes, viewing and reviewing, searching for patterns in my behavior that assisted or hindered student performance during the dialogues. I then determined how I would change my behavior for the next dialogue, what practices to eliminate, what to retain, and with what modifications.

Approximately six months later, I was effectively engaging the students in responsive dialogue. For fully half of the instructional period, the students were talking. The dialogue was conceptually cohesive and logically structured, with each person participating as a member of a team and exploring questions related to the text they were studying. From a Vygotskian perspective, critical thought was occurring "between people (interpsychological)":

> Every function in the child's cultural development appears twice: first, on the social level, and later, on the individual level; first, between people (interpsychological), and then inside the child (intrapsychological). This applies equally to voluntary attention, to logical memory, and to the formation of concepts. All the higher functions originate as actual relations between human individuals (Vygotsky, 1978).

STAGE THREE OF THE RESEARCH: A PROCESS ANALYSIS OF BECOMING A RESPONSIVE TEACHER

Consistent with the theoretical principles of Marxist dialectic, Vygotsky (1978) called for the integration of developmental analysis with the methods of experimental psychology. He labeled as "process analysis" the detailed examination of the unfolding of a psychological development. Moreover, he urged researchers to determine the causal dynamic basis of higher psychological functions by tracing their development from the initial stages. These methodological considerations were especially useful during the third stage of the present study, in which I examined the process of my becoming a responsive teacher.

The transcripts were analyzed to identify and document specific changes in my behavior patterns, as teacher, and in those of the students. My journal and field notes were studied and coded for patterns in thought that related to my teaching in general as well as to the results of the transcript analysis. In the following pages I describe the cognitive and behavioral changes that took place in myself and how those changes affected student performance.

A FUNDAMENTAL CHANGE IN PERSPECTIVE

Before any important changes occurred in my own behavior, I found that I had to alter my view of the roles of time, curriculum, and critical thought in a classroom dialogue, or in what I then called a responsive discussion. In my journal entry and field notes for one class session, dated January 17, I recorded the following:

JOURNAL—

Since my first discussion on December 6, I have conducted several responsive discussions. When I started this session I felt much more confident than I did in December.

When I first started these sessions I purposely allowed a short time for discussion. Today I made every effort to allow for more time because I've learned that there is no problem filling time. The dead silences I had been concerned about haven't occurred. In fact, I need more time than I have.

FIELD NOTES—

Another difference from December 6 is that the reading material was not the primary organizer. I had a set of questions regarding the major points. We referred to the reading, but we did not move through it chronologically, but topically instead. It was not so much a review of what had been read as on December 6, but an examination of the literal meaning and its application to the French Revolution as well as to life at any time. I was focused more on students' comprehending.

As these notes show, a preoccupation with the passage of time and the structure of the curriculum had given way to concern for the students' comprehension and their ability to think critically during these dialogue sessions. As I studied curriculum materials, logically related major questions became the foci for the dialogues. I kept these questions in mind. Movement from one question to the next was not timed, not hurried. Students were given time to think, to respond, to question, which sometimes resulted in not addressing every major question. The dialogue time was valuable because the students were showing the cognitive ability to "step back" from their own reading to gain perspective about what we were studying and to integrate it into their own experiences.

This kind of cognitive processing and responsive teaching through dialogue obviously takes time. In the early dialogue sessions my teaching was chiefly shaped by concerns for time and covering curriculum, whereas six weeks later it was shaped by trying to enhance children's cognitive processing through effective dialogue. Self-observation and reflection, as well as observation of students, led to understanding the value of effective dialogue. Schön referred to this as "reflection in action":

Usually reflection on knowing-in-action goes together with reflection on the stuff at hand. There is some puzzling, or troubling, or interesting phenomenon with which the individual is trying to deal. As he tries to make sense of it, he also reflects on the understandings which have been implicit in his action, understandings which he surfaces, criticizes, restructures, and embodies in further action.

It is this entire process of reflection-in-action which is central to the "art" by which practitioners sometimes deal well with situations of uncertainty, inability, uniqueness, and value conflict (Schön, 1983).

Dialogue does not obviate the need for curriculum nor for considerations of time. There may be occasions when recitation, silent reading, lecturing, and note taking are appropriate for covering a set of facts.

On the other hand, the superiority of dialogue as a method of instruction is clearly more appropriate when one or more students are confused about a concept or when the teacher wants to teach the students how to think critically by analyzing, interpreting, forming logical conclusions and opinions, and going "beyond the information given" (Bruner, 1973a; Bruner, 1973b).

The responsive teacher, an effective dialogist, aims to teach students how to think. When children are confused during recitation or when a teacher wants students to think critically, dialogue needs to begin.

Through dialogue, the focus is placed on the students' skills, intellect, understanding, and confusion which, in turn, dictate curriculum, teacher response, and instructional time—the teacher's responses to her students. The curriculum does not dictate the activities of the responsive classroom teacher, nor does time. Catherine Snow's advice to parents (1979) applies equally to teachers: "Watch what he's doing, listen to what he's saying, and then respond."

We know from previous research that many teachers respond in ways that compromise their effectiveness as dialogists (Goodlad, 1984; Hoetker & Ahlbrand, 1969; Shavelson & Stern, 1981). Based on this work and on the self-observation conducted in connection with this study of responsive teaching using dialogue, the following behavioral changes are recommended for teachers:

1. REDUCE TEACHER TALK TIME

Hoetker and Ahlbrand (1969) found that the average teacher's talk time occupies 75 percent of class time. In this research, teacher talk time was reduced to as little as 40 percent of the total talking time for the class session. However, the discussions in which teacher talk time was approximately 50 percent were more responsive to student need and more successful in directing discussion. The discussions in which I talked less than 50 percent of the time became disjointed and lacked the conceptual cohesiveness essential for productive, responsive dialogue. This suggests a minimum limit below which further reduction of teacher talk time inhibits effective dialogue. The aim of the responsive teacher is to maintain a balance between observation, listening, and responding to the students.

2. PROPERLY BALANCE AND SEQUENCE LITERAL AND FIGURATIVE QUESTIONS

The studies of Hoetker and Ahlbrand (1969) and Goodlad (1984) found that teachers tend to ask questions that are primarily literal as they focus on literal rather than figurative meaning. Building on these findings, the present research suggests that the problem of balance between literal and figurative questions is less a matter of number than of sequence. When I simply increased figurative questions and reduced literal questions, the discussion became disjointed and failed to respond to student need. Rather, increasing the number of questions multiplied perspectives and opinions with no consistent, logical tie between them. However, when I focused on question order, keeping in mind the importance of figurative questions, the discussion was more responsive to student need. For example, posing the broadly conceived figurative question, "Why did the author write this story?" to open the discussion of a short story, prompted little student response. Rather, when I began the discussion with a series of logically related, literal questions to review the short story, students were much more responsive. Then I could pose a figurative question which was also conceptually tied to the discussion. If the students had difficulty answering, I would pose an additional series of logically related, literal questions leading to the figurative questions to assist the performance of the students.

Even in the best combination of literal and figurative questions I found that I was still asking more literal questions. Over the period of the self-observation, I increased the number of figurative questions asked during discussion, but literal questions remained dominant. The data support that, if students comprehend literal information first, they can better respond to figurative questions. Higher order thought is the conceptual tie between literal ideas and their figurative implications.

3. ELIMINATE TEACHER AND STUDENT INTERRUPTION

Among the important conditions of successful dialogue is the observance of dialogic protocol, which proscribes verbal interruption. During the course of the present study, such interruption by both the teacher and the students was particularly intrusive. Interruption of speech rarely occurs without the interruption of thought, which interferes with the conceptual flow of the discussion. Observing the negative consequences of such interruption in our discussions, I systematically eliminated my interruptive behavior by making a conscious as well as a conscientious effort to wait my turn, to listen, to allow others to complete their thoughts before speaking. I became a model of appropriate turn taking.

In order to reduce and even eliminate student interruptions, I ignored such behavior. This response was effective; student interruptions were almost eliminated by June. Once the interruptive behavior was checked, the coherence of classroom dialogue increased.

4. REFINE QUESTION-ASKING TECHNIQUE

a. *Rephrase Questions.*   Because the reduction of literal questions and the increase of figurative questions was not sufficient to produce consistent responsive teaching, it was also necessary to refine question-asking techniques. When the students were confused I sought to rephrase questions, rather than simply to repeat them. Eventually, I learned to simplify figurative questions, separate the component concepts, and question students about those concepts, thereby leading them to the original figurative question.

b. *Pause (Wait Time).*   Pausing before, between, and after questions enhanced my ability to formulate questions. Pausing also gave the students time to apprehend the content of questions and time to respond. Pausing also supported the students' impression that I valued their participation in the discussion and, hence, they regarded their own participation in the dialogue more positively.

5. LEARN TO CONNECT EPISODES AND STATEMENTS CONCEPTUALLY

I came to prize, and sought to foster, coherence in dialogue. With the elimination of interruptions, I was able to pursue this coherence more easily. However, it became necessary that I also learn how to tie conceptually each of my statements and many of the students' statements to those which preceded them. Eventually, the students began to tie their own comments to those of each other, after repeatedly experiencing this conceptual tying process as a teacher-led activity, as can be seen Figure 8–1.

The transcripts of the taped dialogue sessions were coded for conceptual connections between episodes. When the focus of the dialogue shifted, a

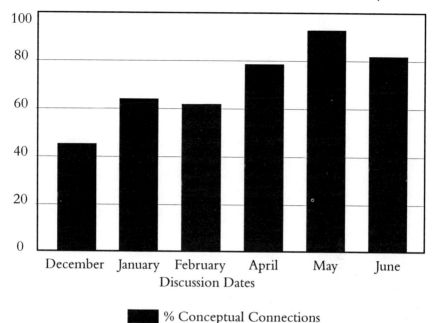

FIGURE 8-1
% Conceptual Connections within and between Episodes

new episode was marked and coded to identify whether or not there was a conceptual tie between the preceding episode and the new one. The result of this analysis showed a steady increase in the percentage of episodes which were conceptually connected, a clear indication of the increasing coherence of the dialogue sessions.

This habit of coherent thinking contributed to the intellectual unity of the class. In contrast, the early discussions were more disconnected, consisting of an accumulation of individual perspectives and opinions, rather than a coherent group effort to examine the major questions addressed.

6. LEARN TO ASSIST PERFORMANCE

Each of the teacher and student behavioral changes described herein was part of the process designed to assist student performance. In the present study, three types of assisted performance were identified specifically. Type 1 was used to assist the performance of the individual who was directly engaged in dialogue with the teacher (direct individual assistance).

Type 2 was used to assist the performance of two or more students (direct group assistance). Finally, Type 3 was used to assist the performance of one or more students through dialogue between the teacher and other students who had demonstrated an understanding of the concept or skill to be learned (indirect assistance). Those students whose performance was to be assisted indirectly had the opportunity to observe the dialogue between the teacher and the more capable student(s).

As these specific types of assisted performance were identified, I understood more clearly the role of assisted performance. I could see that assisted performance often serves more than a single purpose, more than a single person. It is a method used to meet directly the specific developmental needs of the individuals one has engaged in dialogue and/or to meet indirectly the needs of others in the class.

As dialogue strategies developed, assisted performance Types 2 and 3 became predominant. By February, only one assisted performance sequence in five was a Type 1 sequence. This appears to have been a natural extension of the "team" effort during responsive discussion.

The increase of Types 2 and 3 assisted performance challenged the dialogic coherence. There was a greater tendency to pursue tangential questions, and I had to monitor this carefully to prevent a loss of coherence. I also struggled to decide which students should be called on during these group-assisted performance sequences. Who would benefit most and who would be most helpful at particular points in the dialogues? I began to see that the group and individuals within the group benefited more when I clearly identified the students' respective cognitive needs; this became the important element in deciding who would participate and when. Seeing that all students had an equal number of questions or an equal amount of time in a given class period became less important. Rather, the issues were whether I balanced my choice of students over time, and in addition to this consistently sought to identify the students' cognitive needs, assist the performance of students who did not understand, and solicit the help of students who did understand in assisting the performance of their peers. Dialogues as assisted-performance sequences became longer as I learned how to better identify student need and to lead them to correct answers through the questioning process. Assisted-performance sequences also increased in frequency when I learned how to identify when students were confused or did not fully comprehend a particular idea and when I actually assisted the students directly. Previously, I had ignored students when they could not respond and simply moved on to other students who I presumed would be able to respond correctly.

The relationship between increased assisted performance and increased conceptual connection is shown in Figure 8–2. Transcripts of the taped dialogue sessions were coded and then counted for both kinds of teacher-pupil interaction. As is evident in Figure 8–2, the relationship between the two is consistent throughout the period of the study. The two skills are intricately tied to one another, each encouraging the other. The two skills are essential parts of effective responsive teaching. The development of responsive teaching techniques, including the ability to assist performance and to conceptually connect student and teacher turns, benefited both the teacher and the students as individuals and as members of a group.

TEACHING RESPONSIVELY: A DIFFICULT CHALLENGE

This paper has explored the similarities and differences between home and school as teaching places and between parental and classroom teaching styles. It has provided a detailed analysis of the responsive teaching process in a classroom. The results of this research point to three particular challenges related to teaching responsively through dialogue. First, responsive teaching in a classroom of 30 is much more demanding than responsive teaching with a

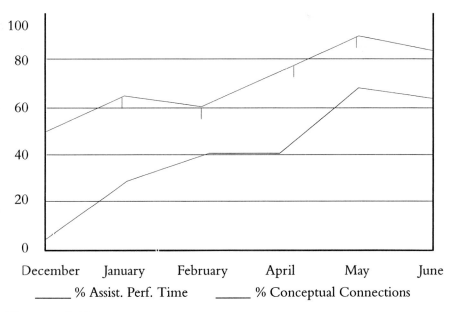

FIGURE 8-2

Assisted Performance and Conceptual Connection Compared

single child in the home. Given the typically large number of students, the constraints of time and curriculum, and the multiple roles of the classroom teacher, responsive teaching requires exceptional teacher effort. Second, because responsive teaching is more complex in a classroom than in a home, teachers should be formally prepared in the process. Responsive teaching does not evolve naturally and is more difficult to learn than more direct styles of teaching. Finally, recitation, the predominant direct style of teaching, is less psychologically demanding for the teacher. Given these challenges, I next look at ways teacher education might respond.

For responsive teaching to become a focus in teacher education, changes regarding the role of the classroom teacher are necessary. The classroom teacher must be viewed not only as one who disseminates knowledge, but also as one who orchestrates learning and teaches students how to think well through responsive teaching. This dialogue research is one important step in our growing understanding of the responsive teaching process, both the role that it plays and the place that it has in classroom life and learning.

REFERENCES

Adler, M. J. (1983). *Paideia: Problems and possibilities.* New York: Macmillan.

Bruner, J. S. (1973a). Going beyond the information given. In J. M. Anglin (Ed.), *Beyond the information given* (pp. 218–238). New York: W. W. Norton and Company.

Bruner, J. S. (1973b). The growth of representational processes in children. In J. M. Anglin (Ed.), *Beyond the information given* (pp. 313–324). New York: W. W. Norton and Company.

Cazden, C. (1986). Classroom discourse. In M. Wittrock (Ed.), Handbook of research on teaching (pp. 432–463). Chicago: American Educational Research Association.

Goodlad, J. I. (1984). *A place called school.* New York: McGraw Hill Book Company.

Greenfield, P. M. (1984). A theory of the teacher in the learning activities of everyday life. In B. Rogoff and J. Lave (Eds.), *Everyday cognition* (pp. 117–138). Cambridge: Harvard University Press.

Hoetker, J., & Ahlbrand, W. P. (1969). The persistence of the recitation. *American Educational Research Journal, 6,* 145–167.

Hyland, J. T. (1984). *Teaching about the constitution: Relationships between teachers' subject matter knowledge, pedagogic beliefs, and instructional decision-making.* Unpublished doctoral dissertation, University of California, Los Angeles.

Schneider, P., Hyland, J., & Gallimore, R. (1985). The Zone of Proximal Development in 8th Grade Social Studies. *The Laboratory for Comparative Human Cognition Newsletter, 7*(4), 113–119.

Schön, D.A. (1983) *The reflective practitioner*. New York: Basic Books.

Shavelson, R., & Stern, P. (1981). Research on Teachers' Pedagogical Thoughts, Judgments, Decisions, and Behavior. *Review of Educational Research*, 51, 455–498.

Snow, Catherine. (1979). Conversations with children. In P. Fletcher & M. Garman (Eds.), *Language acquisition*, (pp. 363–375). Cambridge: Cambridge University Press.

Tharp, R., & Gallimore, R. (1988). *Rousing minds to life*. Cambridge: Cambridge Press.

Vygotsky, L. S. (1978). *Mind in society: The development of higher psychological processes*. Cole, M., John-Steiner, V., Scribner, S., & Souberman, E. (Eds.). Cambridge: Harvard University Press.

Zukow, P. G. (1983). *Caregiver practices in a rural-born population in central Mexico*. Unpublished manuscript, University of California, Los Angeles.

Processes: Implications and Reflections

LESLIE HULING-AUSTIN
W. ROBERT HOUSTON

CRITIQUE/APPLICATION

The topic of diversity in the processes of instructional analysis perhaps has more to do with a mind-set than research methodologies. Griffin (1985) comments on the need to use multiple approaches in creative combinations to better understand the complexities of schooling and the teaching/learning process:

> To understand the interactions around and within complex contexts such as schools, I believe it absolutely necessary that we make much more vigorous use of methodologies that blend and explain, that answer and provide needed detail, and that name and describe. This blend is only possible when complementary although basically different conceptions of scientific inquiry can be used in tandem (p. 45).

The importance of mind-set can be illustrated through the analogy of the journey versus the destination. If one's view of the goal of the journey is to arrive at a destination (the best approach(es) to the study of teaching), then one fails to recognize the elusive, ever-changing nature of the teaching/learning enterprise and is destined to experience frustration over never achieving the goal. However, if one's view is that the purpose of the journey is to continually find better ways of teaching and studying, then the emphasis shifts to one of progressive change and each successive change becomes the "norm" rather than an inconvenience.

A mind-set which embraces progressive change in how we approach the study of teaching is critically important if we hope to advance our understanding of schools, the teaching/learning process, and the preparation and development of teachers. Rather than arguing the benefits of quantitative versus qualitative methods, naturalistic versus controlled studies, or what types of inquiry really "count" as research, we can advance more quickly if we adopt a "progressive change" mind-set to the study of teaching and develop ways of scrutinizing individual studies and bodies of literature for the purpose of gleaning what they have to contribute to our understanding of the educational enterprise and/or ways of studying it.

The four studies included in this division serve as excellent models through which to analyze diverse approaches to studying teaching. The studies can initially be analyzed at different levels involving research questions (purpose and content), and research approaches (source and subjects, setting, scope and duration, construct, process, and procedures). Figure PII–4 graphically demonstrates this analysis. Additional analyses can then be undertaken to examine key findings, the strengths and shortcomings of each study, and the interactive relationship between approaches and findings. Finally, the studies can collectively serve as a catalyst to launch us into additional questions related to diverse approaches to the study of teaching.

RESEARCH QUESTIONS

As a group, these studies address some of the more intriguing and perplexing questions that face teachers and teacher educators. The *purpose* of three of the studies (Rowley and Hart, Kagan and Tippins, and Reiman and Parramore) was to deal with the central question of how to structure a teacher preparation program so that it is meaningful to the preservice teachers and promotes the acquisition of necessary knowledge, skills, and values in the most expeditious ways possible. The purpose of the other study (Johnson) focuses on the function and effects of classroom dialogue and how the amount and quality of teacher talk can be altered through a systematic self-observational process analysis.

In regard to *content*, each of these studies addresses complex questions that have far-reaching implications. Johnson examines the role of the teacher in classroom dialogue and compares the "responsive" teaching style of parents to that of teachers, which tends to focus more on recitation and teacher-dominated instruction. The approach Johnson is advocating is radically different than typical current practice. If future studies bear out that such a method is a superior instructional approach, the challenge for teacher educators would be to respond by preparing a generation of teachers not to teach as they have been taught, but rather to teach a totally different way. Although past efforts to do this have not experienced great success, the real payoff, which would come two generations down the line, could be great. When students who have been taught by teachers using responsive dialogue become teacher prospects themselves, they most likely will approach "responsive" teaching as if it is their native language. Johnson's research question obviously has the potential of far-reaching effects.

Reiman and Parramore are dealing with the questions of the relationship between the psychological maturity of teachers and success as a teacher and

	JOHNSON	REIMAN AND PARRAMORE	ROWLEY AND HART	KAPPAN AND TIPPINS
Purpose	improve own practice	improve preservice	improve preservice	improve preservice
Content	classroom dialogue	moral development of prospective teachers	effects of case studies and expert teacher dialogue on aquisition of expertise	the use of case writing to capture and reflect teacher growth
Source & Subjects	classroom teacher as participant/ observer; N = one classroom	teacher educa-tors as external rcscarchcrs; N = 26 teacher education students	teacher educators as external re-searchers; N = 46 teacher education students	teacher educators as participant/ observers; N = 12 student teachers
Setting	middle school classroom	teacher prepara-tion program including field experiences	college classroom	student teaching experiences in two states at elem. and sec. schools
Scope & Duration	all class discus-sions during one semester in middle school classroom	pre/post tests in freshman and sr. years; 2 semes-ters of field experiences and tutoring	two paired college classes of 90 minutes each	one semester data collection consist-ing of responses to three case writing assignments
Construct	natural setting (mid. school classroom)	natural setting (teacher prep. program)	two simulated treatments in paired classes	natural setting (student teaching)
Process	structured self-analysis resulting in qualitative and quantitative findings	structured analy-sis of qual. meas-ures resulting in qual. and quan. findings	unstructured analysis of qualitative data	unstructured anal-ysis of qualitative data
Procedures	audiotapes; videotapes; journal entries	Defining Issues Test; Paragraph Completion test; Constantinople test	open-ended questionnaires	case studies generated by student teachers

FIGURE PII–4

Studies Can Be Compared and Contrasted Through Cross-Study Analysis how to foster the development of psychological maturity. These questions are of paramount importance because they question the very foundation of the teacher-preparation program. If the teachers we turn out lack the maturity to apply their knowledge and skills in a classroom situation with children, then what good does it do to teach them the knowledge and skills? The answers to the types of research questions being dealt with here may ultimately tell us the answer is not so much in program revision as it may be in determining better methods for recruiting and selecting teacher candidates.

Rowley and Hart, like Reiman and Parramore, are grappling with the question of how you get novice teachers to think and behave more like successful veteran teachers. The question is a difficult one. As Peterson and Comeaux (1987) explain, simply telling novices what experts know will not produce expertise because telling a novice, for example, how an expert opens the classroom lesson does not tell the novice how the expert arrived at the decision to do it in that way or why. "Unless the explanation is broken down in such a way that the novice can assimilate and retain the information and unless the novice is given many different opportunities to practice the procedure, it is unlikely that 'expert' information will have any impact on the novices' schema or on his/her acquisition of expertise." (p. 330). Rowley and Hart are essentially asking whether the use of case studies, combined with input from experts via technology, is effective in helping novices break down, assimilate, and retain information that experts possess.

Kagan and Tippins are also using cases studies, this time to gauge professional growth among student teachers. Their study actually addresses a dual question: What professional growth occurs through student teaching and to what degree do case studies produced by student teachers capture and reflect this growth? Their research approach also leads to a logical cause-and-effect question of "Does the writing of case studies not only indicate growth, but does it also cause professional growth?" These important questions are very complex and can lead to changes in how preservice teacher-education programs are structured and delivered.

The idea of using case studies as a teacher-preparation strategy is one that is growing in popularity. Authors like Shulman (1986) and Carter (1987) have been advocating their use to model step-by-step how experts go through the problem-solving process. More recently, the September/October 1991 issue of *Journal of Teacher Education* was devoted to case methodologies in teacher education and two national competitions focused on case methods are now under way. One effort is a national case competition for teams of prospective teachers from programs across the United States and Canada, while the other is a case-writing competition for people interested in teacher-education curricula.

RESEARCH APPROACHES

The variety of approaches used in these four studies is a testimonial to the need for multiple approaches to investigate complex phenomena. In regard to the *source and subjects* of these studies, Johnson was a participant/observer, as were Kagan and Tippins. The other two studies were conducted by researchers collecting data from other parties. All of the studies use relatively small sample sizes ranging from $N = 1$ (Johnson) to $N = 46$ (Rowley and Hart). The Kagan and Tippins study involved twelve student teachers and the Reiman and Parramore study involved twenty-six undergraduates enrolled in a teacher-education program. Two of the studies involved a comparison group (Reiman and Parramore, and Rowley and Hart).

There was a great deal of diversity in the *setting* and *scope and duration* of the data collections in the four studies. In the Rowley and Hart study, actual data were collected in two 90-minute class periods, although preparations for the study entailed months of selecting case material and producing videotapes of case scenarios and expert teacher reflections. In the Reiman and Parramore study, pretest data were collected in the first month of the freshman year and posttest data were collected in the last month of the senior year. Data collections in the other two studies spanned approximately six months. In terms of *construct*, Rowley and Hart simulated two treatments, whereas the other researchers collected data from actual events and activities as they occurred naturally.

Data collection *processes* and *procedures* also varied greatly. In the Johnson study, the investigator engaged in self-observational process analysis utilizing audio- and videotapes, transcripts of classroom interactions, and journal and field notes. Two other studies analyzed the written work of study participants. Kagan and Tippins analyzed the case studies written by student teachers at the beginning, middle, and end of their student teaching experience, whereas Rowley and Hart examined the responses of students to focusing questions administered at three points during a 90-minute class period in which a case study was being analyzed.

Finally, it is interesting to note that only Reiman and Parramore used formal measures for data collection in that they used well-recognized instruments focused on cognitive and moral development, the Defining Issues Test, the Paragraph Completion Method test for conceptual level, and the Constantinople test of ego development. The fact that the other studies did not utilize traditional measures may indicate that many contemporary researchers are attempting to investigate questions for which there are currently no formal measures available for use. In the past, that absence of validated instruments was seen as a "red flag" that made research results "questionable" at best. The challenge today is to maintain academic rigor while entering new territory and asking new research questions in new ways. While this in no way advocates an "anything goes" approach to educational research, it is probably true that if we insist on looking at things only the way we have always looked at them, we are undoubtedly going to see only what we have always seen.

FINDINGS

Each of the four studies produced important and useful findings. The Johnson study, which focused on the dynamics of classroom interactions, was the most complex study and produced the most detailed set of findings. One finding, which was not explicitly mentioned by the author, is the clear revelation that changing teacher behavior in an area as complex as classroom dialogue is a very involved, time-intensive, and labor-intensive process. While it certainly can be done, there is little likelihood of its being accomplished as a result of short training sessions or sessions that involve teachers with less than high commitment to changing classroom dialogue.

For persons concerned about understanding in detail the dynamics of classroom interactions, this study offers many interesting insights. For example, in the area of teacher talk, it is estimated that in the typical classroom, teacher talk accounts for approximately 75 percent of the classroom talk (Hoetker and Ahlbrand, 1968), and Goodlad and others have indicated the importance of reducing teacher talk time. However, Johnson's findings indicate that in reducing teacher talk time, there appears to be a point of diminishing return. She found that when teacher talk time was reduced to 50 percent, discussions were more successful than when teacher talk time was reduced to substantially less than 50 percent. It is important to remember that the goal is not just for students to talk more, but for classroom discussions to be meaningful for the participants. Johnson also found that, in shifting from more literal to figurative questions, success is highly dependent upon sequencing of questions, not just asking more figurative questions and fewer literal questions. Another exciting finding from Johnson's work is how students learned from a teacher-led activity to tie their own comments to those of each other, thus enhancing the coherence in dialogue. The realization of the need for "connectedness" among comments and the ability to make these connections is undoubtedly at the essence of meaningful dialogue, and appears, from Johnson's work, to be a "teachable skill."

Finally, Johnson's findings related to the role and function of assisted performance in class discussions are very thought-provoking. She found that assisting students in their comments often served more than a single purpose, and more than a single person. In identifying what she called "zones of proximal development," she introduced the idea that not all students have to participate in all aspects of discussions and that, in fact, students can benefit more from observing other students operating in their respective zones than having the class discussion become disjointed because specific students were not able to contribute meaningfully in discussions involving advanced complexity.

The other three studies focus on teacher-preparation strategies and each contributes valuable information related to how novice teacher development can be facilitated and studied. Reiman and Parramore's findings, like those of Kohlberg (1969) and Rest (1986), support the proposition that the development of moral reasoning can be facilitated through "role-taking" experiences. Further, one can conclude that certain field experiences and tutoring experiences, coupled with guided reflection, are activities that enable students to take another's point of view. While it is commonly recognized among teacher educators that field experiences serve many functions, it is interesting that most would probably not nominate the "role taking" that takes place among prospective teachers as a primary goal of field experiences. With these new findings and others like them, it is possible that as teacher educators work to conceptualize and implement field experiences, greater attention can be given to the "role-taking" function of field experiences in order to better facilitate the development of moral reasoning. This approach to teacher preparation would certainly be in line with Goodlad's view (1990) that teaching is fundamentally a moral enterprise (p. 255).

The remaining two studies examine the use of case studies in teacher preparation. The Rowley and Hart study utilizes the case study in an attempt to promote the acquisition of expertise among prospective teachers. Specifically, the study compares a nontechnological approach to an approach that integrates the use of videotapes and the discussions of "expert" teachers. Their findings suggest that the use of video in presenting a teaching case does enhance student understanding and their ability to generate more and better suggestions to address the problem presented through the case. It stands to reason that the integrated use of video makes the case more interesting and helps it "come alive" for participants. Furthermore, by observing how experts go through the problem-solving process, novices learn to look at the causes, and not just the symptoms, of problematic situations in the classroom. The Rowley and Hart findings also suggest that observing how experts solve problems helps novices come to value the need to resolve their own problems through autonomous action or peer collaboration as opposed to referring problems to superordinates. This suggests that input from experts is enormously helpful in teacher preparation and that technology can help make this happen when immediate face-to-face contact between notives and experts is not feasible.

In the Kagan and Tippins study, the case study is used primarily to study teacher growth, as opposed to facilitating teacher growth, although it is likely that some of the latter occurred. Kagan and Tippins based their study on the belief that classroom cases reflect their authors' cognitions and perceptions and their findings supported this belief in that the cases written by participants tended to get more complex with increased experience in field settings. These findings support the value of having students write cases (as well as study already prepared cases) in the preparation phase of learning to teach. Through the cases written by participants in their study, they identified that secondary students may have special needs and concerns related to classroom management and discipline that need to be addressed through special interventions on the part of teacher educators. Also, their study identifies an important contribution that student teaching makes to the teacher-preparation process. Participants in this study exited student teaching with the understanding that there are many important things teachers cannot fix. Such an understanding is very important in combatting what Veenman (1984) terms as the "reality shock" that contributes to the demise of many beginning teachers.

INTERRELATIONSHIPS BETWEEN APPROACHES AND FINDINGS

The challenge the researcher faces in selecting investigative approaches to answer a specific research question is much like the challenge the classroom teacher faces in selecting the best teaching strategy once he/she has determined the content to be taught. In both cases, numerous approaches are possible, and each approach has both strengths and drawbacks. In most cases, there is not a single, best approach, and in every case, the results are highly dependent upon the approach selected.

Every study has the potential to contribute to our understanding of the teaching/learning process and to our understanding of investigative processes. Sometimes, our biases (either positive or negative) related to one factor or the other overshadow our view of the other. For example, if one questions the research approach being used in a specific study, then one might totally discount the findings of that study even though some or all of them may be valid. Similarly, if the findings of a specific study appear to be insignificant, the tendency is to discount the value of the study even though the investigative processes might be groundbreaking. It is important to consider the dual functions of research efforts and to value contributions in both the areas of findings and methodologies.

These four studies provide the opportunity to analyze the interrelationships between research approaches and findings. These analyses are presented to model an ongoing process of critical analysis and reflection that we believe to be an important part of the research enterprise, and should not be interpreted as criticisms of these studies, as many of the points we make here are acknowledged by the authors themselves as study limitations.

The self-observational process analysis attempted by Johnson is an extremely difficult and time-consuming research approach. Most teachers report that it is difficult to focus on the technical aspects of teaching while engaging in teaching. Johnson has relied on technology (audio- and video-tapes) to help with this process. However, an analogy that is often used is that the classroom observer, through observation and feedback, is like someone "holding up a mirror" that helps the classroom teacher see his/her own performance. Johnson did not have the benefit of "a mirror" in this study and it is reasonable to question how the findings might have been different if viewed with one or more additional set(s) of eyes. In addition, since teacher growth was the primary purpose of this study, if Johnson had had a partner who was also attempting to modify his/her own classroom dialogue, Johnson would have had not only the benefit of another set of eyes observing her, but would also have benefited from being able to "see" firsthand the techniques she was focusing on and to discuss this through feedback sessions both as an observer and one being observed. Our point here is not to draw into question all self-analyses, but to suggest that the researcher carefully consider both the advantages and drawbacks of such an approach in determining whether or not this is the best approach to utilize in any specific research endeavor.

Both the Kagan and Tippins study and the Rowley and Hart study probably could have been strengthened through more rigorous data-analysis procedures. In each study, two researchers began data analysis independently without a common data analysis framework or coding system. While this approach may have promoted greater diversity of interpretations, it is unclear what may have "fallen through the cracks" as a result of sorting the data using undefined categories. While we believe it is important to maintain some flexibility throughout the data-analysis process, in these cases we believe some attempt at a common coding system and perhaps even striving for some degree of interrater reliability might have strengthened the end product.

The Kagan and Tippins study also included a confounding variable that is quite problematic. This study involved elementary student teachers at the University of Georgia and secondary student teachers at the University of Alabama. While interinstitutional collaboration and research hold much promise for improving practice, in this study it is unclear whether differences are primarily the result of elementary versus secondary differences or Institution A versus Institution B differences. The study would have been much improved if it could have included both elementary and secondary student teachers at both institutions, or student teachers at the same level at both institutions. If this had been the case, results could have been discussed in terms of similarities and differences between elementary (or secondary) teachers at both institutions and between student teachers at Institution A and Institution B, regardless of level.

Also, in the Kagan and Tippins study, the researchers reported major differences between elementary and secondary student teachers. While these differences may be present, we believe the researchers may be premature in trying to speculate why these differences exist. For example, the researchers noted that secondary student teachers are more concerned with discipline than elementary student teachers, presumably because the elementary student teachers have made more progress in understanding the complexity of student problems and how this influences the classroom situation. While this may be true, an alternative explanation might be that secondary student teachers are more concerned with discipline than elementary student teachers because an unruly secondary student may in fact be considerably more threatening (and harder to deal with) than an unruly elementary student. We suggest that instead of prematurely explaining these differences, the researchers perhaps should only note the differences and cite a need for additional studies to investigate in detail the dynamics of the elementary and secondary teaching experience in an attempt to understand why these differences exist.

As mentioned earlier, the Reiman and Parramore study involved the longest data collection period of any of the studies and was the only study to use established measures for data collection and analysis. While these factors may be strengths on the one hand, they might also be study limitations on the other. Because the amount of time that elapsed between the pretest and posttest was so great (four years), there is a greater possibility that influencing factors other than those being investigated have intervened and are partially or totally responsible for the differences in moral reasoning gains experienced by treatment subjects. In addition, because the measures were formal and standardized, the opportunity to get other, possibly valuable data, is precluded. In other words, if one were to have an informal discussion with study subjects about moral reasoning, could the subjects themselves give alternative explanations for any changes that may have occurred? This study could perhaps have been strengthened by the collection of periodic data throughout the study and by combining informal, qualitative measures along with the formal measures used.

ADDITIONAL QUESTIONS

Our analyses of these studies lead us to some additional questions related to diversity in the study of teaching. While all of the questions addressed in these four studies are important and intriguing, we wish to single out a few that we believe are especially critical at this time.

The role of technology in teacher education is a research question that has only begun to be addressed. Technology has the potential to change teacher education as we know it. For example, college classrooms can be linked interactively with public school classrooms miles away, allowing the pre-service teacher-education student earlier and more timely access to classrooms than has previously been the case. As teachers begin to teach in classrooms with more sophisticated technology (interactive videodisk players, computers networked with a variety of subscription services, and so on), the way we prepare teachers to teach and to use technology must change radically. The challenge before us is to incorporate technology, not for technology's sake, but in ways that allow us to accomplish meaningful ends that are consistent with a developmental view of learning to teach.

Perhaps one of the most difficult questions we face in teacher education today is the issue of adult/moral development as it relates to teacher preparation. Although few people have been bold enough to ask, a fundamental question of importance to teacher education is whether or not, as a group, young adults (persons in the early to mid-twenties) possess the psychological maturity to be successful in the classroom. If the answer ultimately is found to be that, by and large, they do not, the question then becomes whether or not learning experiences can be structured to help significant numbers develop the level of psychological maturity needed by the time teacher preparation is completed. Ultimately, if this cannot be accomplished, a total rethinking and restructuring of teacher-preparation programs will be required to target a different population than the typical college undergraduate. Obviously, such radical changes could have serious repercussions related to teacher recruitment, teacher supply and demand, and the structure and function of traditional university-based teacher education programs.

Our final question relates to how the study of teaching if viewed. One way to view the study of teaching is in terms of research questions and research approaches. This is somewhat similar to viewing teaching in terms of subject matter and pedagogy. In the past, it was assumed that an individual with a firm grasp of subject matter and pedagogy was fully equipped to teach. However, in recent work (Grossman and Richert, 1986), it has been suggested that teachers actually develop through experience something called "pedagogical content knowledge," which enables them to conceptualize the subject matter as a series of connected learning events or classroom activities. It occurs to us that, similarly, the study of teaching may be more than just research questions and research approaches. Instead, part of our mind-set might be to recognize the study of teaching as a systematic series of investigations that link together and build toward a deeper understanding. Without this broader view, our overall research efforts might resemble a classroom in which daily lessons are unrelated to one another and therefore outcomes are significantly diminished. We believe individuals should consider this broader view both in terms of their own work as it evolves over a period of years and how their work interrelates with that of other researchers. Currently, much research exists but it is as if much of it is "floating" in midair. Grimmett and his colleagues (1990) discuss a process of knowledge validation that allows practitioners to recast, reframe, and reconstruct past understandings in such a way as to generate fresh appreciations. To be utilized effectively, research needs to be linked to the broader field in both logical and creative ways, and we believe this to be the greatest challenge facing researchers and practitioners in our profession today.

REFERENCES

Carter, K. (1987). Using cases to frame mentor-novice conversations about teaching. *Theory into Practice, 27*, 214–222.

Goodlad, J. I. (1990). *Teachers for Our Schools.* San Francisco: Josey-Bass.

Griffin, G. A. (1985). Teacher induction: Research issues. *Journal of Teacher Education, 36* (1), 42–46.

Grimmett, P. P., Erickson, G. L., Mackinnon, A. M., & Riecken, T. J. (1990). Reflective practice in teacher education. In R. T. Clift, W. R. Houston, and M. C. Pugach (Eds), *Encouraging Reflective practice in education: An analysis of issues and programs* (pp. 20–38). New York: Teachers College Press.

Grossman, P. L., & Richert, A. E. (1986). Unacknowledged knowledge growth: A reexamination of the effects of teacher education. *Teaching & Teacher Education, 4*, 53–62.

Hoetker, J. & Ahlbrand, W. (1968). The persistence of the recitation: A review of observational studies of teacher questioning behavior. Washington, D. C.: Office of Education.

Kohlberg, L. (1969). Stage and sequence: The cognitive-developmental approach to socialization. In D. Goslin (Ed.), *Handbook of socialization theory and research*, Chicago, IL: Rand.

Peterson, P. L., & Comeaux, M. A. (1987). Teachers' schemata for classroom events: The mental scaffolding of teachers' thinking during classroom instruction. *Teaching and Teacher Education, 3*, 319–331.

Rest, J. R. (1986). *Moral development: Advances in research and theory*. New York: Praeger.

Schulman, L. S. (1986). Those who understand: Knowledge growth in teaching. *Educational Researcher, 15*, (2), 4–14.

Veenman, S. (1984). Perceived problems of beginning teachers. *Review of Educational Research, 54* (2), 143–178.

Division III

Diverse Perspectives on Communication

Communication: Overview and Framework

Virginia P. Richmond
James C. McCroskey
West Virginia University

Virginia P. Richmond is Professor and Coordinator of Graduate Studies in the Department of Communication Studies at West Virginia University. She has authored over 10 books and 80 journal articles and book chapters relating to communication. Her current research interests focus on nonverbal immediacy teacher behaviors and impact on student motivation and on student affective and cognitive learning.

James C. McCroskey is Professor and Chairperson of the Department of Communication Studies at West Virginia University. He has authored over 25 books and 200 journal articles and book chapters relating to communication. His current research interests focus on comparisons across cultures of the impact of teacher communication behaviors on student affective and cognitive learning.

Teachers are professional communicators. Teacher educators are responsible for preparing prospective teachers to enter the profession. To the extent that teachers enter the profession less than fully competent to communicate with their students, their students' parents, their colleagues, their administrators, and the general public of the communities where they teach, the teacher education program has failed them.

Unfortunately, if we were to judge most of our programs by this standard, failure would be the norm. Even the majority of teacher *educators* have little or no formal training in the field of communication. For elementary and secondary teachers who have had a course in the field, the course they are most likely to have taken is public speaking. While such courses can be useful, they typically do not even introduce the student to the process of human communication as it exists in typical classrooms. As any experienced teacher knows, most teachers do very little public speaking as such, but they are involved in communication virtually all day, every day. In a very real sense, there is no teaching without communication.

While there are those of us who are both instructional communication specialists and teacher educators, we are relatively few in number and our influence, for good or ill, is not widely felt in teacher-education programs across the country. While there are a few books available in this area (for example, McCroskey, 1992; Richmond, 1992; Richmond & McCroskey, 1992), these are not required reading for students in most teacher-education programs. Hence, it came as a very pleasant surprise to us to learn that one of the four sections of this volume was to be devoted to communication and that we were selected to introduce this section and comment on the top papers that were chosen to appear here. ATE's decision to place this emphasis on communication is a very important step toward creating a wider understanding of the important role communication plays in the teaching profession. To facilitate this objective, therefore, let us begin by providing an overview of some of the areas within the study of communication, which may have direct bearing on the teaching profession.

AREAS OF STUDY IN COMMUNICATION

The field of communication is very broad and, depending on how one chooses to define its parameters, includes such vastly divergent concerns as theater, speech, telecommunications, journalism, advertising, television production, packaging, audiology, and insect communication. For our purposes here we can focus on a somewhat smaller range of concerns. The areas that we have identified as highly associated with the teaching profession include general communication theory, nonverbal communication, organizational communication, communication problems of children (and adults), mass-mediated communication, interpersonal and relational communication, persuasion and social influence, and intercultural communication. We will briefly consider each of these and attempt to indicate how each might provide useful information for teachers, and hence, teacher educators.

General communication theory.   This is a broad area of scholarship that draws on both philosophical and empirical scholarship in the pursuit of understanding how the communication process actually occurs, what are the components of the process, what variables operate within the process, how communication happens, and what are its effects. "Instructional" communication theorists seek to apply general communication theory to the specific instructional context in order to generate specific theories relating to instruction. Testing of such theories in actual classrooms permits the refinement and amplification of the theories to the point that they can provide a substantive base for instruction of preservice and in-service teachers.

Nonverbal communication.   While most of the emphasis on communication in our educational system is on *verbal* communication, most of the human communication that occurs is *nonverbal* communication. Although many people believe one can "read a person like a book," as was suggested by the title of a popular book, the facts suggest the contrary. Nonverbal communication is an extremely complex process and one that has an important impact in the instructional process. Unfortunately, very few teachers have any formal instruction in this area and most are prone to make mistakes in producing or interpreting one or more of the categories of nonverbal behaviors—eye behavior, facial expression, touch, gesture, movement, interpersonal spacing, use of territory, vocal behavior, use of time, scent, and so on. Understanding intercultural differences in communication behavior is virtually impossible without a firm understanding of the nonverbal aspects of communication. It is these nonverbal differences that are most likely to cause problems between people with different cultural backgrounds.

Organizational communication.   It has been said that more teachers leave the profession because of their inability to get along (communicate effectively) with their supervisors than any other reason. Whether that is the case or not, the relationship of a teacher with her or his supervisor has a pervasive impact on that teacher's behavior and success as a professional. The study of organizational communication within the context of the school system helps the teacher understand the source and impact of power in communication with superiors and parents, as well as with his or her own students, the nature of conflict and its management, the formal and informal communication systems, and the identification of communicative roles and rules in educational systems. Being able to communicate in organizationally sensitive ways can be a teacher's most important survival skill.

Communication problems of children.   For several decades, most teacher education programs have introduced prospective teachers to information relating to some of the problems that their students may have with communication, information concerning such common problems as articulation disorders, voice disorders, stuttering, and hearing loss. More recently identified, or at least more commonly recognized, problems have been added to some programs—dyslexia, autism, various reading problems, and problems stemming from various diseases. But most teachers are not exposed to information on the most common communication problem of all, one that has only become widely recognized in the last decade. This is the problem of chronic communication apprehension and avoidance, a problem confronted by one person in five in the United States, both children and adults—including teachers. Research has indicated that most teachers, as a function of their desire to help these children, will do precisely the things that are most *harmful* to them. Much research is needed on how teachers can communicate more effectively with those students with communication problems, and how to help those students overcome their problems.

Mass-mediated communication.   Contemporary children live in a mass-media dominated world. The impacts of the media on children have a major impact on how they relate to teachers and the instructional process. Teachers with an understanding of how the media work and how they impact children can use this information to advantage in working with children. Even the commercial media provide many, many opportunities for the astute teacher. But there is still much about how children relate to the media that is unknown, and as the media change, new questions continue to arise for educators. We particularly need research on prosocial uses of the media that can be employed by classroom teachers. Even video games have the potential for prosocial uses.

Interpersonal and relational communication.   The study of interpersonal communication involves, among other things, the ways people develop relationships through communication. Positive teacher-student relationships, particularly in the early grades, are critical to student learning. In large measure, students learn what they want to learn, and if they have a positive relationship with a teacher they are more likely to want to learn from the teacher. Research has indicated that when student/teacher relationships are positive, there is a substantial reduction in student misbehaviors and a much greater likelihood of student compliance with teacher requests.

Persuasion and social influence.   Concern with persuasion and social influence has an extremely long tradition in the field of communication, stretching back into antiquity. For well over 2,000 years, scholars have sought to identify means by which one person can obtain the cooperation and/or compliance of others through communication. Teachers' concerns with discipline, classroom management, and time-on-task are directly related to the concerns with persuasion and social influence. The classical study of persuasion was motivated by the desire to use communication as a prosocial alternative to coercion of others. As it was then, it is today. Teachers who lack communication competence in the area of persuasion and social influence are often left with nothing but coercive techniques to control student behavior, the use of which will produce no long-term behavior change but will create negative teacher/student relationships. One of the papers that follow is specifically concerned with planning communication in this kind of situation, so we will address this concern again later.

Intercultural communication.   The study of communication between people with differing cultural backgrounds is the most rapidly growing area in the field of communication. Teachers today confront intercultural communication problems not even dreamed of by teachers a decade or two ago. Although the norm in the past was a teacher with a group of students from the same cultural background as the teacher, that no longer is the case in many areas of the country. Today it is not uncommon to find a group of students from one culture with a teacher from a very different culture. An even more difficult situation exists in some areas: a classroom with a half-dozen or more cultures represented. We even know of one middle school that has identified thirty-seven distinct cultural groupings within its student body. Since two of the papers that follow relate to intercultural concerns, we will address this concern again later.

CONTEMPORARY RESEARCH TRENDS

We do not presume that most teacher educators are going to become major communication researchers as a result of our discussions here. However, many may wish to know what kinds of research efforts have been conducted in the recent past and how to find summaries of that research which may be useful. Thus, this section will be devoted to reviewing some of the areas that have received attention and noting references where additional work can be surveyed.

Conceptualizations of communication. Many people make serious errors in communication simply because they do not understand its basic workings. In our work with teachers we have administered a simple 10-item, true-false test covering some of the most common misconceptions about communication. Less than one-fourth of those tested achieve a passing mark on the test. This is not a consequence of teachers being unintelligent. Rather, it is because they have learned misconceptions that are commonly espoused in our schools and in our society. If one starts off in the wrong direction, it is hard to get where one wants to go. These misconceptions are what lead many otherwise bright and well-intentioned people to make unnecessary communication blunders. Discussion of these conceptual issues is included in many introductory books concerned with communication in instruction (for example, McCroskey, 1992, Chs. 1 and 2).

Teacher/student affinity. "Affinity" is the student's liking for the teacher, the rapport the teacher has with the student. In general, the higher the student's affinity for the teacher, the more likely it is that the student will engage in behaviors recommended by the teacher, that the student will like the subject matter the teacher teaches, and that the student will learn that subject matter. This body of research, as summarized by Daly & Kreiser (1992), represents a direct application of interpersonal communication research to the classroom context. Earlier work identified twenty-five techniques that one person could use to enhance affinity with another in an interpersonal context. The research investigating the applicability of this research to the instructional arena has indicated that many of the same techniques work in this context, but it also identified several that were inappropriate for classroom use. Teachers who use the appropriate affinity-seeking techniques have been found to be better liked by their students, to produce higher motivation in those students, and to increase student learning in both the cognitive and affective domains.

Teacher immediacy and nonverbal behavior. "Immediacy" is produced by communication behaviors that increase a perception of psychological or physical closeness on the part of others. If we perceive a person as immediate, we feel closer to that person. In our summary of this research (McCroskey & Richmond, 1992) we have noted the very strong impacts of teacher immediacy on affective and cognitive learning. Recent research has provided strong indications that such effects are mediated by the impact of immediacy on student motivation. Essentially, teacher immediacy behaviors result in increased student motivation, which produces heightened student learning. Whereas immediacy research has focused primarily on nonverbal behavior, research related to verbal aspects of immediacy indicates that such behaviors are also associated with positive motivation and learning outcomes.

Teacher power and behavior-alteration techniques.   The study of power in human relationships has drawn attention from scholars in most of the social sciences and several of the humanities. Power is a central fact of life in organizations. It is no less so in organizations devoted to teaching. Power is something that is negotiated by the participants in the instructional process—by the teachers and the students. When instruction is at its best, questions of power fade into oblivion. When instruction is at its worst, the battle for power becomes central. Recognizing this, communication researchers have sought to determine what communication approaches lead to teacher effectiveness and reduction of "power wars" between teachers and students. The early research confirmed that the impacts of various bases of power in the instructional environment were not unlike those in other organizational contexts (Richmond & Roach, 1992). That is, use of coercive and assigned power tends to reduce cognitive and affective learning, whereas use of referent and expert power tends to have a positive effect on both cognitive and affective learning.

Subsequent research (Plax & Kearney, 1992) generated a wide variety of specific communication techniques designed to alter the behavior of others. This work was applied to the specific context of teacher/student communication. The results of these efforts indicated that use of several of the techniques had severe negative impacts on students' affective responses, techniques that were rooted in punishment or the threat of punishment or associated with the presumed authority of the school system to regulate student behavior. In contrast, a substantial number of techniques were found to be usable by teachers without the negative impacts found for the others. These "prosocial" communication techniques, then, were seen as methods for teachers to use to manage student behavior in positive ways leading to student learning.

Student resistance to teachers.   As an outgrowth of the above research, efforts have been made to determine what factors tend to lead students to resist the teacher's efforts at controlling and directing their behavior and what forms this resistance may take (Kearney & Plax, 1992). One of the outcomes of this research has been the realization that teacher immediacy has impact in this area as well as in the more direct ways noted above. It was found that students are much less likely to resist the influence attempts of immediate teachers and, it would seem, the students may not even recognize some of these efforts as being attempts to control their behavior.

Communication apprehension and avoidance. One of the most extensive research efforts in the communication field has been directed toward the problem of communication apprehension and avoidance. As a result, we now know that the impact of apprehension and/or avoidance can be much more severe in the instructional context than was first believed. Even the threat of having to talk in a classroom may substantially retard the learning of many students. Some teaching techniques involving student interaction and/or participation—long thought to be advantageous to all students—now are known to present severe problems for some students. Such popular instructional assignments as show and tell, oral reading, oral book reports, oral current events, group projects, and individual science projects need to be tempered with other alternatives for some students. Since problems of apprehension and avoidance have their roots in both genetic and experiential factors, these problems are very difficult or impossible to overcome in the normal classroom context, although they are amendable to treatment with behavior therapy techniques. Hence, teachers need to be aware of how to be of what help they can to students with these problems without making the problems worse. Two recent books summarize this work and provide guidance for interested teachers and teacher educators (M. Booth-Butterfield & S. Booth-Butterfield, 1992; McCroskey & Richmond, 1991).

Teacher images. No verbal or nonverbal message is interpreted apart from its source. In fact, the source/message relationship is so strong that receivers will create a source in their minds if the real source is unknown. Thus, the image of the teacher in the student's mind often determines the effectiveness of that teacher's messages. Factors that influence the images of sources have been studied for over 2,500 years. Recent research has applied the findings of such efforts to the classroom context and learned that the credibility of the teacher helps determine whether students learn the content, the attractiveness of the teacher helps determine whether students are willing to take the teacher's class, and the degree of homophily (similarity) the teacher has with the students sets the tone for the "culture" of that classroom (for example, McCroskey, 1992, Ch. 7). This factor is explored in the context of a multicultural classroom in one of the following papers.

Intercultural instructional communication theory. This final area is identified with an intentional misnomer. There really is no such thing today as intercultural instructional communication theory. The overwhelming majority of instructional communication research and theory is like most communication research and theory and most educational research and theory. It is heavily impacted by the ethnocentric orientations of the dominant culture of this society. Intercultural tests of the generalizability of our instructional communication theories have only recently begun. We trust this section of future books in this series will be able to note significant advances in this important area.

THREE RESEARCH REPORTS

The three research reports that follow are very different from each other and address very different kinds of issues. The first is an experimental study that examines the complexity of teachers' planning for dealing with student misbehaviors. The second, also an experimental study, investigates the effectiveness of a persuasive effort to increase cultural sensitivity embedded within an undergraduate basic communication course. The third paper is an ethnographic analysis of the teacher/student interaction in a highly successful college-prep program for Hispanic students in a large public high school. Each of these studies addresses different kinds of issues with differing degrees of relevance to communication instruction.

REFERENCES

Booth-Butterfield, M., & Booth-Butterfield, S. (1992). *Communication Apprehension and Avoidance in the Classroom*. Edina, MN: Burgess Publishing Group.

Daly, J. A., & Kreiser, P. O. (1992). Affinity in the classroom. In V. P. Richmond and J. C. McCroskey (Eds.) *Power in the Classroom: Communication, Control, and Concern*, (pp. 121–143). Hillsdale, NJ: Lawrence Erlbaum Associates.

Kearney, P., & Plax, T. B. (1992). Student resistance to control. In V. P. Richmond and J. C. McCroskey (Eds.) *Power in the Classroom: Communication, Control, and Concern* (pp. 85–100). Hillsdale, NJ: Lawrence Erlbaum Associates.

McCroskey, J. C. (1992). *An introduction to communication in the classroom*. Edina, MN: Burgess Publishing Group.

McCroskey, J. C., & Richmond, V. P. (1991). *Quiet Children and the Classroom Teacher*, 2nd ed. Bloomington, IN: ERIC Clearinghouse on Reading and Communication Skills; and Annandale, VA: Speech Communication Association.

McCroskey, J. C., & Richmond, V. P. (1992). Increasing teacher influence through immediacy. In V. P. Richmond and J. C. McCroskey (Eds.) *Power in the Classroom: Communication, Control, and Concern* (pp. 101–119). Hillsdale, NJ: Lawrence Erlbaum Associates.

Plax, T. G., & Kearney, P. (1992). Teacher power in the classroom: Defining and advancing a program of research. In V. P. Richmond and J. C. McCroskey (Eds.) *Power in the Classroom: Communication, Control, and Concern* (pp. 67–84). Hillsdale, NJ: Lawrence Erlbaum Associates.

Richmond, V. P. (1992). *Nonverbal communication in the classroom.* Edina, MN: Burgess Publishing Group.

Richmond, V. P., & McCroskey, J. C. (1992). *Power in the Classroom: Communication Control and Concern.* Hillsdale, NJ: Lawrence Erlbaum Associates.

Richmond, V. P., & Roach, K. D. (1992). Power in the classroom: Seminal studies. In V. P. Richmond and J. C. McCroskey (Eds.) *Power in the Classroom: Communication, Control, and Concern* (pp. 47–65). Hillsdale, NJ: Lawrence Erlbaum Associates.

CHAPTER 9

Complexity in Teacher Plans for Managing Teacher- and Student-Owned Classroom Misbehaviors

JOSÉ I. RODRÍGUEZ
Michigan State University

TIMOTHY G. PLAX
PATRICIA KEARNEY
California State University

JOSÉ I. RODRÍGUEZ is a doctoral student at Michigan State University. His research interests include teacher planning, classroom management, and the importance of social cognitive perspectives to understanding interpersonal encounters in and out of the classroom.

TIMOTHY G. PLAX is a Professor of Speech Communication at California State University, Long Beach. His primary areas of research are communication in instruction and applied communication. In particular, he studies classroom management, teacher planning, student resistance, teacher misbehaviors and power in the classroom.

PATRICIA KEARNEY is a Professor of Speech Communication at California State University, Long Beach. Her primary area of study is communication in instruction. She does research on student embarrassment, teacher sex-role egalitarianism, classroom management, student resistance, teacher misbehaviors and power in the classroom.

ABSTRACT

This study examined the relationship between the complexity in teachers' plans for managing in-class student misbehaviors and teachers' attributions regarding the ownership of a particular misbehavior. Teacher plans for managing teacher-owned misbehaviors were hypothesized to be significantly more complex than those plans constructed for managing student-owned misbehaviors. Experienced teachers ($N = 224$) composed a plan for managing one of several varieties of either a student-owned or a teacher-owned student misbehavior. A MANOVA computed on the coded data resulted in a significant complex interaction for student gender and problem ownership on plan complexity. Providing support for the hypothesis, simple effects and multiple comparisons indicated that for three of six measures of complexity, teachers constructed the simplest plans for managing a male student engaging in a student-owned misbehavior. The implications of these findings of prospective and novice teachers are discussed in terms of the importance of the target students' gender, problem ownership, and complexity in experienced teacher plans.

Students come in all shapes and sizes. Some are advanced learners; others need remediation. Some are willing and eager to learn; others remain reluctant or defiant. In response to such individual needs and concerns, teachers have successfully devised and executed carefully conceived instructional plans (Clark & Petersen, 1986; Leinhardt & Greeno, 1986; Naff, 1987). Teacher planning, as we know it, has focused historically on those plans that attempt to efficiently and effectively organize and present information to students. Investigations in this area have examined teachers' weekly plans, daily plans, unit plans, long-range plans, lesson plans, short-range plans, yearly plans, and term plans (Clark & Petersen, 1986). Noticeably absent from the planning research are studies examining teacher plans for the management of disciplinary interactions with students in the classroom.

In this study, we recognize that planning is an important antecedent to effectively managing the diversity of students we continually face. Classroom management doesn't just happen; teachers must plan for appropriate preventive measures and intervention techniques. This investigation explores the planning activity of experienced teachers in their projected management of various types of student classroom misbehaviors. Specifically, this project explores the complexity of teachers' plans for managing particular student misbehaviors based on diverse, but potentially relevant, student characteristics: problem ownership and student sex.

In explanation, this investigation examines the degree to which teacher plans for handling misbehaviors vary in complexity as a function of who they perceive as actually "owning" (or who is responsible) for a particular misbehavior. Ownership in this investigation then, refers to assigned responsibility or blame for the problem misbehavior. In other words, is the student misbehaving because she/he is simply willful and uncontrollable, or is it because the teacher is boring, disinterested, and confusing? In this study, we reason that teachers will devise plans differently when the misbehavior is assigned teacher versus student ownership.

TEACHER PLANNING

Since the work of Miller, Galanter, & Pribram (1960), the study of plans has contributed to understanding how actions are eventually produced by actors (Brand, 1984; Bruce, 1980; Dixon, 1982; Flower & Hayes, 1982; Galambos, Abelson & Black, 1986; Lichtenstein & Brewer, 1980; Sacerdoti, 1975; Schank & Abelson, 1977; Schmidt, 1976; Wilensky, 1983). According to Miller et al. (1960), "A plan is any hierarchical process in the organism that can control the order in which a sequence of operations is to be performed" (p. 16)[1]. In terms of classroom management, such plans refer to the deliberating process that teachers employ in their efforts to anticipate and define the steps necessary for handling student problems in the classroom.

Plans can vary in degrees of abstraction and complexity. Highly abstract plans have been conceptualized as general and extremely flexible cognitive representations concerning the order and syntax of potential actions (Berger, 1987). Individuals who devise detailed rather than abstract plans tend to make finer distinctions regarding potential actions. Thus, detailed plans differ from abstract plans in that they provide the planner with more calculated steps toward goal attainment.

Within the structure of a detailed plan, a planner may include strategies for achieving a goal(s). The number of strategies that planners project for achieving their goals are usually indicative of plan complexity. For instance, complex plans have been defined by the number of alternatives, the number of steps, and the number of conditional actions within them (Berger, 1988; Berger & Bell, 1988; Berger, Karol, & Jordan, 1989). Conditional actions are if-then statements like: "If the student says *no* when I ask her to stop talking, then I will give her detention."

Researchers use the planning concept[2] to create models for explaining how humans process information. For instance, Hayes-Roth & Hayes-Roth's (1979) opportunistic planning model indicates that plans are the first step in a two-step problem-solving process (p. 276). The second step is control. According to the model, plans specify the actions that will be taken; control involves the monitoring and adjusting of the execution of a plan in order to move successfully toward goal attainment.

Planning is not enough for effective goal attainment, however. Adjustments must be made to external variables in order for plans to be successful.

Hayes-Roth and Hayes-Roth explain that planners can alter the course of a plan during execution by making and acting on decisions at any point during attempted goal fulfillment. One way that planners handle potential variables encountered during execution is by devising plans that contain numerous alternative actions. According to Berger and his colleagues (1987, 1988, in press), plans containing alternative actions for goal attainment are more complex than those with only one method for goal achievement.

Researchers exploring teacher plans report that expert, as opposed to novice, teachers regularly engage in planned routines that facilitate student learning (Leinhardt & Greeno, 1986). For Leinhardt and Greeno, teacher routines are, in fact, *familiar teacher plans*. A teacher who uses the same plan every day to conduct a lesson will be so familiar with that plan that it becomes routine. It is because of such planned routines that expert teachers are able to identify student difficulties with the subject matter and help students learn.

Leinhardt & Greeno's (1986) research corroborates conclusions regarding classroom management. For instance, Kounin's (1970) research illustrates that teachers who are effective at reducing student misbehavior are able to quickly identify and stop such misbehaviors in the classroom. Like Leinhardt and Greeno's, Kounin's research shows that effective teachers were able to recognize student behaviors that are counterproductive to learning and handle them efficiently. In explanation of these complementary findings, all of these researchers argued that effective teachers develop plans that allow them to quickly identify and control counterproductive behaviors.

Similarly, investigations on classroom management have examined the specific control strategies that teachers employ to gain the compliance of misbehaving students in the classroom (Kearney, Plax, Richmond, & McCroskey, 1984, 1985; Kearney, Plax, Sorensen, & Smith, 1988; McCroskey, Richmond, Plax, & Kearney, 1985; Plax, Kearney, McCroskey, & Richmond, 1986; Plax, Kearney, & Sorensen, 1990; Plax, Kearney, & Tucker, 1986). According to Plax et al. (1986), effective classroom management occurs as a consequence of thoughtful and specific teacher behaviors that encourage students to remain on task, reduce disruptions to student learning, and maximize classroom resources. These researchers also suggest that such behaviors are a function of the strategies that teachers devise to accomplish their management goals. Importantly and as indicated earlier, such strategies are important components of teachers' plans. Teachers' plans play a critical part in their ability to effectively manage a classroom.

Viewing teachers' "mental representations" or schemes as cognitive functions that influence teacher plans provides for a meaningful link between the plan and classroom management literatures. In keeping with these perspectives, teachers' schemes (as defined by Applegate, 1982; Clark & Delia, 1977; Delia, 1977; Greeno, 1980; Piaget, 1954, 1963, 1970; Rumelhart & Ortony,

1977) may be seen as the perceptual frames with which teachers construct their plans. Teacher plans are composed of conceptual, interdependent hierarchies outlining the order, sequence, and number of steps a teacher proposes to use in fulfilling his or her goal(s).

Kearney & Plax (1987) and Kearney et al. (1988), for example, argue that teachers' mental representations concerning student control may be viewed as schemes. Using the social cognition perspective as their framework, Kearney et al. (1988) hypothesized that expert teachers should have more sophisticated schemes for handling student misbehaviors than novice teachers. To test their hypothesis, Kearney et al. (1988) asked expert and novice teachers to select the control strategies they would use to manage particular misbehaviors. Expert teachers reported using a greater number of both reward-based and punishment-based strategies for controlling student misbehaviors than did novice teachers. In terms of plans, these results indicate that with a greater number of possible response options, the plans of expert teachers for controlling student misbehaviors are likely to be more complex than those of novice teachers.

PROBLEM OWNERSHIP

Also important to the reasoning of the present study, researchers probing the management of student classroom misconduct classify student misbehaviors as either teacher-owned or student-owned (Brophy & Rohrkemper, 1980a, 1980b, 1980c; Kearney, Plax, & Burroughs, 1991). Teacher-owned student problems are conceptualized as problems or incidents that either teachers or students perceive as being caused by and/or primarily attributable to the teacher (Kearney et al., 1991). In other words, a particular student problem/misbehavior is perceived as being the responsibility of the teacher.

Unlike teacher-owned problems, student-owned misbehaviors are conceptualized as problems or incidents that arise for reasons associated with or attributable to the individual student (Kearney et al., 1991). For a student exhibiting this type of misbehavior in the classroom, a teacher would attribute the responsibility for the problem directly to the student. Recent research affirms (Kearney et al., 1991) this distinction in problem ownership and the influence of perceived ownership on teachers' management decisions and students' responses to teachers' attempts at classroom control.

RATIONALE

Researchers investigating teacher strategies for controlling student misbehavior indicate that experienced teachers possess sophisticated schemes when making decisions regarding classroom discipline. In this way, they can be described as complex in the ways they process and organize information concerning classroom control. Linking the teacher plan perspective to the conclusions concerning teachers' information processing suggests that experienced teachers' effectiveness at managing a classroom is, to a large extent, a function of the sophistication (complexity) of their schemes and/or plans. The plans constructed by teachers with sophisticated schemes about classroom control then should illustrate an ability to recognize which specific student misbehaviors are the responsibility of the student, and which are truly the responsibility of the teacher.

Teachers who perceive that they are primarily responsible for a particular student's misbehavior (teacher-owned) should attempt to search (through their schemes) for a multitude of sequential strategies (complex plans) to manage that student because of their desire to obtain control. Thus, teachers may construct complex plans for managing students enacting teacher-owned misbehaviors to ensure that they actually manage the student.

Conversely, teachers who perceive that they are not primarily responsible for a particular student's misconduct (student-owned) might disassociate themselves from the problem by blaming the student. As a consequence, teachers should experience a low sense of obligation. With a low sense of obligation, teachers are likely to experience a minimal desire to actually pursue their goal (control the student), and thus are less committed to planning for that goal. That is, teachers should experience a low desire to search through their sophisticated schemes, and instead, construct relatively simple plans to deal with a problem that they perceive is attributable to the student. Based on this rationale then, the following hypothesis was advanced:

Teacher plans for managing teacher-owned student classroom misbehaviors will be significantly more complex than those plans constructed by teachers for managing student-owned misbehaviors.

METHODS

Participants. Two hundred and twenty four (37 males, 187 females) elementary and secondary teachers with one or more years of full-time experience participated, representing all levels of K–12 instruction (K–3 = 57; 4–6 = 35; 7–9 = 37; 10–12 = 52; 43 did not indicate their level). Instructors were taking graduate classes at a large Eastern university.

Procedures. Teachers' projected plans were anchored to specific student misbehaviors. Before constructing their plans, participants indicated their sex, grade level taught, and years of teaching experience. Teachers were then presented with one of four different student misbehavior scenarios. The scenarios depicted either a male or female student engaging in a common type of misbehavior. Additionally, problem ownership was embedded within each scenario. Both student sex and problem ownership were rotated across scenarios so that 57 teachers responded to a male student engaging in a student-owned misbehavior; 53 responded to a male student engaging in a teacher-owned misbehavior; 59 were exposed to a female student engaging in a teacher-owned misbehavior; and finally, 55 were exposed to a female student engaging in a student-owned misbehavior.

After reading their particular scenarios, teachers were instructed to assume that the student was in his or her current classroom "and engaging in the behaviors described." Teachers were asked to construct a plan for dealing with or managing the misbehaving student. Specifically, participants were asked to indicate "what STEPS you would go through and what you would actually SAY to this student?" Additionally, teachers were encouraged to "please be as specific as you can in writing down statements you would communicate, and what you would actually say to this student at each step."

Student Scenarios.   Four student misbehavior scenarios were devised to serve as anchors for teacher plans. Scenarios were revised versions of the student misconduct vignettes developed and validated by Brophy and Rohrkemper (1980a, 1980b, 1980c). Each vignette described a target student exhibiting a common in-class misbehavior. To enable teachers to easily imagine themselves interacting with the students depicted in the vignettes, no references were made "to facilities, equipment, or individuals (school psychologists, social workers) that might be familiar to some teachers but not others" (Brophy & Rohrkemper, 1980c, p. 5). Correspondingly, no references were made to age, race, ethnicity, or social class of the students described in the vignettes. These omissions "avoid confounding the behavior depicted in the vignettes with various status characteristics of students" (p. 5).

Specific to the scenarios employed, two of the vignettes were revised so that the target student blamed the teacher for her/his behavior (teacher-owned; see Table 9–1 for the scenarios). For instance, a student blaming the teacher for her/his behavior may say that "the work is boring and you (the teacher) don't make it very interesting." This manipulation, then, was used to determine how teachers would plan to handle a student who blames the teacher for her/his misbehavior.

Similarly, two other vignettes were revised so that they described a student misbehaving for reasons attributable to the student (student-owned). A student exhibiting this type of behavior might say that "her/his mind is on other more important things, like her/his friends and family or a popular T.V. show or movie." This manipulation then, probes how teachers would plan to handle student misbehaviors that seem to be a function of the teacher's actions, not the student's.

Coding Procedures and Complexity Categories.   A codebook developed to content-analyze the complexity of teacher plans was constructed from an examination of the teacher-plan protocols collected in the present project and

TABLE 9–1
Student Misbehavior Scenarios

SCENARIO 1: STUDENT-OWNED

Carl can do good work, but he seldom does. He will try to get out of work. When you speak with him about this, he makes a show of looking serious and pledging reform, but his behavior does not change. Just now, you see a typical scene: Carl is reading a comic book when he's supposed to be reading his assignment for class.

SCENARIO 2: TEACHER-OWNED

Roger has been fooling around instead of working on his project (or paper) for several days now. Finally, you tell him that he has to finish or stay after school and work on it then. He says, "I won't stay after school!" and spends the rest of the period sulking. At the sound of the bell, he quickly jumps up and heads for the door. You tell him that he has to stay and finish his assignment. He retorts, "You don't care about me, so why should I care about what you want?" and continues out the door.

SCENARIO 3: STUDENT-OWNED

Barbara often seems to be off in her own world, but today she is watching you as you lead a discussion. Pleased to see her attentive, you ask her what she thinks. However, you have to repeat her name and she looks startled when she realizes you have called on her. Meanwhile, you realize that she has been immersed in daydreams and only appeared to be paying attention. In the past, whenever you confronted her about her inattention, she claimed to have her mind on other more important things, like her friends and family or a popular T.V. show or movie.

SCENARIO 4: TEACHER-OWNED

Nancy is oriented toward peers and social relationships, not schoolwork. She could be doing top-grade work, but instead she does just enough to get by. She is often chatting or writing notes when she is supposed to be paying attention or working. When you confront her about this, she complains that the work is boring and that you don't make it very interesting. During today's lesson, she has repeatedly turned to students on each side of her to make remarks, and now she has a conversation going on with several friends.

from the coding procedures reported in the literature on plans. Coding procedures provided the conceptual and operational definitions for six codable categories of plan complexity. The first category dealt with the loquacity or length of the plan. Plan length was examined to determine the relative size of the teacher plans. Lengthy plans have been associated with plan complexity, and complex plans have been positively associated with effective goal achievement in previous research (Berger, 1987, 1988). Coders assessed the length of the teacher plans by counting the number of words included in the plan. The second category was the number of action units reported in the plan. Action units (AU) are the sentences, phrases, or clauses that depict a single action (Berger, 1987, 1988). Each and every time a planner indicated a separate, discrete active attempt to modify the student's behavior, a separate action unit was coded. Action units included verbs such as talk, speak, walk, discuss, call, take, and so on. Coders counted the action units reported in each plan. Plans with large numbers of action units are defined as complex (Berger, 1987, 1988).

Third, plan complexity was determined by the number of alternatives depicted in each plan. Alternatives are defined as phrases or clauses that depict an action a planner proposes to enact AFTER the planner has made some evaluation, decision, or judgment. Alternatives are the THEN part of an IF-THEN statement. Fourth, conditional statements were indexed by a planner's use of IF-THEN statements. In other words, every IF-THEN statement was counted as one conditional statement. Conditional statements (CS) were also indexed occasionally by the planner's use of the word OR (when OR was used to signify a decision-making instance regarding a host of potential options). By definition, conditional statements are not counted as action units (see Berger 1987, 1988). Fifth, steps consisted of units of behavior or thought that were self-contained in a chronological or sequential order. Steps were operationalized as the sum total of action units and conditional statements (STEPS = AUs + CSs). This was done to ensure the most accurate measurement of all the individual actions [cognitive (CSs) and behavioral steps (AUs)] that comprised each plan. Finally, coders evaluated the over all complexity of the plan by responding to a 1 to 5 global scale (1 = complex, 5 = not complex).

The six categories of plan complexity were assessed initially by a single coder who had been familiarized with the data and trained in the use of the codebook. To asses coder reliability, a second coder reanalyzed 20 percent of the sample units from each of the categories in order to compute an index of coder agreement. Percent of unit-by-unit agreement between the original and the second coders ranged from 92 percent to 100 percent. Overall intercoder agreement, assessed by unit-by-unit agreement, was 96 percent.

RESULTS

Treatment Checks.   After participants completed their respective plans, they responded to three 7-point Likert-type scales. The first scale assessed the "imaginability" of each scenario. Participants indicated "How easy is it for you to imagine yourself dealing with a situation or student of this type?" Response options ranged from 1 (Easy to Imagine) to 7 (Hard to Imagine). The second scale indexed how often the teacher dealt with that particular type of misbehavior. Participants were asked, "How frequently have you had to deal with this particular type of problem/student in your class over the past three years?" Response options ranged from 1 (Frequently) to 7 (Infrequently). The third scale assessed how irritating the particular misbehavior was to the respective teacher. Participants were asked, "How irritating are problems of this type for you to deal with?" Response options ranged from 1 (Very Irritating) to 7 (Not at all Irritating).

With the means for the first treatment check all below 2.5, we confirmed that for each scenario teachers could imagine themselves actually interacting with a student exhibiting each type of student misbehavior (condition 1 = male/student-owned, $M = 1.84$; condition 2 = male/teacher-owned, $M = 2.42$; condition 3 = female/student-owned, $M = 2.22$; condition 4 = female/teacher-owned, $M = 1.54$). Similarly, the means for the second check (all above 3.0) indicated that teachers perceived that the student misconduct illustrated in each scenario occurred with some degree of frequency in their actual classrooms (condition 1, $M = 3.61$; condition 2, $M = 4.41$; condition 3, $M = 3.80$; condition 4, $M = 3.05$). The means for check three suggested that teachers viewed each student problem depicted in the scenarios as sufficiently irritating to warrant potential planning (condition 1, $M = 4.05$; condition 2, $M = 3.77$; condition 3, $M = 3.8$; condition 4, $M = 3.66$).

Finally, we tested whether or not teachers in our sample perceived the ownership of the misbehaving student consistent with those teachers who participated in the original development of the vignettes (Brophy and Rohrkemper, 1980a, 1980b, 1980c). We asked planners to indicate ownership for their respective scenarios: "Who do you believe is primarily responsible for the student's behavior described in your scenario?" Teachers' open-ended responses to this item confirmed the manipulated ownership as belonging primarily to the teacher (conditions 2 and 4) or the student (conditions 1 and 3). Taken together with the validational findings of Brophy and Rohrkemper then, our results support those attributions represented in the scenarios.

Tests of the Research Hypothesis.   To test the research hypothesis, a 2 x 2 multivariate analysis of variance was computed on the plan data. The MANOVA produced a significant overall complex interaction for student sex and problem ownership on the six measures of plan complexity (Wilks = 0.889, Approx. F = 4.493, df = 6/215, p < 0.0001, accounting for 13 percent of the variance in the dependent variable set).

Simple tests of the interaction resulted in three significant and three nonsignificant effects. Student sex by problem ownership was nonsignificant on the number of alternatives generated in the plans, the number of conditional statements reported in the plans, and the overall measure of plan complexity (all Fs < 1). Power estimates for all nonsignificant simple effects produced within our MANOVA were about .99 for a medium effect at alpha = .05 and a sample of 200.

For significant findings, student sex by problem ownership was significant on the number of action units generated in the plans (F = 16.67, df = 1/220, p < 0.0001). Table 9–2 presents the means and standard deviations explicating this result. Follow-up Tukey-HSD multiple comparisons indicated that conditions 2 and 3 were significantly different from condition 1. That is, teachers who constructed plans for managing a male student exhibiting a teacher-owned misbehavior (Condition 2) and teachers who devised plans for managing a female student exhibiting a student-owned misbehavior (Condition 3) used significantly more action units to construct their projected plans than those who devised plans to handle a male student exhibiting a student-owned misbehavior (Condition 1).

Second, student sex by problem ownership was significant on the total number of words (loquacity) used to generate the plan (F = 4.85, df = 1/220,

TABLE 9-2
Number of Action Units Used to Construct the Plans

	STUDENT-OWNED MISBEHAVIOR	TEACHER-OWNED MISBEHAVIOR
	Condition 1	Condition 2
Male	M = 5.18	M = 8.21
Student	sd = 2.65	sd = 4.56
	Range = 0–13	Range = 0–27
	Condition 3	Condition 4
Female	M = 7.66	M = 6.68
Student	sd = 3.65	sd = 3.64
	Range = 0–17	Range = 0–18

TABLE 9-3

Number of Words Used to Construct the Plans

	STUDENT-OWNED MISBEHAVIOR	**TEACHER-OWNED MISBEHAVIOR**
Male Student	Condition 1 $M = 93.84$ $sd = 58.07$ Range = 0–269	Condition 2 $M = 128.19$ $sd = 64.91$ Range = 0–338
Female Student	Condition 3 $M = 115.71$ $sd = 78.43$ Range = 0–351	Condition 4 $M = 110.95$ $sd = 62.98$ Range = 0–334

$p < 0.03$). Table 9–3 presents the means and standard deviations explicating this interaction. Follow-up multiple comparisons procedure indicated that condition 2 was significantly different from condition 1. Specifically, teachers who devised plans to manage a male student engaging in teacher-owned misbehaviors (Condition 2) used significantly more words to generate their potential plans than those teachers who constructed plans to handle a male student exhibiting a student-owned misbehavior (Condition 1).

TABLE 9-4

Number of Steps Used to Construct the Plans

	STUDENT-OWNED MISBEHAVIOR	**TEACHER-OWNED MISBEHAVIOR**
Male Student	Condition 1 $M = 6.19$ $sd = 3.34$ Range = 0–17	Condition 2 $M = 9.15$ $sd = 5.07$ Range = 0–28
Female Student	Condition 3 $M = 8.85$ $sd = 4.20$ Range = 0–19	Condition 4 $M = 7.86$ $sd = 4.47$ Range = 0–22

Third, the test of interaction effects demonstrated that student sex by problem ownership was significant on the total number of steps that were employed to devise the plan ($F = 11.56$, $df = 1/220$, $p < 0.001$). Table 9–4 presents the means and standard deviations explicating this result. Follow-up multiple comparisons demonstrated that conditions 2 and 3 were significantly different from condition 1. Specifically, teachers who generated plans for handling a male student exhibiting a teacher-owned misbehavior (Condition 2) and teachers who devised plans for managing a female student exhibiting a student-owned misbehavior (Condition 3) used significantly more steps to construct their projected plans than those teachers who devised plans to handle a male student exhibiting a student-owned misbehavior (Condition 1).

DISCUSSION WITH IMPLICATIONS

The results of this study provided support for the hypothesis when plan complexity was indexed by the number of action units in the plans, the number of steps in the plans, and the number of words used to construct the plans. However, the results did not support the prediction when plan complexity was indexed by the number of conditional statements in the plans, the number of alternatives in the plans, and subjective impressions of overall complexity. For these latter three indexes of complexity that failed to discriminate sex and problem ownership, we might conclude that either the measures were insensitive to those differences or that some degree or type of complexity is evidenced across all experienced teachers' plans to control student misbehaviors.

For the three other measures—action units, steps, and loquacity—teachers' plans varied significantly in complexity as a function of both problem ownership and student sex. In other words, the type of problem the teacher planned to manage and the gender of the misbehaving student significantly impacted the complexity of teacher plans. On both theoretical and practical levels then, the results of the present study illustrate the importance of these two issues in teachers' management plans.

Of additional importance, although plans constructed for the other conditions differed in complexity for one measure or another, no condition was *consistently* associated with either complex or simple plans—except for condition 1: male, student-owned. Thus, our discussion centers primarily on the reasons why experienced teachers might be more inclined to construct their plans differently for male students who engage in student-owned misbehaviors. We draw implications within our discussion for novice or prospective teachers interested in directions for improving their own management plans.

When the complexity of teacher plans was indexed by the number of action units, the number of steps, and the number of words (loquacity) teachers used to construct their plans, our teachers constructed relatively simple plans for managing a student-owned misbehavior attributed to a male student. Plans constructed in relation to the other three misbehavior conditions were all more complex. Based on the arguments advanced in the rationale, these findings indicate that the teachers created a simple plan to manage a male student engaging in a student-owned misbehavior because teachers did not feel ultimately responsible for this particular students' misbehavior. That is, teachers may have disassociated themselves (perceived low obligation) from the student problem. After all, the misbehavior was student-, not teacher-, owned.

Disassociation can be argued further by examining the specific misbehavior under investigation. The student in condition 1 was reading a comic book rather than the assigned text. The fact that he was not disturbing others, he was not aggressing upon others, may have modified any teacher efforts to engage in either overt or persistent desist attempts. An important implication of our interpretation here for prospective and novice teacher planners then, is that low obligation, coupled with minimal desire or commitment to actually correct the misbehaving student, may lead to simple, rather than complex, experienced teacher management plans.

Other findings were not so consistent. When the complexity of teacher plans was indexed by the number of action units and steps teachers used to construct their plans, the teachers constructed relatively complex plans for managing a teacher-owned misbehavior enacted by a male student (Condition 2) and a student-owned misbehavior generated by a female student (Condition 3). Based on our rationale, this finding indicates that teachers must have felt partially or fully responsible (that is, they owned the misbehavior) for these particular student misbehaviors. For the teacher-owned condition, by definition, responsibility for the misbehavior belongs to the teacher, not the student. In fact, the scenario was written so that the student, Roger, blamed the teacher for his behavior by overtly accusing the teacher of not caring about him.

For the student-owned condition, however, assigning blame to the teacher is problematic. Nevertheless, teachers may have felt sufficiently obligated or committed to control the student's misbehavior in this particular instance. Recall that Barbara is caught daydreaming when the teacher calls on her during a class discussion. Unlike Carl who is reading a comic book quietly while others are engaged in reading the assignment, Barbara's behavior is more obvious, more overt, more visible to her peers. Consequently, teachers may experience a strong desire to actually correct Barbara's behavior in their efforts to minimize any modeling or contagion effects. The implication of this perspective for novice planners is that under conditions of high desire and commitment, then, experienced teachers understandably devise complex plans.

When teacher plan complexity was indexed by the number of words teachers used to construct their plans (loquacity), the teachers sampled constructed relatively complex plans for managing a teacher-owned misbehavior generated by a male student. Based on the rationale, this finding also indicates that the teachers used a complex plan because they felt responsible for the student's misbehavior. Compared to all other conditions, teachers may have constructed the most complex plans in this particular instance because the male student enacting the teacher-owned misbehavior was openly rebellious and aggressive. The implication here, which is similar to our last one above, is that experienced teachers may feel a need to devise complex plans when a behavior is not only teacher-owned, but also when the misbehavior is overt and severe. That is, the male student in condition 2 was openly confronting the teacher and, at one point, the student walked out of the room without the teacher's permission. Thus, the teachers in this study may have felt an exceptionally strong desire to actually control the student, and thereby encode a more complex plan.

ENDNOTES

1. Distinguishing among schemes, scripts, and plans is important for understanding the structure and content of plans more generally. A scheme is a *global* or "gestalt" perceptual system an individual has developed to represent the world or universe. Plans are different from schemes in that plans represent a social actor's *specific* knowledge of the sequencing of projected actions. Scripts are developed by planners through the routine use of plans. Once someone uses a plan several times, he or she may convert that plan into a script for accomplishing a specific task. According to Schank & Abelson (1977), a script represents specific knowledge of a standard event sequence. They explain that "Specific detailed knowledge about a situation [a script] allows us to do less processing and wondering about frequently occurring events" (p. 37).

2. Plans have been differentiated from the planning process in that plans are the conceptual representations of action sequences, and planning includes data collection, organization, execution, and revision (Naff, 1987).

REFERENCES

Applegate, J. L. (1982). The impact of construct system development on communication and impression formation in persuasive contexts. *Communication Monographs, 49,* 277–289.

Berger, C. R. (1987). Planning and scheming: Strategies for initiating relationships. In R. Burnett, P. McGhee, & D. Clarke (Eds.), *Accounting for relationships: Social representations of interpersonal links* (pp. 158–174). London: Methuen.

Berger, C. R. (1988). Planning, affect and social action generation. In R. L. Donohew, H. Sypher, & E. T. Higgins (Eds.), *Communication, social cognition, and affect* (pp. 93–116). Hillsdale, NJ: Lawrence Erlbaum.

Berger, C. R., & Bell, R. A. (1988). Plans and the initiations of social relationships. *Human Communication Research, 15,* 217–235.

Berger, C. R., Karol, S. H., & Jordan, J. M. (1989). When a lot of knowledge is a dangerous thing: the debilitating effects of plan complexity on verbal fluency. *Human Communication Research, 16,* 91–119.

Berger, C. R. (in press). A plan based approach to strategic communication. In D. E. Hewes (Ed.), *Cognitive bases of interpersonal communication.* Hillsdale, NJ: Lawrence Erlbaum.

Brand, M. (1984). *Intending and acting: Toward a naturalized action theory.* Cambridge: MIT Press.

Brophy, J., & Rohrkemper, M. (1980a). *Teacher's general strategies for dealing with problem students (Research Series No. 87).* East Lansing, Michigan: Institute for Research on Teaching, Michigan State University.

Brophy, J., & Rohrkemper, M. (1980b). *Teacher's specific strategies for dealing with hostile, aggressive students (Research Series No. 86).* East Lansing, Michigan: Institute for Research on Teaching, Michigan State University.

Brophy, J., & Rohrkemper, M. (1980c). *The influence of problem ownership on teachers' perceptions of and strategies for coping with problem students (Research Series No. 84).* East Lansing, Michigan: Institute for Research on Teaching, Michigan State University.

Bruce, B. C. (1980). Plans and social action. In R. J. Spico, B. C. Bruce & W. F. Brewer (Eds.), *Theoretical issues in reading comprehension* (pp. 367–384). Hillsdale, NJ: Lawrence Erlbaum.

Clark, C. M., & Petersen, P. L. (1986). Teachers' thought processes. In M. C. Wittrock, (Ed.) *Handbook of research on teaching* (pp. 255–296). New York: Macmillan.

Clark, R. A., & Delia, J. G. (1977). Cognitive complexity, social perspective taking and functional persuasive skills in second to ninth-grade children. *Human Communication Research, 3,* 128–134.

Delia, J. G. (1977). Constructivism and the study of human communication. *Quarterly Journal of Speech, 63,* 66–83.

Dixon, P. (1982). Plans and written directions for complex tasks. *Journal of Verbal Learning and Verbal Behavior, 21,* 70–84.

Flower, L., & Hayes, J. R. (1982). The dynamics of composing: Making plans and juggling constraints. In L. W. Gregg and E. R. Steinberg (Eds.), *Cognitive processes in writing* (pp. 31–50). Hillsdale, NJ: Lawrence Erlbaum.

Galambos, J. A., Abelson, R. P., & Black, J. B. (1986). Goals and plans. In J. A. Galambos, R. P. Abelson, & J. B. Black (Eds.), *Knowledge structures* (pp. 101–102). Hillsdale, NJ: Lawrence Erlbaum.

Greeno, J. G. (1980). Psychology of learning 1960–1980: One participant's observations. *American Psychologist, 35,* 713–744.

Hayes-Roth, B., & Hayes-Roth, F. (1979). A cognitive model of planning. *Cognitive Science, 3,* 275–310.

Kearney, P., Plax, T. G., & Burroughs, N. F. (1991). An attributional analysis of college students' resistance decisions. *Communication Education, 40,* 1991, 325–342.

Kearney, P., Plax, T. G., Richmond, V. P., & McCroskey, J. C. (1984). Power in the classroom IV: Teacher communication techniques as alternatives to discipline. In R. Bostrom (Ed.). *Communication Yearbook 8* (pp. 724–746). Beverly Hills, CA: Sage.

Kearney, P., Plax, T. G., Richmond, V. P. & McCroskey, J. C. (1985). Power in the classroom III: Teacher communication techniques and messages. *Communication Education, 34,* 19–28.

Kearney, P., & Plax, T. G. (1987). Situational and individual determinants of teachers' reported use of behavior alternation techniques. *Human Communication Research, 14,* 145–166.

Kearney, P., Plax, T. G., Sorensen, G., & Smith, V. R. (1988). Experienced and prospective teachers' selections of compliance-gaining messages for "common" student misbehaviors. *Communication Education, 37,* 150–164.

Kounin, J. S. (1970). *Discipline and group management in classrooms.* New York: Holt, Rinehart and Winston.

Leinhardt, G., & Greeno, J. G. (1986). The cognitive skill of teaching. *Journal of Educational Psychology, 78,* 75–95.

Lichtenstein, E. H., & Brewer, W. F. (1980). Memory for goal directed events. *Cognitive Psychology, 12,* 412–445.

McCroskey, J. C., Richmond, V. P., Plax, T. G., & Kearney, P. (1985). Power in the classroom V: Behavior alteration techniques, communication training, and learning. *Communication Education, 34,* 214–226.

Miller, G. A., Galanter, E., & Pribram, K. H. (1960). *Plans and the structure of behavior.* New York: Holt, Rinehart and Winston.

Naff, B. E. (1987). *The impact of prescriptive planning models on preservice English teachers' thought and on the classroom environments they create: An ethnographic study.* Dissertation, Virginia Polytechnic Institute and State University.

Piaget, J. (1954). *The construction of reality in the child.* New York: Basic Books.

Piaget, J. (1963). *Origins of intelligence in children.* New York: Norton.

Piaget, J. (1970). *The science of education and the psychology of the child.* New York: Orion Press.

Plax, T. G., Kearney, P., McCroskey, J. C., & Richmond, V. P. (1986). Power in the classroom VI: Verbal control strategies, nonverbal immediacy and affective learning. *Communication Education, 35,* 43–55.

Plax, T. G., Kearney, P., & Tucker, L. K. (1986). Prospective teachers' use of behavior alteration techniques on common student misbehaviors. *Communication Education, 35,* 32–42.

Plax, T. G., Kearney, P., & Sorensen, G. (1990). The strategy selection-construction controversy II: Comparing pre– and experienced teachers' compliance-gaining message constructions. *Communication Education, 39,* 128–141.

Rumelhart, D. E., & Ortony, A. (1977). The representation of knowledge in memory. In R. Andersen, R. Spiro, & W. Montague (Eds.), *Schooling and the acquisition of knowledge,* (pp. 99–135). Hillsdale, NJ: Earlbaum.

Sacerdoti, E. D. (1975). *A structure for plans and behavior.* Amsterdam: Elsevier North-Holland.

Schank, R. C., & Abelson, R. P. (1977). *Scripts, plans, goals and understanding: An inquiry into human knowledge structures.* Hillsdale, NJ: Lawrence Erlbaum.

Schmidt, C. F. (1976). Understanding human action: Recognizing the plans and motives of other persons. In J. S. Carroll & J. W. Payne (Eds.), *Cognition and social behavior* (pp. 47–67). Hillsdale, NJ: Lawrence Erlbaum.

Wilensky, R. (1983). *Planning and understanding: A computational approach to human reasoning.* Reading, MA: Addison-Wesley.

CHAPTER 10

Infusing a Multicultural Perspective into the Basic Communication Course: An Investigation

VIRGINIA H. MILHOUSE
GEORGE HENDERSON
University of Oklahoma

VIRGINIA H. MILHOUSE is an Assistant Professor of Human Relations at the University of Oklahoma, Norman. Her current research interests include: interpersonal competence in intercultural/international contexts; conceptualization of intercultural communication, education and training; and models of institutes of international education and international internship programs.

GEORGE HENDERSON is Chair and Regents Professor of Human Relations at the University of Oklahoma. His current research interests include racial and ethnic relations, international human relations, and the sociology of education.

ABSTRACT

The purpose of this study was to examine student perceptions of the effectiveness of multicultural education and cross-cultural training (MECT) and to determine the ability of the MECT to promote accepting attitudes toward diverse ethnic groups. It was hypothesized that students assigned to a multicultural "treatment condition" (N = 60) would significantly improve attitudes toward diverse groups over students assigned to a "control group"

(N = 60). One hundred twenty subjects completed the Evaluation of Multicultural Objectives assessment and the Survey on Ethnic Groups pretest and posttest scales and, after sixteen weeks, sixty subjects completed the MECT that was provided within three sections of a basic communication course at a large midwestern university. Repeated measures analysis of variance and condescriptive and frequency statistics were used to test three research hypotheses and analyze three research questions. The three hypotheses were concerned with the ability of the training to significantly impact the attitudes of students. The research questions examined the extent to which the program effectively provided for the attainment of multicultural knowledge, effective motivational behavior, and skills. The results indicated that the "treatment group" demonstrated a 30 percent increase in positive attitudes and a 26 percent reduction in nonaccepting attitudes toward diverse cultures or ethnic groups; the attitudinal position of the "control group" showed no significant change over the sixteen-week period.

It was concluded that, when infused into the context of a university communication course, MECT appears to have great potential to develop appreciation of cultural diversity, effective motivational behaviors and communication skills, thereby improving perceptions about diverse cultures/ethnic groups. Implications of this research for teacher educators at the university- and school-based levels are discussed.

By the year 2000, the projected undergraduate enrollment for U.S. colleges and universities will be 30 percent multicultural. An even higher projection can be made for our elementary and secondary schools, whose current multicultural population exceeds 30 percent. These projections are based on the U.S. Department of Education's enrollment statistics for the period 1988 to 1990. They lend credence to the argument that our colleges and universities cannot neglect their responsibility to develop programs for beginning teachers that reflect the multicultural realities of our society and the world (AACTE, 1980).

Infusing diversity (Gudykunst, Ting-Toomey & Wiseman, 1991; Richmond & Gorham, 1988; McCroskey, 1982; Friedrich, 1978) and multicultural education perspectives into teacher preparation and classroom curricula has been the focus of many community-based and national teacher education organizations (Association of Teacher Educators, 1986; AACTE Commission on Multicultural Education, 1973; ASCD Multicultural Education Commission, 1977) over the years. Also, many educators have associated multicultural education with the development of *cultural diversity* (Appleton, 1988; Garcia, 1982; Green, 1989; Kendall, 1983; Sleeter & Grant, 1988), *educational equity*

(Baptiste and Baptiste, 1980), *theory and practice in multicultural learning* (Wurzel, 1988; Bennett, 1990; Banks, 1988), *interpersonal skills* (Banks & Benavidez, 1981) and with the enhancement of *teaching methods* (Wurzel & Holt, 1991).

After an extensive review of related literature, Wurzel and Holt (1991) categorized existing teaching materials and resources into six different but interrelated conceptual models of multicultural education: (1) Single Group/ Ethnic Studies Model, (2) Human Relations Training Model, (3) Social Reconstructionist Model, (4) Intercultural Communication Model, (5) Global Education Model, and (6) the Historical/Reflective Thinking Model. These multicultural perspectives have both the potential to enhance understanding about diverse cultures and facilitate teacher preparation and classroom instruction. However, a review of theoretical and empirical studies in the field indicates that few studies have investigated the effectiveness of multicultural education when infused in a college-level course. Thus, the purpose of this study is to assess the effectiveness of a multicultural education and cross-cultural training model (Milhouse, 1986; Pusch, 1981) when infused into the basic communication course. First, research that explains the various conceptual approaches to multicultural education is reviewed. Second, the multicultural education and cross-cultural training model used in the present study is described. This is followed by a discussion of three research questions that were posed to examine each of the model's objectives. In addition, three hypotheses are presented. These were designed to test the model's overall ability to promote positive perceptions of diverse cultures.

CONCEPTUAL MODELS OF MULTICULTURAL EDUCATION

Single Group/Ethnic Studies Model.   This approach to multicultural education has mainly focused on information about the history, literature, and culture of a particular group—usually racial, ethnic, and religious groups. Within the past ten years, this approach has been expanded to include studies pertaining to gender, sexual orientation, and age groups (Grant & Sleeter, 1989). These large varieties of groups require a variety of disciplines such as history, anthropology, sociology, literature, and psychology to understand them. The expected outcome of the approach is to raise the level of self-esteem of individuals who have not traditionally been positively accepted by the dominant society (Banks & Banks, 1989; Banks, 1988).

Human Relations Training Model.   Utilizing experiential activities designed to prevent or ameliorate conflict between individuals and groups, this approach emphasizes psychosocial factors of intergroup relationships (Appleton, 1988; Lerner, 1986). For example, conflict resolution and mediation strategies are used to reduce racial prejudice. Central to human relations training is a focus on the content and the processes of learning. That is, *how* something is taught is just as important as *what* is taught (Green, 1989; Hernandez, 1989). When successful, this approach has facilitated greater tolerance of individual differences and, relatedly, positive interaction between conflicting parties. The Anti-Defamation League of B'nai B'rith (1986) has authored a seminal book, *A world of difference*, which focuses on human relations and strategies for reducing prejudice in the classroom.

Social Reconstructionist Model. This approach stresses power relationships as the major factor affecting relationships between majority- and minority-group people. Deemphasizing cultural and psychological factors, it incorporates curricular emphasis on active participant involvement in social issues such as racism, sexism, and ageism. Case studies, historical films, and experiential activities characterize this approach (Schniedewind & Davidson, 1983; Sleeter & Grant, 1988). A major goal of this approach is to develop helpful decision-making skills in order for relatively powerless people to acquire power in social relationships.

Intercultural Communication Model. This approach centers on dealing appropriately with cultural differences between groups (Pusch, 1981; Samovar & Porter, 1991). Specifically, the emphasis is on sociocultural conditioning and its influence on communication and intercultural interaction. The range of topics includes values and verbal and nonverbal communication. Videotapes, discussions, simulations, and writing exercises are used to teach participants nonoppressive ways of communicating across cultures.

Global Education Model. This approach is based on the premises that diversity is a foremost characteristic of our global community and that educators must teach students to communicate and interact with people from different cultures (Stubbs, 1976; Tye, 1991; United Nations, 1983). Information on world cultures is taught in history, geography, and comparative education. This approach often uses written, oral, and visual aids. Gibson (1984) stated that effective global educators develop the ability to interact and communicate in different cultural settings.

Historical/Reflective Thinking Model. The major purpose of this approach is to provide information about group relations by examining carefully selected conflict events from a historical perspective (Wurzel, 1988). Basic to this approach is the belief that there are universal human conditions that cross time and geographical boundaries. When successfully implemented, this approach helps participants understand themselves and others within historical and contemporary contexts.

Multicultural Education and Cross-cultural Training Model.   Since the purpose of this research was to (1) explore students' perceptions of the effectiveness of a multicultural education and cross-cultural training model when infused into teacher lesson plans and classroom laboratory exercises and to (2) determine the ability of the model to promote understanding, sensitivity, and skills to communicate with individuals from diverse cultures (that is, Euro-Americans, African Americans, Asian Americans, Hispanic Americans, Native Americans), the researchers relied upon several multicultural and cross-cultural training approaches (Browne & Perez, 1981; Gudykunst, Ting-Toomey & Wiseman, 1991; Hoopes & Pusch, 1979; Milhouse, 1986; Pusch, 1981; Spitzberg & Cupach, 1984) to design the present model. All of these approaches are endorsed by the AACTE Commission on Multicultural Education (1973) and the Association for Supervision and Curriculum Development (1977), which states that multicultural education is mandatory for quality education in that it contains the variety of educational models, alternatives, and opportunities necessary to acquaint students with the total spectrum of society's cultures.

Another reason multicultural education and cross-cultural training was used in this study is that previous research has demonstrated its ability to enhance participants' knowledge and appreciation of diverse cultural and ethnic groups. For instance, the provision of a four-week multicultural education inservice program by Agee & Smith (1974) produced positive changes in the attitudes of participants toward speakers of divergent dialects. Similarly, Amodeo & Martin (1982) found that the utilization of multicultural education and training can be highly effective for increasing participants' awareness and sensitivity to cultural biases.

An equally important reason for employing this model is its relationship to the nature and objectives of the discipline of communication, which seeks to develop students' communication competence, for example, the students' ability to demonstrate appropriate knowledge of communicative behavior in a given situation (McCroskey, 1982). Further, it can be argued that in order to become a competent communicator, one must acquire knowledge and skills that enhance communication in diverse settings (Gudykunst, Ting-Toomey & Wiseman, 1991; Friedrich, 1978). In fact, Gudykunst et al. (1991) argue that introductory courses which are designed to teach effective communication among diverse cultures "ideally should include cognitive, affective, and behavioral components" (p. 275). These components interdependently influence and are essential to communication competence (Spitzberg & Cupach, 1984; Spitzberg & Hurt, 1987). Moreover, Spitzberg and his colleagues' work is the basis for the Relational Model of Intercultural Communication Competence (Imahori & Lanigan, 1989), which also advocates an interdependent relationship between knowledge, motivation, and skills.

In Imahori and Lanigan's model, knowledge (cognitive) refers to awareness and appreciation of interaction rules across cultures, culture-specific and general knowledge, and language. Motivation (affective) focuses on specific thoughts and feelings about diverse cultures (that is, social distance, positive regard, and attitude similarity) and general affectations (that is, ethnocentrism, open-mindedness). The skills (behavioral) component includes the demonstration of respect, interaction posture, empathy, interaction management, and tolerance of ambiguity when interacting with other cultures. These components have been tested in both intercultural and cross-cultural studies (Martin & Hammer, 1989; Milhouse, in press; Olebe & Koester, 1989), which reveal that competence in communication enhances successful relationships within and across diverse cultural groups.

To assess the MECT model's effectiveness to provide knowledge, effective motivational competencies, and skills pertaining to cultural diversity, three research questions were posed. Each question was designed to address the nine triads pertaining to each of the model's componential objectives, activities, and opportunities:

RQ1: To what extent do students perceive the model to achieve its objectives, activities, and opportunities relating to the development of awareness and appreciation of cultural diversity?

RQ2: To what extent do students perceive the model to achieve its objectives, activities, and opportunities designed to motivate positive attitudes and relationships with individuals of diverse cultures?

RQ3: To what extent do students perceive the model to achieve its objectives, activities, and opportunities relating to the development of cross-cultural communication skills?

To determine the model's ability to promote positive changes in students' attitudes about individuals of diverse cultures, the following hypotheses were tested:

H1: Prior to MECT, students in Groups 1 and 2 will hold similar attitudes about diverse cultures as reflected in Pretest ProScale and Antiscale mean scores.

H2: Students exposed to MECT (Group 1) will score lower on both posttest scales (ProScale and Antiscale) than students not exposed to MECT (Group 2).

When used as a teaching tool, an instructional model should be relatively unbiased by variables such as the instructor's or the students' gender (Spitzberg & Hurt, 1987). Also, previous research indicates that cross-cultural experiences might positively influence future cross-cultural interactions (Gudykunst, 1979; Imahori & Lanigan, 1989; Milhouse, in press). Therefore the third hypothesis predicted:

H3: There would be no significant main or interactional effect between the variables of students' sex and the model; or prior contact and the model.

METHODS

Evaluation Instruments. The *Evaluation of Multicultural Objectives (EMO)* questionnaire (a revised version of Harty's 1975 *Evaluation of Program Experiments in Multicultural Living Instructions Instrument*) was used to assess each of the model's nine objectives. It consisted of nine triad sections that allowed students to assess objectives, activities, and opportunities pertaining to multicultural knowledge, motivation, and skills.

First, the students indicated achievement or nonachievement of the objectives by rating them on a 1 (lowest rating) to 5 (highest rating) Likert-type scale. Second, the students assessed the effectiveness of the model's activities by rating them along a continuum that ranges from 1 (ineffective activity) to 5 (very effective activity). Third, the students indicated whether or not enough opportunities were provided them to achieve a given objective. The ratings for this item range from 1 (far too few opportunities) to 5 (more than enough opportunities).

To evaluate a student's score on the *Evaluation of Multicultural Objectives* questionnaire, the following guidelines were used: (1) Students whose scores fell at level 3 were considered to have moderately achieved the objectives. (2) Students whose scores ranged between the levels of 4 and 5 were considered to have achieved a high level of development concerning the objectives. (3) Students scoring 1 or 2 were considered to have obtained low or no development from an objective.

To evaluate the model's goal "to enhance positive attitudes about diverse cultures," a revised version of Shulman & Harding's (1964) *A Survey on Groups*

(SOG) was used as the before and after measure. It elicited students' responses to 48 pairs of statements about diverse cultural groups. Two of those statements are pro (proscale) and two are anti (antiscale) diverse cultures. An example of an item on the proscale is: "Our schools should teach the history of diverse cultural groups." An example of an item on the antiscale is: "Our schools should only teach the history of Euro-American groups." A pro response received a score of 1 point (regardless of the degree of sureness). An anti response, with a degree of sureness of "very sure," received a high score of 5. When an anti response was given with a "moderate" rating of sureness, a score of 4 points was given. When an anti response was chosen at a level of "not very sure," a score of 3 points was given. The lower the score (48 and below), on both scales, the more pro a student/group was considered to be toward diverse cultures. The higher the score (above 48) the more anti a student/group was considered to be toward diverse cultures.

Procedures. Approximately one week prior to the beginning of the 16-week semester, three instructors who were teaching two sections each of the basic communication course were provided the essential instructions and materials needed to infuse and teach Multicultural Education and Cross-Cultural Training (MECT) in their classes. The model was incorporated into the appropriate course units. The basic course curriculum is divided into four units and each unit focuses on different dimensions of communication theory and skills. The units most conducive to the infusion of the multicultural components are: (1) interpersonal communication, (2) small group discussions, and (3) public communication. A complete description of the model and its format is available from the authors upon request.

On the first day of the classes, one hundred and twenty undergraduate students enrolled in the three sections of the communication course were asked to complete the SOG. Sixty of those students were assigned to an "experimental" group and sixty were assigned to a "control" group. The experimental group (hereafter referred to as Group 1) received multicultural education and cross-cultural training. The control group (hereafter referred to as Group 2) received no training. Information was also obtained pertaining to the students' gender, ethnicity, and prior contact with persons from cultures different from their own. A description of the distribution of the participants by these variables is as follows: *Gender:* Group 1 had twenty-seven (45 percent) males and thirty-three (55 percent) females. Group 2 had twenty-six (43 percent) females and thirty-four (57 percent) males. *Ethnicity:* Fifty-three (87 percent) students in Group 1 were Euro-Americans and seven (13 percent) were from other diverse cultural groups (for example, African Americans, Africans, Native Americans, Asians, Asian Americans, and Hispanics and Hispanic Americans). The ethnic distribution for students in Group 2 was similar—fifty-four (90 percent) were Euro-Americans and six students (10 percent) were from diverse cultures. *Prior Contact*: A total of forty-two (70 percent) students in Group 1 had some prior contact with culturally different persons, whereas eighteen (30 percent) students had no prior contact. In Group 2, thirty (50 percent) students had some prior contact and thirty (50 percent) students had no prior contact.

At the end of the semester, the students were informed that they were participating in research to measure the effectiveness of the Multicultural Education and Cross Cultural Training Model that had been infused in the content of the course. They were then asked to complete the *Survey on Groups* (posttest) measure.

RESULTS

To examine the research questions, condescriptive and frequencies procedures were used. These procedures provided the following descriptive statistics (mean score, standard deviations, and distribution characteristics) for the experimental group on each of the three research questions:

Research Q1: In reference to the model's effectiveness at facilitating awareness and appreciation of cultural diversity, forty (67 percent) students responded at levels 4 or 5. The majority believed the training was highly effective. Sixteen (27 percent) students answered this question at level 3 (moderate achievement), whereas only four (6 percent) indicated "inadequate" to "no achievement" of

TABLE 10-1

Means and Standard Deviation Scores for RQ1

QUESTION	N	$\bar{X}$	SD
RQ1: What extent do students perceive MECT to develop their awareness and appreciation of cultural diversity?			
(O) 1. No awareness (1) to a great deal of awareness (5)	60	3.91	0.98
(A) 2. Activities were not effective (1) to very effective (5)	60	3.63	0.90
(P) 3. No opportunities (1) to sufficient opportunities (5)	60	3.50	0.89

O = Objective; A = Activities; P = Opportunity; RQ = Research Question awareness of cultural diversity. Mean scores and standard deviations for each triad item appear in Table 10–1. All items received mean scores of 3.50 or better—indicating an overall favorable rating for the training in achieving the stated objective (mean = 3.91; s.d. = 0.98), and in providing effective activities (mean = 3.63; s.d. = 0.90) and enough opportunities (mean = 3.50; s.d. = 0.89).

Research Q2: Forty-three (71 percent) reported they perceived the model as highly effective (intervals 4 or 5) at changing negative and nonaccepting attitudes toward individuals from diverse cultures. Thirteen (22 percent) students scored the model at interval 3 (moderate obtainment of the objective) and only four (7 percent) students reported the training as being ineffective in motivating them to change their attitudes. Table 10–2 provides a summary of mean scores and standard deviations for all triad items. The model's objective received a mean value of 3.85 (s.d. = 0.82). In addition, above average mean scores of 3.75 (s.d. = 0.93) and 3.56 (s.d. = 0.83) were obtained for quality of program activities and quantity of program opportunities, indicating that most students perceived these factors as beneficial to the achievement of the objective.

Research Q3: The model was rated highly effective in developing skills in communicating and relating with individuals of diverse cultures. Twenty-seven (45 percent) students responded to this question at intervals 4 or 5, indicating that they developed high levels of cross-cultural communication skills. Eighteen (30 percent) students reported at interval 3, indicating moderate development and fifteen (25 percent) students indicated that the training provided

TABLE 10–2
Means and Standard Deviation Scores for RQ2

QUESTION	N	$\bar{X}$	SD
RQ2: What extent do students perceive MECT to help identify forms of stereotyping, prejudice and discrimination?			
(O) 1. Provides no help (1) to a great deal of help (5)	60	3.85	0.82
(A) 2. Activities were not effective (1) to very effective (5)	60	3.75	0.93
(P) 3. No opportunities (1) to sufficient opportunities (5)	60	3.56	0.83

O = Objective; A = Activities; P = Opportunity; RQ = Research Question

TABLE 10–3

Means and Standard Deviation Scores for RQ3

QUESTION	N	$\bar{X}$	SD
RQ3: What extent do students perceive MECT to develop skills at maintaining positive relationships with individuals of diverse cultures?			
(O) 1. No development (1) to a great deal of development (5)	60	3.70	0.89
(A) 2. Activities were not effective (1) to very effective (5)	60	3.58	0.91
(P) 3. No opportunities (1) to sufficient opportunities (5)	60	3.50	0.83

O = Objective; A = Acitivities; P = Opportunity; RQ = Research Question

below average to no development of cross-cultural interaction skills. Table 10–3 reports above-average mean scores for Objective 3: (mean = 3.70; s.d. = 0.89) for the quality of program activities (mean = 3.58; s.d. = 0.91) and for the quantity of program opportunities m = 3.50; s.d. = 0.83. This indicates an overall effective rating for the training.

TEST OF THE HYPOTHESES

Prior to the direct test of hypotheses, the relation of the two instruments was examined. Correlational analyses of students' scores from the EMOG with scores from the SOG instrument revealed a significant relationship between the two measures ($r = 0.70$, $p > 0.001$). The reliability coefficient alpha for the EMOQ and SOG was 0.88 and 0.87, respectively. The two hypotheses were each subjected to separate 2 x 2 repeated measures analyses of variance. *Hypothesis I:* As predicted, there were no differences in the attitudes between Group 1 (m = 51.41) and Group 2 (m = 52.37) on the pretest proscale, $[f(1,118) = 1.02 \ p < 0.314]$, or the pretest antiscale, $[f(1,118) = 0.33, p < 0.566]$ toward diverse cultures. *Hypothesis 2* was also confirmed. It appears that students exposed to the MECT (Group 1) scored lower (m = 28.52) on the posttest proscale $[f(1,118) = 10.52, p > 0.002]$ and the posttest antiscale $[f(1,118) = 101.04, p > 0.000]$ than students in Group 2 who were not exposed to the MECT (mf 32.18). Pre- and posttest means and standard deviations scores for both groups are presented in Table 10–4.

TABLE 10–4

Means and Standard Deviation Scores for The Pre- and Posttest Results between Groups

		GROUP 1			GROUP 2	
	N	$\bar{X}$	sd		$\bar{X}$	sd
PreMeasure						
ProScale	120	34.63	2.97		35.28	4.00
AntiScale	120	68.20	9.94		69.46	13.83
PostMeasure						
ProScale	120	28.52	9.52		32.18	4.89
AntiScale	120	50.63	7.83		71.45	13.99

A lower mean score on both the pro and antiscales reflects a positive change in attitude.

Hypothesis 3 was rejected. There were both a *main effect* for gender on the posttest proscale [$f(1,118) = 8.28, p > 0.05$] and the posttest antiscale [$f(1,118) = 3.20, p > 0.05$], and an *interactional effect* with gender and training on the posttest proscale [$f(3,116) = 5.51, p > 0.05$]. As for prior contact, only a *main effect* was obtained on the posttest proscale [$f(1,118) = 12.26, p > 0.05$]. Table 10–5 presents main and interaction effect means for the variable of gender and gender with training. Means and standard deviations for prior contact are presented in Table 10–6.

DISCUSSION

The results of this research suggest that a multicultural perspective can be successfully infused into teacher preparation and classroom curricula, thereby developing students' competence in multicultural education. Analysis of the data indicates that 80 percent of students enrolled in three sections of the basic communication course sections where MECT was infused rated it as highly effective (levels 4 and 5) in improving their levels of knowledge, motivation, and skills.

Although all of the competence objectives were important in influencing students' ratings, the most significant were those pertaining specifically to knowledgeability and appreciation of cultural diversity, effective motivational behaviors, and cross-cultural communication skills. Moreover, it was hypothesized that students exposed to MECT would demonstrate improved attitudinal behaviors (for example, thoughts, feelings, and sensitivity toward diverse

TABLE 10-5

Means and Standard Deviations for Gender and Gender with Training

| | | MAIN MEANS | | | |
| | | Male | | Female | |
Scale	N	$\bar{X}$	sd	$\bar{X}$	sd
PreProScale	120	35.07	2.97	34.20	3.88
PostProScale	120	32.09	6.46	29.32	4.65
PreAntiScale	120	69.04	10.84	68.81	12.93
PostAntiScale	120	62.27	10.71	59.68	11.24

| | | INTERACTION MEANS | | | | |
| Dependent Measures | | MALE | | | FEMALE | |
	N	$\bar{X}$	sd	N	$\bar{X}$	sd
Group 1						
PreProMeasure	27	34.93	2.57	33	34.48	3.19
PostProMeasure		30.19	8.88		24.82	5.72
PreAntiMeasure	27	69.19	8.43	33	67.39	11.08
PostAntiMeasure		51.59	7.97		49.85	7.75
Group 2						
PreProMeasure	34	35.21	3.36	26	35.92	4.57
PostProMeasure		34.06	4.03		33.81	3.57
PreAntiMeasure	34	68.88	13.25	26	70.23	14.72
PostAntiMeasure		72.94	13.45		69.50	14.72

groups) when compared with students not exposed to MECT. Analysis of students' (Group 1) responses to the posttest proattitudinal measure indicates a 30 percent increase in positive attitudes; whereas the posttest antiattitudinal measure showed a 26 percent decrease in nonaccepting attitudes.

These results are consistent with other studies which indicate that cognitive, affective, and behavioral teaching methods are important to diverse cultural education. According to Gudykunst et al. (1991), it is important that all three factors be addressed in introductory courses that offer intracultural or intercultural communication emphases. Similarly, Spitzberg (1989) maintains that communication competence does not change given different cultural contexts, but that competence depends on the interrelationship of all three factors. Finally, Imahori and Lanigan (1989) posit that the most ideal condition (that is,

TABLE 10–6

Means and Standard Deviations for Prior Contact

	N	$\bar{X}$	sd	$\bar{X}$	sd
		PRIOR CONTACT		NO PRIOR CONTRACT	
GROUP 1					
PreProScale	60	34.21	2.77	36.05	2.86
PostProScale		26.57	7.97	29.05	7.07
PreAntiScale	60	68.97	10.03	66.47	10.04
PostAntiScale		50.95	7.04	49.23	8.70
GROUP 2					
PreProScale	60	33.60	3.57	35.60	4.06
PostProScale		32.23	3.32	35.66	3.50
PreAntiScale	60	75.16	10.41	63.76	14.60
PostAntiScale		64.90	12.37	61.04	15.45

learning, interactional) of intercultural communication competence occurs when participants demonstrate high degrees of knowledge, motivation, and skills. Thus, overall MECT appears to be an extremely useful tool for instructors who wish to infuse multicultural perspectives into the content of their courses. However, some unexpected results arising from this research also deserve discussion.

It was expected that the student variables such as gender and prior contact would not influence their responses to the attitude measures. However, both variables produced either significant main and/or interactional effects on the instructional model. This suggests that the significant differences found might have been mediated by student gender, particularly the females, whose scores were significantly lower than the males' on the proattitude and antiattitude measures. Other researchers have concluded that under conditions where expressions may depend on empathy, females may be more accepting than males. For example, Bochner and Yerby (1977) stated that, depending on the condition, females are more likely than males to score higher on measures of perception such as those that require reflection of feelings, thoughts, self-disclosure, and empathy. Similarly, Spitzberg and Hurt (1987) reported that female students in their study perceived themselves as more competent than their male counterparts in terms of other-oriented behavioral skills such as speaking about others, body lean, vocal variety, and the use of encouragement.

Another possible explanation of gender differences may be the fact that females were mentioned in a number of the statements contained in the *Survey of Groups* questionnaire. This may have interfered with their being totally objective or remaining "detached" while responding to the statements and, therefore, more "pro" than "anti" cultures/ethnic groups.

As for prior contact, O'Brien, Fiedler, & Hewitt (1971) reported that multicultural training is more effective for subjects who have had prior contact with the target culture than for subjects who have not. Similarly, Imahori and Lanigan (1989) posit that past positive intercultural experience produces positive expectations of future intercultural interactions. Students in both groups of our study indicated some prior contact with persons of different cultures or ethnic groups.

Two additional factors that should be identified as possible explanations are facilitator gender and ethnicity. It is possible that the instructors' gender and ethnicity had some influence on the students in our study. They may have scored higher because of the positive information they received about females and ethnic minorities. If those interactions were positive, the respondents may have been more acceptant of cultural and gender differences. However, without controlling for effects of instructor gender and ethnicity, we can only presume that those factors were partial contributors to the significant findings in our study. The importance of those variables warrants research about their impact upon MECT.

IMPLICATIONS FOR PRESERVICE TEACHER EDUCATION

This research offers significant implications for programs designed to train prospective educators to function successfully in both university- and school-based multicultural classrooms. First, scientific data are provided which indicate that a multicultural perspective can be successfully infused into existing classroom curricula. These data are important in the conception and design of multicultural preservice and in-service teacher education. For preservice educators who will need to learn how to design and develop courses with a multicultural perspective, this study offers a viable model because it can be used by educators and/or programs to help them do so. The model is especially useful to preservice graduate students who teach the introductory-level communication, sociology, psychology, history, or political science course.

On the other hand, it provides in-service teachers with a body of knowledge about cultural diversity in our society that can be objectively imparted to their students. Also, this research provides a systematic examination of the most effective activities, methods, and techniques that can be used by prospective educators and educators already responsible for teaching diversity in the classroom. Further, the multicultural education and cross-cultural training model in this study is useful to teacher education because it can be interwoven throughout a program's course or a sequence of courses. The need for such interweaving is argued by many educators, including Hunter (1974) who posits that it is significant to the development of student teaching and field-based practicums, graduate teaching, and in-service programs. Finally, the MECT model incorporates the three components (that is, knowledge, attitudes, and skills) which Gay (1977) believes are essential to curriculum designs for multicultural teacher education.

In conclusion, when infused into the context of a university communication course, MECT appears to have great potential for developing appreciation of cultural diversity, for affecting motivational behaviors, and for developing helpful communication skills, thereby changing negative perceptions about diverse cultures/ethnic groups. Even so, more research is needed to investigate and control the extent to which the MECT model differentiates gender and prior contact of subjects, and the effect of the gender and ethnicity of instructors. Also, other factors such as the content and context of the instruction should be more closely controlled.

REFERENCES

American Association of Colleges for Teacher Education (AACTE) Commission on Multicultural Education. (1990). *Multicultural Teacher Education: Preparing Educators to Provide Educational Equity*, Vol. I.

AACTE Commission on Multicultural Education. (1973). No one model America. *Journal of Teacher Eduction, 24*, 264–265.

Agee. W. H., & Smith, W. (1974). Modifying teachers attitudes towards speakers of divergent dialects through inservice training. *Journal of Negro Education, 43*(1), 82–90.

Amodeo, L. E. & Martin, J. (1982). A study of the effects of multicultural training on the factual knowledge and attitudes of elementary and secondary teachers. (ERIC Document Reproduction Service No. ED 213 686).

The Anti-Defamation League of B'nai B'rith. (1986). *A world of difference.* Boston: Author.

Appleton, N. (1988). *Cultural pluralism in education: Theoretical foundations.* New York: Longman.

ASCD Multicultural Education Commission. (1977). *Multicultural education: Commitments, issues and applications.* Washington, DC: Association for Supervision and Curriculum Development.

Association of Teacher Educators Annual National Conference, Atlanta, GA, 1986.

Banks, G. P., & Benavidez, P. L. (1981). Interpersonal skills training in multicultural education. In H. P. Baptiste, M. L. Baptise, & D. M. Gollnick (Eds.), *Multicultural teachers education: Preparing educators to provide educational equity.* (pp. 177–201). Washington, DC: Association of Colleges and Teacher Education.

Banks, J. A. (1988). *Multiethnic education: Theory and practice* (4th ed.). Boston: Allyn and Bacon.

Banks, J. A., & Banks, C. A. McGee (Eds). (1989) *Multicultural education: Issues and perspectives.* Boston: Allyn and Bacon.

Baptiste, P. H., & Baptiste, M. L. (1980). *Multicultural teacher education: Preparing educators to provide educational equity.* Washington, DC: American Association of Colleges for Teacher Education.

Bennett, C. I. (1990). *Comprehensive multicultural education: Theory and practice* (2nd ed.). Boston: Allyn and Bacon.

Bochner, A., & Yerby, J. (1977). Factors affecting instruction on interpersonal competence. *Communication Education, 26,* 91–103.

Browne, J., & Perez, P. (1981). *Multicultural education course of study for grades kindergarten through twelve.* California State Department of Education.

Friedrich, G. W. (1978). Effect of teaching behavior on the acquisition of communication competencies. Paper presented at the meeting of the American Educational Research Association, Toronto.

Garcia, R. L. (1982). *Teaching in a pluralistic society: Concepts, models, strategies.* New York: Harper and Row.

Gay, G. (1977). Curriculum design for multicultural education. In C. A. Grant (Ed.), *Multicultural education, commitments, issues, and applications.* Washington, D. C.: ASCD.

Gibson, M. A. (1984). Approaches to multicultural education in the United States: Some concepts and assumptions. *Anthropology and Education Quarterly, 15,* 94–119.

Grant, C. A., & Sleeter, C. E. (1989). *Turning on learning: Five approaches for multicultural teaching plans for race, class, gender, and disability.* Columbus, OH: Merrill.

Green, M. F. (1989). *Minorities on campus: A handbook for enhancing diversity.* Washington, DC: American Council of Education.

Gudykunst, W. B., Ting-Toomey, S., & Wiseman, R. L. (1991). Taming the beast: Designing a course in intercultural communication. *Communication Education, 40,* 271–285.

Hernandez, H. (1989). *Multicultural education: A teacher's guide to content and process.* Columbus, OH: Merrill.

Hoopes, D. S., & Pusch, M. D. (1979). Teaching strategies: The methods and techniques of cross-cultural training. In M. D. Pusch (Ed.) *Multicultural education: A cross-cultural training approach,* pp. 106–121. Yarmouth, ME: Intercultural Press.

Hunter, W. A. (1974). *Multicultural education through competency-based teacher education,* (Ed.). Washington, DC: AACTE.

Imahori, T. T., & Lanigan, M. L. (1989). Relational model of intercultural communication competence. *International Journal of Intercultural Relations 13,* 269–286.

Kendall, F. E. (1983). Diversity in the classroom: A multicultural approach to the education of young children. New York: Teachers College.

Lerner, E. (1986). *Cultural conflicts: Case studies in a world of change.* Portland, ME: J. Weston Walch.

Martin, J. N., & Hammer, M. R. (1989). Behavioral categories of intercultural communication competence: Everyday communicators' perceptions. *International Journal of Intercultural Relations, 13,* 303–332.

McCroskey, J. E. (1982). Communicative competence and performance: A research and pedagogical perspective. *Communication Education, 31,* 1–7.

Milhouse, V. H. (1986). *The effectiveness of multicultural education and cross cultural training: The Student Perspective.* Unpublished Ph.D. dissertation, University of Oklahoma, Norman, OK.

Milhouse, V. H. (In press). The applicability of interpersonal competence to the intercultural context. An investigation. *International and Inter-cultural Communication Annual.*

O'Brien, G. E., Fiedler, F. E., & Hewitt, T. (1971). The effects of programmed culture training upon the performance of volunteer medical teams in Central America. *Human Relations, 24,* 305–315.

Olebe, M., & J. Koester (1989). Exploring the cross-cultural equivalence of the behavioral assessment scale for intercultural communication. *International Journal of Intercultural Relations, 13,* 333–347.

Pusch, M. D. (Ed.) (1981). *Multicultural education: A cross-cultural training approach.* Yarmouth, ME: Intercultural Press.

Richmond, V. P., & Gorham, J. (1988). Language Patterns and gender role orientation among students in grades 3–12. *Communication Education,* 37, 142–149.

Samovar, C. A., & Porter, R. E. (1991). *Intercultural communication: A reader.* (6th ed.). Belmont, CA: Wadsworth.

Schniedewind, N., & Davidson, E. (1983). *Open minds to equality: A sourcebook of learning activities to promote race, sex, class and age equity.* Englewood Cliffs, NJ: Prentice-Hall.

Sleeter, C. E., & Grant, C. A. (1988). *Making choices for multicultural education: Five approaches to race, class, and gender.* Columbus, OH: Merrill.

Spitzberg, B. H. (1989). *Handbook of interpersonal competence research.* Springer-Verlag.

Spitzberg, B. H., & Cupach, W. R. (1984). *Interpersonal Communication Competence.* Beverly Hills, CA: Sage.

Spitzberg, B. H., & Hurt, H. T. (1987). The measurement of interpersonal skills in instructional contexts. *Communication Education, 36,* 28–45.

Stubbs, M. (1976). *Global education: From thought to action.* Alexandria, VA: Association for Supervision and Curriculum Development.

Tye, K. A. (Ed.). (1991). *Global education: From thought to action.* Alexandria, VA: Association for Supervision and Curriculum Development.

United Nations. (1983). *World concerns and the United Nations: Model teaching, units for primary secondary and teacher education.* New York: Center for Teaching International Relations.

Wurzel, J. (1988). *Toward multiculturalism: A reader in multicultural education.* Yarmouth, ME: Intercultural Press.

Wurzel, J., & Holt, W. (1991). Teaching aids for multicultural education. *Communication Education, 40,* 287–290.

CHAPTER 11

Meeting the Needs of Multicultural Classrooms: Family Values and the Motivation of Minority Students

JEANNETTE ABI-NADER
Gonzaga University

JEANNETTE ABI-NADER is an Associate Professor in the Teacher Education Department at Gonzaga University. Her research interests are the motivation of minority students and preparation of teachers for multicultural classrooms. She is currently conducting a study of teaching writing on an Indian reservation, which will have implications for teacher education.

ABSTRACT

The concept of *familia* is central in cultural descriptions of Hispanic people. Studies of culture and cognition have probed the link between patterns of cultural socialization and cognitive development, of affiliation motivation and achievement, and of family authority structures and adaptation to mainstream ideals of autonomy. This study of a teacher's motivational strategies demonstrates how the cultural concept of family can shape instruction and create a sensitive classroom environment. The Hispanic high school students in this study attribute their decisions to finish high school and enroll in college to the effective integration of their cultural values into everyday classroom interactions. This study suggests that teacher educators need to incorporate the results of this research into preservice training. Implications for field experiences and faculty inservice are discussed.

The best thing I like about this class is that we all work together and we all partici-pate and try to help each other. We're family! (Student Survey).

Although statistics reveal a rapidly growing minority population in the United States, the teacher work force is, by and large, white middle class. Motivational strategies, classroom management routines, and teaching styles, once effective with most students, are failing. This dilemma is especially evident in inner-city schools where minorities have become the majority student population. The literature suggests that teachers daily enter a culture they admit is foreign to them and practice a pedagogy just as foreign to their students. The dearth of minority teachers discourages hopes of matching cultural teaching and learning styles. We are left with a mismatch of culturally based goals, perspectives, and frames of reference that gridlock efforts to meet students' academic, emotional, and social needs in American schools. The current focus on the failures of teachers and the deficiencies of minority students, however, ignores real successes that occur and from which we can all learn.

This inquiry focused on a special academic program in which up to 65 percent of the participants complete high school and enroll in college. By all current statistics, the inner-city Hispanic adolescents in the program, most of them children of single mothers on welfare and with few models of academic success, should not accomplish such a record. The program's success for the 11 years preceding the study merited inquiry and led to the formulation of the following questions: What motivated these students to succeed in school? Is the special program related to their success? How was student motivation evident in this setting? What emerged as crucial in the investigation were the motivational strategies of the teacher whose deliberate, focused use of the cultural concept of "family" shaped instruction and the environment for learning. *Family* is identified as the overarching metaphor that weaves through teacher/student interaction and instructional activities and permeates the structure and function of the academic program. Examples from observations, surveys, and interviews demonstrate how the teacher's strategies in incorporating the family concept support the development of achievement motivation. This study has implications for helping preservice and in-service teachers gain awareness and skills to create effective instruction for the diversity of cultural backgrounds in their classrooms.

THEORETICAL FRAMEWORK

The theoretical framework upon which this study is based recognizes the influence of culture on cognitive development. Meaningful inquiry into achievement motivation among minority students draws on research in both culture and cognition. Indeed, there is no way to meaningfully separate culture from cognitive functions. Cognitive structures and cognitive processes, such as achievement motivation, are inferred from what people say and do (Rueda, 1987). How they say and do is shaped by the social and historical forces that make up their world. Understanding and interpreting this world and the meaning of the activities and events that comprise a person's experience of it is the domain of ethnographic studies in culture and cognition (Erickson, 1986).

Influencing much of ethnographic research today is the sociohistorical approach developed by Vygotsky (1978) and his followers. Vygotsky's approach effectively integrates the study of cognition with studies of how human activity is organized in a culture (Cole, 1985). In developing a sociohistorical/sociocultural theory of human cognitive development, Vygotsky proposed that individual development is mediated by social interaction in a culture-specific, historical setting. The analysis of this development is achieved by examining the external activities in which the individual engages and manifests cognitive behavior. Cole summarized the "common ground" on which culture and cognition can be studied:

1. There is a basic unit common to the analysis of both cultures' and individuals' psychological processes.
2. This unit consists of an individual engaged in goal-directed activity under conventionalized constraints. This unit is variously designated an "activity," a "task," an "event."
3. In the main, particularly where children are concerned, these activities are peopled by others, adults in particular.
4. The acquisition of culturally appropriate behavior is a process of interaction between children and adults, in which adults guide children's behavior as an essential element in concept acquisition/acculturation/education (Cole, 1985, p. 158).

Identifying and analyzing activities, tasks, and events that occur naturally in the life of the community provides insights into how culture and cognition interact. Language, for example, is a set of cultural activities experienced by the child externally through social interaction with peers and adults and gradually internalized. The child first imitates sounds and gestures, discovers the utility of these moves in accomplishing certain objectives, internalizes this information, and transforms it for practical use on other occasions. This cycle is influenced by the cultural and historical context in which it occurs and is shaped by contextual exigencies (Vygotsky, 1978). By fusing the study of context and social interaction with that of the cognitive functions of learning and problem solving, Vygotsky's theory provides a framework for considering how culture influences motivation and other cognitive processes. The wellspring of a child's experience of and participation in culture is the family. In the context of family, a child is introduced and socialized into the systems of belief, communication, self-perception, and world definition of a culture. Ethnographic researchers probe these systems as they are experienced in social interaction and offer interpretations of their effects on cognitive development and motivation.

One of the outstanding characteristics of the Kamehameha Early Education Project (KEEP) is the practice of allowing the children to overlap each other's speech as in the familiar patterns of the Hawaiian "talk story" (Au & Jordan, 1980). The "talk story" is the telling of a story by more than one narrator overlapping each other's speech and with similar overlapping responses from the audience. The use of this structure allowed the children to participate in storytelling by overlapping their comments with the storyteller's in a manner that resembled their native cultures. The third year of using this strategy resulted in 67 percent improved reading achievement. KEEP researchers met with an entirely different response on the Navajo reservation, however, where they conducted studies similar to those done in Hawaii (Tharp, 1989). Here the effective strategy resembled the Native American participation pattern of the "talking circle," that gives each person the floor uninterruptedly for long discourses. Navajo children seemed more comfortable when the teacher read a story straight through before beginning discussion.

Ways with Words (Heath, 1983) details another study of students' home linguistic and participative structures and how they affect cognitive functioning in school. Heath's study of language acquisition and use in two communities in the mill towns of the Carolinas reveals the diverse patterns imprinted by socialization practices, child-rearing customs, and the environment of human interaction. Children of Black families in Trackton, for example, learned different ways of perceiving and responding to questions posed by adults. Trackton children did not experience questions as directives, nor did they experience questions as requests for displays of analytic or descriptive skills or as questions for which answers were already known to the questioner. Heath's study showed that making teachers aware of these differences and of their own culture-based interaction patterns resulted in innovative adaptations in classroom instruction.

In a study of student teachers' communicative failures in multicultural classrooms, Kleifgen (1988) observed that when the student teacher approached a Korean boy in a style typical of American classrooms—stooping down to the boy's level, repeatedly questioning him about the task—he was able to elicit only a whispered response from the child. The experienced "cooperating teacher," on the other hand, understood the boy's need to maintain a culture-specific personal space and his reluctance to respond in English until he felt secure in his mastery of the words.

When we examine studies of motivation from the perspective of cognitive psychology research, we learn that motivation is inextricably tied to considerations of meaning and context (Maehr, 1984), emotional states (Weiner, 1984), and individual self-perceptions (Schunk, 1989). These qualitative aspects of motivational studies evolve inevitably toward integration with sociocultural investigations of the meanings and interpretations that influence motivation in a cultural context.

'FAMILY' AS A CULTURAL CONCEPT

The concept of *familia* is central to cultural descriptions of Hispanic people. In a study of 85 Puerto Rican, Mexican, Cuban, and Venezuelan families living in the United States, Cintrón de Esteves and Spicola (1982) found family to be the "first priority in life" (p. 5). Social engagements were essentially family get-togethers around traditional religious and family holidays. Family roles and socialization patterns were consistent across the four groups.

The Mexican Family Attitude Scale used to elicit responses about family values showed that Mexican Americans made significantly higher scores when compared with Anglo Americans on such items as

6. For a child the mother should be the dearest person in existence.
9. More parents should teach their children to have unquestioning loyalty to them.
13. Some equality in marriage is a good thing, but by and large, the husband ought to have the main say-so in family matters. (Ramírez, 1967, p. 5)

Studies exploring the link between affiliation and achievement motivation have determined that "achieving for others" is a strong component of Hispanic family relationships (Ramírez, 1967). In a comparison of Anglo, African American, and Mexican American children on the basis of a test of achievement motivation, Ramírez and Price-Williams (1976) found that "the Mexican American and (African American) groups seemed to encourage children to identify with the family early in life and to remain so identified, while the Anglo group seemed to encourage children to consider themselves as separate individuals early in life" (p. 57). In reviewing sociocultural studies of motivation, Tharp (1989) concludes that

> In many immigrant groups, parents emphasize the welfare of the family as a whole, and students assume the moral burden of succeeding for the whole family, if not the whole community. . . . Although testing often shows Black, Hispanic, and Hawaiian children to have less need for achievement and more need for affiliation, they do not lack motivation for accomplishment, recognition, and reward. But achievement is more often sought in a context and for the purpose of family and peer-group solidarity and identification, rather than for individual and independent attainment (p. 354).

The characteristics of "family" that surface in these and other studies include a sense of acceptance and belonging that extends beyond the nuclear family to embrace grandparents, cousins, aunts, uncles, and in-laws. This large "web of kinship (brings) obligations of mutual assistance and reciprocal favors. Outside the nuclear family, relationships to individuals in kinship roles may be viewed as variations on themes set up in the roles of father, mother, son, daughter, brother, and sister" (Brussell, 1971, p. 172). The individual's response to this unconditional acceptance by family and the expectation of support in hard times is loyalty, service, success, and leadership in preserving and extending the life of the family.

Studies show that culture deeply affects the cognitive development and achievement motivation of minority students and does so in a familial mode that differs from the mainstream American emphasis on individualism (Suarez-Orozco, 1989). Research that probes the link between patterns of cultural socialization and cognitive functioning predicates "the social and cultural basis for knowledge acquisition on the indivisibility of the psychological and sociocultural functions of the family and social group" (Trueba, 1988, p. 280).

AN ETHNOGRAPHY OF FAMILY VALUES AND ACHIEVEMENT MOTIVATION

In this investigation of a successful college prep program for Hispanic high school students, I focused on teacher/student interaction. The personality of the teacher and the almost universal opinion of him as "a great motivator" interested me and raised questions about what made his program effective. From the beginning of data gathering, the concept of "family" kept recurring in observations and interviews as the most common descriptor of the program.

Method

A large public high school in a metropolitan area in the northeastern United States was the site for the study. Of the 1,700 students enrolled in "Heritage High," 81 percent were minorities, including 21 percent Hispanic. Heritage High is a magnet school that, in addition to the regular program of a comprehensive high school, offers advanced courses in television production and photography, and thus attracts students from all over the city. The inquiry focused on an elective program called "Program: Learning According to Needs" (PLAN), which was designed under a Title VII grant in 1975 to prepare Hispanic students for college. (Pseudonyms are used for all persons, places, events, and programs.) PLAN offers a three-year sequence of elective courses in reading, writing, and public speaking for sophomore, junior, and senior Hispanic students who are "college material" but may have never imagined themselves in college. The students meet in separate grade-level groupings for 50 minutes each day and then attend other classes in either bilingual or monolingual English programs. Curriculum materials include workbooks in reading, spelling, grammar, and vocabulary that provide exercises to improve comprehension, note-taking, and writing skills. Scholastic books and magazines with current events, stories, and plays are read aloud or dramatized in class. Students in PLAN prepare short speeches and TV commercials for videotaping and playback. In addition, seniors prepare a newscast for videotaping, research a topic of their choice for a term paper, and write a personal essay to accompany their college application.

The People in PLAN

The study focuses on Don Bogan, the teacher/director of PLAN, who spent several years as a Peace Corps volunteer in Puerto Rico and Honduras. This experience initiated him into Hispanic culture and was the source of his commitment to raise academic success levels for Hispanic students. He often tells stories of his Peace Corps experiences and compares his efforts to adapt to new cultures to his students' challenges in American schools. Although Anglo, he speaks Spanish and is perceived by his students as knowing their culture and being totally dedicated to their personal and academic welfare. They describe him as "father, brother, and friend to us." He is especially appreciated by bilingual teachers and by parents who see him as an ally in their struggles to make a better life for their children. Bogan's administrators and colleagues characterize him as "a terrific motivator," as "good with Hispanic families," "successful because he completes the triangle of home, the student, and the school. He's helped Hispanics to trust educators." Even those who dislike him acknowledge his high expectations for Hispanics and describe him as "fierce" in the demands he makes for his students to excel. Admissions counselors from local colleges regularly visit PLAN classes to recruit because they know "Bogan's kids have a better grasp of what they need to do to make it—confidence, skills, and ambition" (Interview with admissions counselor).

Ten students and four graduates of PLAN comprise the roster of student informants. Most of the students in PLAN are from families headed by single mothers on welfare. They live in the projects and other low-income housing in three large neighborhoods surrounding the school. Many are the first in their families to stay in high school or to consider college. Of the student and graduate informants, two were born in the United States of Puerto Rican descent; seven were born in Puerto Rico; one is Colombian; one is from Honduras; one is from the Dominican Republic. Two students who were not Hispanics, but wanted to be in PLAN, were from Cape Verde and Jamaica.

THE SOCIAL CONTEXT OF PLAN

Field notes, interviews, and taped classroom sessions yield a rich description of the social context of PLAN. From this description it is possible to identify episodes, speech events, and activity settings as units of analysis. Typical patterns of interaction in and about the program include implicit as well as explicit references to and expressions of the family-like structure of PLAN, to family values, and to affiliation motivation.

'FAMILY': THE CENTRAL METAPHOR IN PLAN

The model of family that emerges from the data encompasses traditional cultural understandings as well as specific descriptions of what family means to PLAN participants. Three aspects of the cultural concept of family characterize PLAN: a feeling of belonging; a sense of responsibility for the well-being of all members; and a commitment to extending the life of the family physically and socially.

PLAN, like the families the students come from, provides a place and a welcome for everyone and a promise of stability and permanence. Students are there for each other. Older students help younger ones by tutoring, mentoring, and modeling behaviors that lead to success. In introducing PLAN to the sophomores, Bogan explains their special relationship to the juniors and seniors.

> The students in this program stick together. We're family. You're going to see that. The juniors and seniors will help you. I'll find the student who is good in geometry, who will help you make a schedule . . . meet you in the library. That's how much they want you to make it. The same thing I'll ask of you when you're juniors and seniors and you're good in one subject. I'll ask you to do the same thing for the sophomores. That's the way it works. We help each other.

Family values of caring and mutual support are expressed in one of the ground rules for class participation familiar to everyone in PLAN, "We never laugh at each other's mistakes." This rule is stated early and reiterated often in all levels of the program.

> People in this room have picked a risk, and it is a risk. When I ask you to take the risk of coming up and giving an oral presentation, I promise you one thing, nobody will laugh at you. If anybody starts to laugh at you, I promise you, they'll be out the door. Right out the door. I say that strongly. However, we might laugh with you. That's different.

Instructional methods emphasize cooperation and support. Although cooperative learning as a formal strategy is not used, students often work in pairs or small groups. Interdependent learning activities such as role playing, dramatized skits and plays, and communications games that require group decision-making and consensus are frequently used.

The earliest expression of mutuality and care in the data occurs when the seniors present their first public speaking assignment. They are understandably nervous before their peers and clutch wrinkled half-sheets of paper or index cards. The topic is "My Three Wishes." Students are to introduce their topic, develop it, and make a concluding statement. A long introduction by Bogan assures them that public speaking is the "number one phobia of all people." He models enthusiastic clapping for each presenter and encourages the class to add compliments to his positive evaluations. However hesitant and nervous the performance, Bogan finds something to praise. "You have a nice voice. You'll be a good storyteller for your children. But I had to strain to hear you. Just make it louder." This type of feedback characterizes Bogan's interaction with students in PLAN. He embeds high expectations and exhortations to improve in warm expressions of acceptance and support. The students internalize this behavior, which then characterizes their relationships with one another. They urge each other on when someone stumbles over words or hesitates in speech-making. In this encouraging atmosphere, the seniors articulate their dreams for the future.

The seniors' "Three Wishes" speeches support the notion of "achieving for others" (Ramírez, 1967) that characterizes affiliation motivation attributed to the family orientation of Hispanic students. The wishes for success and material wealth are not just for themselves but for the family: ". . . good health for my parents . . . I want to go back to my country and help my people because they are in terrible need of education . . . I want to go to Puerto Rico and visit my father . . . I want to help my parents, to be the best success I can for them." Affiliation also challenges members to reciprocate through service and leadership and to extend the life of the "family" by recruiting new members for PLAN. Some seniors accompany Bogan on recruitment visits to local middle schools where he shows slides of Heritage High, and the students talk about the academic and social opportunities they enjoy in PLAN. When I went back the year after the study for a follow-up visit, Bogan had enlisted the cooperation of all his classes in "adopting" five Central American orphans, one from each of the countries most represented in PLAN. The students donate money each month for the orphans' support and take great pride in showing visitors the pictures and biographies of these new additions to their extended family. Bogan recognizes this as a replication of values they learn at home. "When someone gets sick or dies," he says, "other family members, no matter how poor they are, take the children in. *Nothing* with six (children). Now *nothing* with nine." When spirits sag under weighty assignments, Bogan points to UNICEF posters of orphaned Latino children and reminds his students to "learn to read well for them if you don't want to read for yourselves." Bogan also challenges them to gain public speaking skills because "When you're at a school meeting and your children aren't getting the right education, you might be the only one to speak up." These experiences in cooperation and solidarity are meant to develop into a lifelong commitment to service and leadership on behalf of the Hispanic community.

When the students talk about PLAN, family is the most common descriptor. "PLAN means to me coming together and learning as a family." "The things about the program that I like best are that everybody is like a family. We help each other and trust each other, and most important, we're there to help our friends when we're needed." "That class is like family to me because, we met only one year but he has us like family." In a group interview with a Dominican student and her friends from Cape Verde and Jamaica, family themes and their translation into PLAN characterize their talk. They refer to the discomfort they feel in other classes where they are ridiculed for their accent by some teachers and classmates. The Jamaican student explained,

Yeah, especially when we speak (in PLAN classes) we don't be shy when we say things 'cause kids so friendly with each other, they don't laugh at you. We laugh together. It's great. We be nervous but we know we gonna be together. It's not like when we say something and they all laugh at us.

Linda, a sophomore, describes Bogan as different from all her other teachers. "He's like a real close friend, you know. He helps us out, really a lot. And any problem, you know, outside of school, he's like a big brother to us." Another student says:

> He's aware of our background. How we were back there. He was there so he knows everything that we've been through, our families, you know, he knows everything we're about. It's not like some people, "Oh, they come from Puerto Rico" but not all of us are. He knows where we're coming from. He understands everything that we go through.

Other students refer to the level of trust and sharing that characterizes their relationships in PLAN. "(PLAN) means friendship, fun, and being able to express and share your ideas with different people with different cultures and perspectives." "In Mr. Bogan's class I feel especially good because, you know, it's like, I'm with Hispanics and we all treat each other like a big family, trust each other."

Evidence that students are motivated by strategies that recognize their family values rests partially on their own words. In interviews, they share their thoughts and ideas about specific decisions they are able to make because of the support of their teacher or of their friends in PLAN.

> Mr. Bogan helped me a great deal . . . I don't think I would have been able to do so many things nor to plan my future so good. This class helps you be independent and more mature towards life. The best thing I like about this class is that we all work together and we all participate and try to help each other. We're family.

Traditional family values surface in interviews with parents as well. "I have been talking to him (Roberto)," one mother says, "and advising him that after he graduates he has to go to college and get an education to help the community and his family."

"Achieving for others" is invoked to motivate students in instructional activities, such as an outlining exercise in geography. Students read passages in their workbooks that describe several continents with information about the countries and their characteristics. The exercise requires students to outline the information, putting the facts into appropriate subtopics. Bogan tells them about a TV news item that reported low scores for high school seniors who took a test on the locations of countries and cities prominent in current events. He talks about the importance of knowing geography, not to pass a test, but for the following reasons:

> We should know where our brothers and sisters live around the world and what's happening there; what's happening in El Salvador today affects all of us; they're our brothers and sisters, all right? They're our brothers and sisters and more so even you guys because they're your Latin brothers and sisters, my brothers and sisters also. But you know this is your culture and that's why again so many people know what's happening because they get involved and they help them out.

PLAN also imitates the authoritarian structures present in descriptions of traditional Hispanic families (Brussell, 1971; Ramírez, 1967). In his rules for completing homework assignments, meeting deadlines, following directions for group work, and participating in PLAN activities, Bogan demands total compliance. He sees himself as the "director" and his students as "actors." His method for correcting their English is reserved for public speaking and reading—never for conversation or class discussion. He does this by insisting on unquestioning imitation as he models correct pronunciation, inflection, and intonation patterns.

> You are the players and I'm the director. And as director, you have to allow me to tell you the things I think you can improve on. I'm not criticizing, you got to understand; I'm going after you guys because you're good, and you could be better.

Students typically show him the same respect accorded the father of a family. They lower their heads when being admonished and use the title "sir" in accepting his advice and criticism.

Because these strategies gain Bogan his students' confidence, he is success-ful in helping them adjust to the demands of mainstream culture. For instance, Bogan is keenly aware of the deleterious effects on women who, more than men, are caught in a cycle of unemployment and poverty because of family responsibilities and lack of education. He encourages his female students to think of their futures and plan careers that will allow them to be independent. "If you have a profession, your life doesn't have to stop. Prepare yourself now." Without denigrating the *ama de casa* or housewife role that Hispanic women are expected to fulfill, Bogan presents the alternative of education as a key to success in the mainstream culture. He visits the homes of female students, talks to parents about the value of a college education and allays their fears about their daughter leaving home to live on a strange campus. Pregnancies and early marriages pose an even greater threat than parental rejection of higher education for their daughters. A PLAN graduate reflected on this dilemma.

> I think we're all scared of the future. What do I do after high school? So it's like, well, get married, have a family. Isn't that what everybody else does? It's like we're scared to go out there and go to school because in the Hispanic homes they're always pushing the boys to achieve academically. But the girls, it's like they slack back and they don't (go to school). It's really something that girls just don't do in our culture, you know. It's like you're expected to be, you know, less than your husband because he's going to support you so you don't have to worry about all this.

This attitude is reflected in the absences of female students who are sometimes kept home to care for the babies, accompany family members to the doctor, or even to clean the house. In a short story Bogan selected for class reading and discussion, the conflict between an immigrant mother's attachment to traditional female roles and her daughter's dreams of going to college and having a career is explored in the context of "new world" challenges. In the discussion, Bogan tells the senior girls, "You're not in Tegucigalpa; you're not in Guatemala City. Things are different here. I want the best for my daughter; I want no less for you."

These examples demonstrate that acceptance, mutual support, trust, and affiliation motivation that characterize the cultural concept of "extended family" also shape and influence relationships in PLAN. The students feel "like a family" in his classes and accept Bogan's directives for adapting traditional values for greater success in the mainstream culture. When he speaks Spanish with his "gringo" accent and demonstrates his familiarity with their traditions, they know that he, too, had to adapt while in the Peace Corps in order to succeed in their culture. Bogan's motivational strategies in PLAN are grounded in his knowledge and appreciation of the students in his program and echo for them the familiar voices of family and culture.

DISCUSSION

The concept of "family" functions as both an instrumental and a structural model in PLAN; it is the means for achieving motivational objectives, and the goal to which the objectives lead. Strategic use of this concept unites the students and gives them a sense of belonging. The teacher infuses his classroom environment and curriculum with the motivating power with which Hispanic culture endows the notion of family ties and obligations. "Family" also provides a structural model for what PLAN students look to in the future, a goal for their educational and professional endeavors. It provides clues to future roles and relationships that are to be characterized by service and leadership in the larger Hispanic family. Bogan's efforts to help his students plan for the future and redefine their self-image (Abi-Nader, 1990, 1991) are firmly grounded in the cultural context of "family" as experienced by the students themselves. The supportive community the students find in PLAN is both the seedbed and the harvest. Through education, self-discipline, hard work, and mutual caring for one another, they recreate a climate that promotes confidence in risk-taking and in goal-setting.

In "family," the social interaction, central to Vygotsky's theory of cognitive development, can be integrated with concepts of motivation from cognitive psychology. For example, the organismic model developed by Ryan, Connell, and Deci (1985) is useful in relating the motivational strategies used by Bogan and attributions of their effectiveness by the students in PLAN. Ryan and his associates propose that intrinsic motivation results from the satisfaction of basic psychological needs for competence, autonomy, and relatedness. When these needs are satisfied in an optimal educational environment of support and involvement, the student experiences engagement and success. Data gathered on Bogan's strategy of creating a family atmosphere in PLAN support this model and demonstrate that when students' need for relatedness is satisfied in a culturally familiar and appropriate way, they indeed exhibit high levels of engagement and achievement motivation.

CONCLUSIONS

What can teacher educators and classroom teachers learn from this account of PLAN? Clearly, direct imitation of Bogan's strategy could result in an inadequate and perhaps harmful parody. The underlying principle, that Bogan's approach to teaching is shaped by the direct experience of his students' culture, does have something to say to teacher education and in-service programs. Although it is not possible for everyone to gain firsthand experience in the Peace Corps or similar projects, learning from immersion in a culture is a component of professional education that is sorely lacking. Limited immersion, however, is better than relying solely on accumulating secondhand information about cultures. A range of options needs to be explored, from designing field experiences for preservice teachers that provide them with prolonged contact with diverse populations in school settings to cultural awareness workshops that expose participants to the dynamics of cross-cultural communication. Ethnographic experiences like those Heath (1983) designed for her teachers struggling with cultural conflicts in a desegregated South can orient teachers, new and old, to the communities in which their students live. Collaboration with parents and community members in shaping the curriculum and environment of school brings the context of the students' lives to bear on the teaching/learning experience. Teacher education programs need to require multicultural field experiences in courses besides the "token" multicultural course. This is even more important in culturally homogeneous areas where experiences of diversity may need to be imported or students transported to multicultural settings. Field experiences and collaboration with multicultural communities can inspire commitment to and imagination in meeting the academic needs of diverse classrooms.

It is fruitless to think about motivation without awareness of the students' frame of reference. As Díaz, Moll, and Mehan (1986) state:

> It is possible to capitalize on children's social, linguistic, and academic strengths to change teaching and learning situations. To do so, we need to view students' backgrounds and life styles, not as a hindrance to educational advancement that must be corrected or circumvented, but as legitimate and powerful resources for improving students' performance in schools, and, as a consequence, improving the process of schooling itself. (p. 225)

REFERENCES

Abi-Nader, J. (1990). "A house for my mother": Motivating Hispanic high school students. *Anthropology & Education Quarterly*, 21, (1), 41-58.

Abi-Nader, J. (1991). Creating a Vision of the Future: Strategies for Motivating Minority Students. *Phi Delta Kappan*, 72. (7), 546-549

Au, K. H., and Jordan, C. (1980). Teaching reading to Hawaiian children: Finding a culturally appropriate solution. In H. T. Trueba, G. P. Guthrie, & K. H. Au (Eds.). *Culture and the bilingual classroom: Studies in classroom ethnography* (pp. 139-152). Rowley, MA: Newbury House.

Brussell, C. B. (971). Social characteristics and problems of the Spanish-speaking atomistic society. In J. C. Stone & D. P. DeNevi (Eds.). *Five heritages: Teaching multi-cultural populations.* (pp. 169-196). New York: Van Nostrand Reinhold.

Cintrón de Esteves, C., & Spicola, R. F. (1982). *Four Hispanic groups: Oral and social traditions, education and play implications for educators.* (Report No. RC 013 872). Chicago, IL: International Reading Association. (ERIC Documentary Reproduction Services ED 226 897).

Cole, M. (1985). The zone of proximal development: Where culture and cognition create each other. In J. V. Wertsch (Ed.). *Culture, communication and cognition: Vygotskian perspectives.* (pp. 146-161). New York: Cambridge University Press.

Díaz, S., Moll, L. C., & Mehan, H. (1986). Sociocultural resources in instruction: A context-specific approach. In *Beyond language: Social and cultural factors in schooling language minority students* (pp. 187-230). Los Angeles: Evaluation, Dissemination and Assessment Center.

Erickson, F. (1986). Qualitative research on teaching. In M. C. Wittrock (Ed.), *Handbook of research on teaching* (3rd ed.), (pp. 119-161). New York: Macmillan.

Heath, S. B. (1983). *Ways with words: Language, life, and work in communities and classrooms.* New York: Cambridge University Press.

Kleifgen, J. A. (1988). Learning from student teachers' cross-cultural communicative failures. *Anthropology & Education Quarterly*, 19 (3), 218-234.

Maehr, M. L. (1984). Meaning and motivation: Toward a theory of personal investment. In R. E. Ames & C. Ames (Eds.), *Research on motivation in education: Student motivation*, Vol 1. (pp. 115-144). New York: Academic Press.

Ramírez, M., III. (1967). Identification with Mexican family values and authoritarianism in Mexican-Americans. *The Journal of Social Psychology*, 73 3-11.

Ramírez, M., III., & Price-Williams, D. R. (1976). Achievement motivation in children of three ethnic groups. *Journal of Cross-Cultural Psychology*, 7 (1), 49–60.

Ryan, R. M., Connell, J. P., & Deci, E. L. (1985). A motivational analysis of self-determination and self-regulation in education. In C. Ames & R. E. Ames (Eds.). *Research on motivation in education: The classroom milieu*, Vol. 2 (pp. 13–52). New York: Academic Press.

Rueda, R. (1987). Social and communicative aspects of language proficiency in low-achieving language minority students. In H. T. Trueba (Ed.), *Success or failure?* (pp. 185–197). New York: Newbury House Publishers.

Schunk, D. H. (1989). Self-efficacy and cognitive skill learning. In C. Ames & R. E. Ames (Eds.). *Research on motivation in education: Goals and cognitions* Vol. 3 (pp. 13–44). New York: Academic Press.

Suarez-Orozco, M. M. (1989). *Central American refugees and U.S. high schools: A psychosocial study of motivation and achievement.* Stanford, CA: Stanford University Press.

Tharp, R. G. (1989). Psychocultural variables and constants: Effects on teaching and learning in schools. *American Psychologist*, 44 , 349–359.

Trueba, H. T. (1988). Culturally based explanations of minority students' academic achievement. *Anthropology & Education Quarterly*, 19, 270–287.

Vygotsky, L. S. (1978). *Mind in society: The development of higher psychological processes.* Cambridge, MA: Harvard University Press.

Weiner, B. (1984). Principles for a theory of student motivation and their application within an attributional framework. In C. Ames & R. E. Ames (Eds.). *Research on motivation in education: Student motivation*, Vol. 1 (pp. 15–38). New York: Academic Press.

Communication: Implications and Reflections

JAMES C. MCCROSKEY
AND
VIRGINIA P. RICHMOND

The three research papers represent very different research methodologies, topic areas, and degrees of association with communication concerns. Thus, comparisons among the papers will, for the most part, be of little value. We will, however, address the same issues in our comments on each paper: (1) the appropriateness of the methodology, (2) the relationship of the study to communication concerns, (3) the importance or usefulness of the topic, (4) conclusions we can draw from the research, (5) directions for future research, and finally, (6) implications for classroom teachers.

COMPLEXITY IN TEACHER PLANS

Researchers generally engage in one of two general approaches to research. We have chosen, possibly because of our rural roots, to label these the "honeybee" approach and the "hybrid farmer" approach. Honeybee researchers flit from one topic to another, barely stopping on one topic long enough to extract a bit of sweetness before buzzing on to an unrelated topic. While occasionally this approach to research extracts a finding of importance to a field, most such efforts barely receive passing notice from the significant scholars and practitioners in that field. Hybrid-farmer researchers, in contrast, stay with a topic area until they have generated significant new understandings, new contracts, and/or new ways of doing things. They put things together in ways not examined before and bring forth ideas that did not previously exist. Then, and only then, do they move to a new topic of study. Usually that topic is not wholly unrelated to the previous topic. This is the approach to research that generates most of the important knowledge in any field. It is the work of these researchers that draws most of the attention of the significant scholars and practitioners in that field.

This paper is the interim product of hybrid-farmer researchers who have been pursuing the topic of student resistance of teachers and student misbehavior. This paper explores the association of type of misbehavior with the complexity of plans generated by teachers for coping with that misbehavior. This is part of an overall program of research, but the first study directly looking at teacher planning behaviors. Hence, we must look at the paper in this broader context.

Methodological appropriateness.   We are not generally positively disposed toward simulation research methodologies because of their usually low ecological validity. However, in this instance the simulation methodology employed is quite appropriate. The use of real in-service teachers is an important strength of this study. The use of simulation is most appropriate when the researcher(s) is exploring a new branch of a topic, as is the case here, and is not certain what to expect. Creating student misbehaviors in a naturalistic classroom environment is not something one should do without being very certain one can keep the situation under control. Hence, initial experimental work with student misbehavior, of necessity, should be outside the natural environment.

The simulation methodology has a major advantage in that it permits creation of conditions which might be very difficult to find in a natural classroom environment, and it permits combinations of conditions which might be even more difficult to study in that environment. Thus, the researchers in this instance were able to cross student sex with type of misbehavior. Presumably in the attempt to create greater generalizability, different student names were used in the two male conditions as was the case in the female conditions. Also, each type of misbehavior was represented by a different example in each of its two conditions. Had the results of the study produced a significant main effect for sex, or a significant main effect for type of misbehavior, or both, everything would have been fine. Unfortunately, the worst possible result, in terms of interpretation, was the result obtained—an interaction of sex and misbehavior type. Nothing in the previous literature should have led the researchers to expect such a result; hence we have an example of Murphy's law at work!

In a clean design of this study, the student name and description in each male condition would have been the same; similarly the student name and description in each female condition. The student misbehavior described in each "teacher-owned" condition would have been identical, and the student misbehavior in each "student-owned" condition would have been identical. Then if an interaction had been observed, it could have been interpreted to be a function of misbehavior type interacting with student sex. Since neither of these circumstances existed—there were four different students identified, and four different misbehaviors—the results cannot be interpreted unambiguously. For all we know, the results in condition 1 could have been because teachers just don't like people named Carl! Or maybe it is just that comic books cause teachers to make plans quickly. We use these comparatively silly explanations not to suggest that they are likely to be the real reason for the results, but to indicate that even silly conclusions cannot be ruled out by the design of the study. The only way to know how to interpret the present results is to do the study over with consistent manipulations across conditions in place of the inconsistent ones used in the present study.

Communication concerns. This concern with communication in this overall research program is strong. However, in the present study the focus is mostly on types of student misbehavior and their effect on teacher planning for dealing with those misbehaviors, plans which presumably would involve communication.

Topic importance. Student misbehaviors and teachers' response to and prevention of those misbehaviors are of major importance. This is a very important topic and the research program likely will produce valuable information for teachers and teachers educators.

Conclusions. As we noted previously, we are not able to draw firm conclusions from this study. However, when additional research is completed, we anticipate important conclusions will be possible.

Future research. As we suggested above, the immediate follow-up research should unconfound the sex and misbehavior types considered in the present study. Beyond that, we believe the researchers should consider the possibility of expanding their typology of student misbehaviors, an effort they have touched upon in previously published efforts. We doubt that "student-owned" and "teacher-owned" classifications do justice to the complexity of the issue of misbehaviors, although this distinction does seem to us to be quite important. Although previous research provides considerable communication-based guidance for teachers to *prevent* misbehaviors (for example, employ immediate behaviors, use a variety of affinity-seeking strategies, avoid antisocial control techniques), even the best teacher will sometimes confront misbehaviors. It is important to determine if different communication strategies are needed for different types of misbehaviors, and that necessitates development of a solid typology of recognizable student misbehaviors and testing various communication strategies for dealing with those problems.

Implications for teachers. Although the design and results of this study do not permit us to draw implications for teachers, as this program of research progresses important implications should be forthcoming.

INFUSING A MULTICULTURAL PERSPECTIVE

This paper reports a study designed to test the effectiveness of a program to develop more positive attitudes toward cultural diversity in a college student population. The approach of the program is chosen from a variety of approaches which are described in the paper.

Methodological appropriateness.   The general design of the study is a classic pretest, posttest experiment with one experimental group and one control group. The students were assigned to the two groups on the first day of class in a basic communication course (sixty to each group) and were not informed they were in an experiment until the end of the course. Remarkably, all sixty in each group were still present at the end of the semester and all completed both the pretest and the posttest. It is not specified how the students were assigned to groups nor how it was possible to retain all subjects for the entire semester, a feat we have never been able to accomplish.

It would appear that the design and execution of this study was flawless, until the very last day. Then, the researchers made a critical error. They report the students were debriefed and told they were part of a study designed to measure the effectiveness of the training program that had been included in their class, and *then* the subjects were asked to complete the posttest measure.

The exact nature of that debriefing is not reported, but the students in the experimental condition would certainly have known they were in a class that really stressed cultural concerns. Similarly, the students in the control group would have known they did not have any training that emphasized cultural concerns. Hence, it is most likely the obtained results were at least in part, if not entirely, a function of the students trying to behave like good subjects. On the primary measure, the experimental students raised their prodiversity scores about twice as much as the control group (6 points to 3 points) and on the antidiversity scores their change was about 18 points in the positive direction, whereas the control group change was about 2 points in the negative direction. Clearly the students in the experimental group did not want to identify with negative statements about diversity after being in a training program to get them not to agree with such statements.

It would be satisfying to believe that these results indicate the effectiveness of this program. However, in these days of "political correctness" on college campuses, it would be a naive student indeed who would complete an attitude questionnaire expressing antidiversity attitudes right after being told he/she had just completed a course designed to get her/him not to express such attitudes. This would be particularly the case if he/she has to put her/his name on the questionnaire (or code number) so the researcher could match it with the same questionnaire collected at the beginning of the semester.

Unfortunately, the inappropriate timing of the debriefing in this study precludes our drawing any meaningful conclusions about the tested program. We can only recommend the study be redone with the debriefing held until all data on the Survey of Groups instruments have been collected.

Communication concerns.   The concern of this study was with a program to change student attitudes of matters of cultural diversity. Although the persuasive campaign was embedded in a basic communication course, this was not a communication study. No communication variables or processes were involved as study targets. While the training program itself could be viewed as a composite of communication strategies for producing attitude change, these concerns were not the focus of this study.

Topic importance.   Matters of cultural diversity and the acceptance of such diversity are a major concern for all educational systems. However, this does not make such concerns *communication* concerns. The development of methods for teaching students to accept people from other cultures and their diverse ways is necessary if we are to have a society in which there is harmony among the various groups of people composing the society. However, we should take care that we do not impose such instruction at the cost of not meeting other educational objectives. It was most interesting to us that in the present study, no effort was made to determine whether the cultural diversity program's introduction into the basic communication course had any impact on the primary objectives of that course. Such courses are not adopted because of a primary objective of facilitating cultural diversity, so it is important to learn if the real objectives of the course were meet better with the new program, there was no difference, or some course objectives had to be sacrificed in the name of education about cultural diversity. Clearly, the researchers in this instance did not care one way or the other. In the future, we hope such insensitivity to the objectives of the established system will not be present. Even if the results of the present investigation were not confounded by the design, we still would not know what we lost in order to gain these results.

Conclusions.   As we noted above, the design of the study does not permit us to draw firm conclusions.

Future research.   As we noted previously, this study needs to be redone with appropriate timing for the debriefing. It also is important that this research program examine what is *lost* as well as what is gained by substituting the MECT program into an ongoing course. If the basic course studied is so poorly designed that several days of it can be eliminated with no cost to the students with regard to meeting the objectives of that course, that is one thing. If, however, the course is well designed, with clearly stated objectives and appropriate measures to determine whether those objectives are met, the students in the experimental group *should* show a deficit in meeting the regular course objectives compared to the control group. The well-designed study should be able to identify both the gains in terms of knowledge and/or affect related to cultural diversity and the losses in terms of knowledge and/or affect related to communication. With this information available, those administering and teaching the basic communication course will be in a better position to determine whether the new approach should be retained over the old one. An alternative, of course, is that the new unit be added to some other course in the university (sociology, political science, history) rather than the communication course. At any rate, tests of innovative instructional systems should always be grounded in the normal reality of educational systems—there is a finite limit on instructional time, hence the addition of one instructional package presumes the elimination of another instructional package. When that is not the case, such must be proven. When it is the case, the new package and its objectives must be proven superior to the old one and its objectives.

Implications for teachers.   Since we cannot draw firm conclusions from the present study, there are no direct implications of the study for teachers. However, future research with an appropriate design may indicate that the MECT program is an effective method for enhancing prodiversity attitudes in college students.

MEETING THE NEEDS OF MULTICULTURAL CLASSROOMS

This paper is much different from the other two papers we have examined. It focuses on a highly successful program designed to help Hispanic adolescents prepare for college in an attempt to identify the factors which make that program successful.

Methodological appropriateness.   This paper reports an ethnographic study drawing on the theoretical position that Hispanic children are instilled with a very high value for the family and achieving for the family. The teacher/student interaction in the classroom is observed to determine the use of these values to motivate Hispanic children in the program. While ethnographic methods are somewhat less precise than experimental methods, such as those discussed in the previous papers, a study of a successful program often benefits from the added flexibility this methodology provides. With the sacrifice of some precision, of course, comes increased difficulty for the critic to determine whether the observations made were appropriate, were accurately reported, and were not subject to the normal selectivity processes of human beings. Since we have not observed what the writer has observed, we will assume the accuracy and appropriateness of the observations as reported for this analysis.

Communication concerns. A surface reading of this paper would indicate that the only concern with communication in it is the use of the communicative messages of the teacher and students to determine what ideas are being communicated and to what motives the teacher is appealing. A careful reading of the manuscript, however, suggests to us that the writer is identifying as the factor which leads to the success of this program an element long known to be highly associated with effective communication, the element of "homophily."

Homophily can be roughly translated as "similarity." It involves similarity in background (culture), attitudes, values, and perceptions. One of the most solidly substantiated principles in communication theory is the principle of homophily: The more two people are alike, the more effectively they will communicate, and the more similar they will become. In essence, the present paper is a case study illustrating that important communication principle. It is homophily which this study found to be the factor that makes this program for Hispanic youth so successful.

Topic importance. Finding out why successful educational programs are successful certainly is important. While one would think that most successful programs are such because people knew in advance what would work and thus implemented the program in that form, we all know that is not always the case. In this case, many communication specialists would have advised (in advance) that programs for youth in special groups will be more effective if taught by people from those groups or people who at least have extensive experience with those groups. For these people, the results of this study are obvious, and to have found otherwise would be very surprising. We suspect the people who chose to hire an ex–Peace Corps worker with experience working with Hispanic populations expected him to be more successful with Hispanic young people because of his experience.

Conclusions. The bottom-line conclusion of this research is that teacher education programs must find ways to give prospective teachers experiences with the culture or cultures of the students they plan to teach so that they can develop more homophily with those students. We agree fully with that conclusion. However, we must add caution to the recommendation. Preservice teachers may not have any idea what kind of students they are likely to be asked to teach. Thus, their program may give them experiences with the African-American community and then their teaching position may take them to Appalachia and all-Caucasian students of Scottish and Irish descent, or the opposite. The point is that the advice is good, but the implementation of it is difficult, at best. And what if the teacher takes a position where classrooms are really *multi*cultural, where the cultural values of one group may be directly counter to the cultural values of another group. How then is the teacher to adapt to such diversity?

Future research.   The present paper was drawn from a theory related to the importance of family values of "Mexican American" and "African American" children compared to "Anglos." If "Anglo" is used as a referent of only people of English descent, such distinctions may be accurate; we are not certain. However, if it is sued to reference non-Spanish Caucasians, as is characteristically done in Hispanic communities, this theory needs major work. Any time spent in an Italian-American, Greek-American, or Polish-American community would indicate the absurdity of this theory, as would spending time with Irish Americans in the back country of Appalachia. We believe homophily was the factor in operation in making this school program successful, not "familia." "Familia" was simply one of many manifestations of the teacher's adaptations to the students based on his understanding of their culture.

Implications for teachers.   We hope that a reading of this paper will help preservice teachers understand just how difficult it is to communicate effectively with students who are from a culture (or cultures) unfamiliar to the teacher. Young teachers with nothing but positive motivations to help young people from divergent cultural backgrounds often seek teaching positions in schools which serve such students. Only later do they learn that good motivations are not enough to make one an effective teacher. One of the basic principles of communication is that one must know one's receiver and adapt one's communication to that receiver if one is to be an effective teacher of children from a culture other than one's own; one must expend the time and effort necessary to learn about that culture and how to adapt to people from it. Good motivations are useful only if directed in the right ways.

Diverse Issues in School Curricula

Curriculum: Overview and Framework

GAIL MCCUTCHEON
The Ohio State University

GAIL MCCUTCHEON teaches courses in curriculum at the Ohio State University and is writing a book about practices of curriculum development relying on work about the social and individual construction of reality and about deliberation.

INTRODUCTION

This section of the book concerns curriculum matters. This introduction defines curriculum, then discusses how the curriculum becomes what it is in practice and teachers' roles in the curriculum. Finally, it provides an overview of reports contained here about curriculum.

SOME DEFINITIONS

The curriculum consists of what students have opportunities to learn under the auspices of schools. Obviously, people learn from their surroundings, their parents, and television, but curriculum has to do with learnings for which schools are responsible. However, this is not as simple as it first seems. This is because the curriculum consists of two important parts. Part of the curriculum is *overt*, the publicly advertised fare of the content—the skills and knowledge—students are to learn in schools, such as what is listed on report cards. However, another crucial part of the curriculum is *implicit* in the way school is conducted, in the messages contained in curriculum materials (such as textbooks) and in teachers' actions (Eisner, 1985). Some of the implicit curriculum is unintended, whereas other learnings may be intentional. Moreover, it can contain positive and negative learnings such as opportunities for learning patience; patriotism; learning to live in crowds; the work ethic; tolerance of passivity and boredom; racial, gender, and ethnic stereotypes; and particular thinking processes (such as logic over metaphor or creative thinking).

It is important to recognize the strong relationship between curriculum and instruction. In a sense, the curriculum constitutes the *ends* of education, whereas instruction is the *means*, although since ends and means influence each other the division between these fields is neither clean nor clear. However, decisions about what to teach may be the most important ones made about schooling, and many would argue for close, careful attention to those decisions because they are so crucial. Ideally, all other decisions such as those about which instructional strategies to use should flow from the decisions about what to teach. Curriculum problems are practical (not only intellectual) problems because they call for people to make decisions about actions and to apply to those problems many ideas about students, society, and the discipline(s) being taught.

CURRICULUM: WHAT IS IT IN PRACTICE?

In practice, several phenomena interact to shape what students have opportunities to learn in schools. These include curriculum policies that states, school systems, and schools develop; curriculum materials such as kits and textbooks that schools adopt; and each teacher's practical theory of action, which includes beliefs about what students should learn.

Curriculum policies are developed by school systems and consist of policy statements about what is to be taught. State and local school systems and schools develop these lists of what teachers are to teach. A recent phenomenon is that many state or local school systems have also adopted proficiency tests to measure whether students have mastered the skills and knowledge contained in these polices. Many states and school systems develop the curriculum policies in an effort to control what teachers teach to facilitate students' progression from one grade level to the next and to ease problems due to high mobility by attempting to ensure consistency among schools and to hold teachers accountable for what students learn. These policies and testing practices tell teachers what to teach, so they have quite an influence on the curriculum teachers enact.

Curriculum materials also play a role in determining the nature of the curriculum. Private industry develops materials such as kits and textbooks for teachers and students to use. State and local school systems adopt and purchase them from publishers. Like the policies, they carry with them both an overt and an implicit curriculum. Such published materials also control the curriculum to a great extent in many classrooms because in many schools they are virtually the only materials available for teachers and students to use. Lacking alternatives, teachers use them.

Teachers' practical theories of action also shape the curriculum. Through experiences before and during teaching, teachers interpret their experiences and form generalizations about matters such as what to teach, how students learn, how to teach, how to treat people, and other matters related to their role. These practical theories are idiosyncratic because each teacher's experience is unique (Ross, Cornett, and McCutcheon, 1992). This can cause conflict within teachers as they plan and teach because the aim of the curriculum policies and materials is to make the curriculum uniform, but teachers' practical theories of action are individualistic and may be at odds with the policies. This conflict creates a constant balancing act within teachers as they plan and act. For many teachers, their practical theories act as filters sifting policies and materials so that their plans and subsequent actions are consistent and best for their particular students and the disciplines they teach (McCutcheon, 1994, Part I; Ross et al., 1992). This balancing act is the heart of professional judgment.

WHAT ARE TEACHERS' ROLES REGARDING THE CURRICULUM?

Because teachers are ultimately responsible for getting the curriculum to their students, they play several crucial roles and need to be vigilant and professional about their decisions and actions. One obvious role concerns planning what to teach and which instructional strategies to employ to enable the largest number of students to learn the most possible. This means teachers try to create an *optimum* curriculum for their particular students about the disciplines they teach. This requires careful attention to planning, while acting and when reflecting on lessons already taught. In planning, careful attention to what to teach overtly and implicitly is warranted so decisions about instructional strategies will support optimum decisions about what to teach. Vigilance is also needed during lessons because teachers fine-tune their preteaching plans as they observe whether students are paying attention and are understanding the lesson, so they revise that plan while in the act of teaching (for instance, to reteach previous lessons, to relate a lesson to a current event, to enrich a lesson, or to account for unforeseen events). Equally important are reflections about the lesson, because those reflections can have great bearing upon future plans. Reflections about both the overt and the implicit curriculum are important for reshaping future plans and actions.

Because teachers' practical theories are idiosyncratic, a variety exists from one classroom to the next about what students have opportunities to learn. For this reason it is important for teachers to discuss their plans and practices at grade level or departmental meetings. Through such deliberations teachers can develop plans that facilitate students' integration of the curriculum across disciplines and can ease articulation from one grade level to the next. That is, the discussions can help teachers see potential links across various disciplines and among the courses comprising a sequence. Such understanding of potential links can let teachers plan accordingly to enhance students' integration and articulation and hence their success in understanding the curriculum.

Two teachers' roles, then, are lesson planning and deliberating with other teachers to facilitate students' seeing connections among disciplines and from one grade level to the next. A third role consists of serving on various curriculum committees for the school system and school, such as committees to adopt curriculum materials and to develop policies about what is to be contained in the curriculum. In this case teachers also apply their practical theories of action to practical curriculum problems. Serving on such committees seems likely to continue to be important as many school systems try to involve educators in site-based management and democratic forms of decision making. (McCutcheon, 1994, Part II).

Teachers have central roles in curriculum work, and through them teachers apply their practical theories of action to the various tasks they confront so careful, professional decisions are made. These decision-making times are opportunities for highly professional activities as teachers apply what they know and believe about how students learn, what they should learn and how they should be taught. As a result, this has the opportunity of being the most professional work teachers do because they apply their knowledge to solve these practical problems.

THREE RESEARCH REPORTS

This section of the book contains three reports treating important dimensions of curriculum work. One report concerns an issue worth considering so the curriculum can be optimum—providing access to the largest amount of the curriculum for the greatest number of students. Edward's and Tate's report examines language diversity by focusing upon the reading needs of African-American children. Considering this issue when planning the overt curriculum and reflecting on the implicit curriculum is important if we hope to plan an optimum curriculum for many groups of culturally diverse people— Hispanic Americans, African Americans, Appalachians, Asians, and other groups in our culturally diverse nation. Another example of this problem is evident in Yager's report about gender difference. These two chapters point out the necessity of clearly considering the social context and students as well as subject matter when planning the curriculum, adopting curriculum materials, and enacting the curriculum. They further imply the necessity for considering such issues in blending one's practical theory with various curriculum documents when planning how to enact the curriculum.

Jung's report is somewhat different in that it illustrates processes of teachers' involvement in developing a curriculum policy for their school system. The Yager and Edwards and Tate reports concern the nature of the content of schooling, whereas Jung's report considers how the content gets into schools. Jung's report portrays a highly professional activity of teachers that is increasingly evident as people try various forms of site-based leadership in making curriculum decisions. It also illustrates that curriculum is both an end and a means. This is because the goals might be considered educational ends, whereas the curriculum planning teachers do might be considered part of the means of achieving those ends. While educational innovations are frequently highly acclaimed, unless teachers fully understand them they cannot enact them. Involvement in curriculum development projects such as the one Jung describes can afford teachers the opportunity to continue their professional development because, by developing a curriculum, teachers are simultaneously increasing their understanding of it. This serves to help teachers plan its enactment and teach it better than if they are not involved. As schools continue to implement site-based leadership, issues such as updating the curriculum to explore relationships among science, technology, and society and making more of the curriculum more accessible to a wider group of students are important issues to address.

REFERENCES

Eisner, E. (1985). *The Educational Imagination*. New York: Macmillan.

McCutcheon, G. (1994). *Curriculum Decision Making: Solo and Group Deliberation*. White Plains: Longman.

Ross, W., Cornett, J., and McCutcheon, G. (1992). *Teachers' Personal Practical Theories*. Albany: SUNY Press.

Science/Technology/Society and Teacher Education: Solutions for Problems of Diversity and Equity

ROBERT E. YAGER
University of Iowa

ROBERT E. YAGER is Professor of Science Education, Science Education Center, University of Iowa. His current research interests focus on the Science/ Technology/Society (STS) approach to K-16 teaching, especially in science. Student outcomes in six domains are a current focus, namely concepts, processes, applications of both in new situations, creativity, attitude, and world-view.

The failures of typical school and collegiate programs in science are well documented (Comber and Keeves, 1973; Miller, 1989; NAEP, 1978, 1988a; NSB, 1983; Rutherford and Ahlgren, 1989). The problems can be summarized as:

1. Most view science as specialized information that scientists and science teachers would like high school graduates to possess.
2. There is little evidence that anyone actually acquires this information to the point of using it outside the classroom or laboratory in any new situations.
3. Although there have been attempts in school science to focus on the skills scientists use in practice, there is no evidence that learners improve in their knowledge of or their use of these skills across grade levels.
4. Typical programs are ineffective in promoting interest in science and in producing scientifically literate graduates.

Norris Harms, the director of the huge NSF-sponsored synthesis project of the early 80s, summarized the situation when he said:

> A new challenge for science education emerges. The question is this: "Can we shift our goals, programs, and practices from the current overwhelming emphasis on academic preparation for science careers for a few students to an emphasis on preparing all students to grapple successfully with science and technology in their own, everyday lives, as well as to participate knowledgeably in the important science-related decisions our country will have to make in the future?" (Harms and Yager, 1981, p. 119).

Similarly, Alan Voelker, co-investigator on the literacy studies of high school graduates, commented on the problem and the needed correctives when he said:

> If we want a science program that is truly responsive and responsible to the citizen in the scientifically and technologically oriented society, we must elevate current and future citizen concerns. We cannot assume that curricula which emphasize traditional cognitive knowledge and an understanding of the scientific process will lead to an understanding of the science-related issues confronting society. Neither can we assume that such traditional curricula will assist our student-citizens in applying their scientific knowledge and processes to these issues. Some sacred cows of the science curriculum must be eliminated. But the short-term trauma this sacrifice may elicit will be replaced by long-term gains for all citizens (Voelker, 1982, p. 79).

Certainly the calls for reform have intensified during the past decade. Two national reform efforts have emerged as the two largest (in terms of funding and expected duration) and as the best hopes for reform in the current crisis. These initiatives are: Project 2061 (AAAS, 1988) as sponsored by the American Association for the Advancement of Science; and Scope, Sequence, and Coordination (SS&C) as sponsored by the National Science Teachers Association (Aldridge, 1989). Project 2061 was initiated with significant support from private foundations and now by the National Science Foundation (NSF) and the Department of Education (DEd). SS&C has enjoyed support from both NSF and DEd with other support from industrial foundations. Both projects are long-range, with few tangible results that can suggest the features of reforms which can help teachers and schools with current problems now.

Another international effort for reform is commonly called Science/ Technology/Society (STS). It is an effort to capitalize on current research concerning teaching and learning to reduce the curricular barriers that seem to limit learning in most schools. STS has been a major effort in the United Kingdom, the Netherlands, and Israel for fifteen years. It has been an emerging effort in the United States since Harms' use of it as one of five focus groups for Project Synthesis.

Project 2061, SS&C, and the STS movement all aim to resolve numerous problems in science education, including the commonly identified problems associated with underserved and underrepresented populations in science studies and careers. These populations include females, minorities, and disabled persons. However, the STS efforts are the only ones where information is available concerning the resolution of current problems. Project 2061 occurs in but six school districts out of the 16,000 that exist in the United States. The goal is a complete overhaul of the K–12 science, mathematics, and technology programs. It will take years before programs are in place in the six districts and information is available as to successes in resolving problems. SS&C has been in operation only two years in six centers (Alaska, California, Iowa, North Carolina, Puerto Rico, and Texas). The initial focus has been upon curriculum material and teaching strategies for involved schools for grades six through nine. Again, it is too early for assessment and determination of results for possible resolution of current problems.

This leaves STS as the current reform from which results are emerging that provide evidence for directions needed if current problems are to be solved and reforms established. Certainly this includes the problems identified with underserved and underrepresented populations.

A. OBJECTIVES

The objectives of this report include the following:

1. To review the research associated with females and minorities in the study of science.
2. To define STS as a reform effort in science education around the world.
3. To outline the Iowa Chautauqua Program as an in-service sequence to assist K–12 teachers with moves toward STS.
4. To review results with STS and its power in resolving problems with a special focus on its effects with traditionally underserved student groups.
5. To offer some ideas on the implications of STS strategies for resolving problems of diversity and equality in science study and career choices.

B. PERSPECTIVES

Schools today are striving more than ever to create educational programs that are nonsexist and multicultural in their orientation (Oakes, 1990). The concern is for building science programs that will more effectively meet the needs of all students (NSTA, 1990). Educators are faced with the challenge of providing equal opportunity for students in the science classroom. Equity in science education implies fairness in the distribution of services, equal access to programs, and the inclusion of nondiscriminatory teaching practices in science. Since the advent of Title IX in 1972, segregation in our schools on the basis of gender has become a legal as well as moral and ethical issue. Despite the efforts to legislate equal opportunity, sex-bias and gender issues still exist, especially in school science programs. Even though students may have equal access to science courses and extracurricular activities related to science, research shows that students are treated differently based on a number of student attributes and traits, including gender (Good and Brophy, 1987).

The majority of research that has emerged over the past decades on gender issues related to science education has focused on the psychological and developmental explanations to describe differences between male and female learners (Kelly, 1987). A number of factors, including societal and parental pressures and childhood experiences, affect students' attitude toward science (Kahle and Lakes, 1983). Female students have been shown to exhibit less positive attitudes toward science than their male counterparts (Skolnick, Langbort, and Day, 1982). Boys tend to be more confident in their abilities when it comes to science (Kelly, 1987). Girls tend to view science as masculine and impersonal (Keller, 1982). Research has consistently shown that girls do not perform as well as boys in science classes. Interest in science and achievement levels decline for girls between the ages of nine and fourteen (Hardin and Dede, 1978; NAEP, 1978, 1988b). This type of research has provided useful information for science educators in terms of characterizing the learner and defining the problem. This body of research has focused on the internal states of the students. The overriding tendency has been to blame the students if they do not succeed in science or choose not to participate (Kelly, 1987). Students have, for too long, been expected to change to accommodate school science programs. Perhaps the problem does not lie with the student. Many of the gender differences apparent in today's classrooms result from the exclusionary pedagogical techniques that are still in place in traditional science programs. Too often teachers have thought that if only they could get the students, whether they be male or female, to straighten out, they could teach them science. The question may not be so much what is the matter with our students, as how do we incorporate what we know about how male and female learners develop and move toward more productive and inclusionary science practices and pedagogy?

In terms of research related to gender issues, the tides seem to be shifting. More research is being directed toward sociological and structural questions. The hope is to uncover evidence and explanations that will provide for more inclusive constructs and validate a broader spectrum of the population. Our goals for the 1990s and beyond should not be centered on replacing a womenless curriculum with a manless curriculum but rather to transform the curriculum to include all. The hope should not be for gender-neutral science, gender-free science, but perhaps for gender-balanced science. Connecting students to the curriculum and allowing them to construct their own understandings based on personal experiences seem to be critical in creating meaningful science experiences for students, whether they are male or female.

Connections between science and human beings were a very important concern for many learners. Rosser (1990) argued that such connections are vitally important to women and that they could serve as the link to attract more women and people of color and those white men not now attracted to science. Students in the traditional science classroom are the receivers of knowledge and have little opportunity to connect what they are learning to their own personal experiences or the real world. The majority of students in American classrooms today would not fall into the category of the "constructed-knower" and hence would reject science in such a mode. STS approaches seem to offer helpful correctives.

How do we move toward more connected learning for all students? What types of transformations are needed to make all students "constructed-knowers"? Again Rosser states: "Insuring science and technology are considered in their social context with assessment of their benefits for the environment and human beings may be the most important change that can be made in science teaching for all people, both male and female" (1990, p. 92).

There are also numerous reasons given for poor test results and lower academic achievement of minorities. It has been postulated that minority students are confronted with such learning factors as poor self-concept (Ausubel, 1950; Ausubel and Ausubel, 1963; Clark and Clark, 1950; Moreland, 1963), language barriers (Anastasi and Cordova, 1953), lack of sufficient motivation (Hilgard and Atkinson, 1967; Mosteller and Moynihan, 1972; Packard, 1969), and low teacher expectations (Davidson and Greenberg, 1967; Heathers, 1969; Rosenthal and Jacobson, 1968). There is evidence that minorities like female students exhibit significantly higher anxiety toward math and science than do their white male counterparts (Clawson, Firment, and Trower, 1981; Czerniak and Chiarelott, 1985; Payne, Smith, and Payne, 1983).

Blacks, Hispanics, and Native Americans make up approximately 18 percent of the population, but comprise only 2.2 percent of the science and engineering work force (Malcolm, 1985). According to NSF (1984) estimates, females represented 12.2 percent of the doctoral degrees, 24.8 percent of the master's degrees, and 15.3 percent of the bachelor's degrees when all scientists in the labor force were taken into consideration. An NSF report (1980) suggests that males without graduate degrees find careers in science more easily than females with either a master's or a doctorate.

Racial minorities and females have been consistently underrepresented in mathematics and science majors and careers for at least the last five decades (Hill, Pettus, and Hedin, 1990). This fact has led to a growing national concern for increasing the participation of minorities and females in science and technology careers (NSF, 1984).

Researchers on cultural diversity and multicultural education maintain that certain people of color differ in their world views and cognitive styles from those held by the dominant culture (Anderson, 1988; Banks and Banks, 1989; Banks and Lynch, 1986; Burgess, 1978; Gollnick and Chinn, 1990; Hale, 1978; Kagan and Madsen, 1971; Ramirez, 1973; Sleeter and Grant, 1988). These researchers compare the philosophical worldview of certain minority groups with their nonminority counterparts along the different dimensions. See Table 12–1.

Within the context of STS classrooms, the cognitive structure of minority and female students is accommodated through cooperative learning and assessed through the use of portfolios. The integrative, topical curriculum

Table 12–1
Worldview Comparisons

Non-Western	Western
1. Emphasis on group cooperation.	1. Emphasis on individual competition.
2. Achievement as it reflects group.	2. Achievement for the individual.
3. Holistic thinking.	3. Dualistic thinking.
4. Socially oriented.	4. Task oriented.
5. Extended family.	5. Nuclear family.
6. Accept affective expression.	6. Limited affective expression.
7. Religion permeates culture.	7. Religion distinct from other parts of culture.
8. Time is relative.	8. Rigid time schedule.
9. Value harmony with nature.	9. Mastery and control over nature.

and in-depth study of subject matter characterized by the NSTA, science educators, and researchers (Rubba, 1989; Rubba, McGuyer, and Wahlune, 1991; Spector and Gibson, 1991; Wraga and Hlebowitsh, 1991; Yager, 1991) is consistent with several of the philosophical world views of minority students mentioned above, particularly with respect to holistic thinking and integrative disciplines. Also, the STS rationale parallels cognitive psychologists' theories regarding the role of prior knowledge in cognitive structure (Ausubel, 1968; Champagne and Klopfer, 1984; Resnick, 1986) and the effect that sequential organization of subject matter has on the stability and clarity of anchoring ideas for subsequent learning (Ausubel, 1968). The incorporation of new concepts and information into an existing and established cognitive framework is largely influenced by the student's past experiences and the integrative nature of subject-matter discipline (Ausubel, 1968; Champagne and Klopfer, 1984; Yager and MacCormack, 1989).

The research associated with females and minorities adds an interesting dimension for the needed reforms in science education. Certainly the findings provide information about necessary changes. However, when the goals have clearly shifted to serving *all* students better, special cases and programs may not be as vital for females and minority students. There is considerable evidence that current programs are serving no one well, including students who are most successful and those who pursue further study of science in college.

C. METHODS

In 1990 the NSTA Board of Directors unanimously approved a new paper defining STS more precisely and identifying it as a reform effort for the next decade. This new NSTA position defines STS as "the teaching and learning of science in all the contexts of human experience." It represents an appropriate science education context for all learners, including females and minority students. The emerging research is clear in illustrating that learning science in an STS context results in students with more sophisticated concept mastery and ability to use process skills. All students who experience science in an STS context improve in terms of creativity skills, attitude toward science, and the use of science concepts and processes in their daily living and in responsible personal decision making.

There are no concepts and/or processes unique to STS; instead STS provides a setting and a reason for considering basic science and technology concepts and processes. STS means determining and experiencing ways that these basic ideas and skills can be observed in society. STS means focusing on real-world problems that have science and technology components from the students' perspectives, instead of starting with concepts and processes. This allows students to relate, analyze, and apply concepts and processes to real situations. A good program will have built-in opportunities for the students to extend beyond the classroom to their local communities. These activities should be appropriate for the age of the students and be learner-centered. STS should help lay the basis for empowering students so that as future citizens they realize they have the power to make changes and the responsibility to do so.

Basic to STS efforts is the production of an informed citizenry capable of making crucial decisions about current problems and issues and taking personal actions as a result of these decisions. STS means focusing upon current issues and attempts at their resolution as the best way of preparing students for current and future citizenship roles. This means identifying local, regional, national, and international problems with students, planning for individual and group activities that address them, and moving to actions designed to resolve the issues investigated. The emphasis is on responsible decision making in the real world of the student. STS provides direction for achieving scientific and technological literacy for all. The emphasis is on responsible decision making in the real world of the student, where science and technology are components. Curricular and instructional processes might consider the following: Is it a problem or issue? How did it become a problem or issue? What are some alternative approaches to its solution? What are the potential effects of applying the alternatives on individuals and/or society?

STS programs are characterized as those with many of the following characteristics:

- Utilize student identification of problems with local interest and impact as organizers for the course.
- Use local resources (human and material) as original sources of information that can be used in problem resolution.
- Involve students in seeking information that can be applied in solving real-life problems.
- Extend learning beyond the class period, the classroom, the school.
- Focus upon the impact of science on each individual student.
- View science content not as something that merely exists for students to master on tests.
- De-emphasize process skills as the "special" skills that should be mastered because they are used by practicing scientists.
- Emphasize career awareness—especially careers related to science and technology.

- Provide opportunities for students to perform in citizenship roles as they attempt to resolve issues they have identified.
- Demonstrate that science and technology are major factors which will impact the future.

These 10 features illustrate the focus in STS classrooms. Typical instruction is organized around basic concepts of science—usually as they appear in basic science textbooks. Typically curriculum and instructional decisions are based upon those included in the textbook selected for a given classroom/school. There is little variation among the available textbooks for a given grade level (Harms and Yager, 1981). STS, on the other hand, puts students—their interests, their previous experiences, their thinking, their actions—in a central position. The thought is that such a juxtaposition of the role of students in the learning process may reverse the negative results experienced for students in typical classrooms, perhaps especially so for female and minority students.

NSTA has recognized that STS requires that we rethink, restructure, reorganize, rewrite, and revise current materials (for example, curriculum, texts, audiovisuals) used to teach science. STS requires a realignment of goals and objectives and a reallocation of resources. STS requires re-education on all levels from policy makers to teachers to parents. Such reform of science education is essential. The bottom line is that STS must involve all learners in experiences and issues that are directly related to their lives. STS empowers students with skills which allow them to become active, responsible citizens by responding to issues that impact their lives. The experience of science education through STS strategies will create a scientifically literate citizenry for the twenty-first century. Information concerning student learning in a variety of domains provides evidence for STS as reform. A special look at differences such instruction provides for females and minorities is of special interest for this report.

Two other sources of information and perspectives are important in understanding STS and may be the primary factors providing for success with STS approaches. These include findings of cognitive scientists and the perspectives of constructivists. The Constructivist Learning Model (Yager, 1991) is attracting much attention today because it suggests ways that learning can be enhanced and the changes in teaching that are essential for it to occur. The emerging research regarding constructivism is convincing and has prompted many to identify it as a breakthrough that provides a glimpse of needed reforms in science education. Learners who are enthused, and who can *use* the concepts and skills stressed in classrooms in their world outside the school, result more readily and more often when constructivist practices are used. At the same time the Constructivist Model offers assurance to thousands of excellent teachers who use many of the procedures instinctively without having heard of Constructivism. Perhaps the model can help bring science and other teachers together to the benefit of the whole educational enterprise. There is every reason to believe that such practices will serve the underserved in science and result in more females and minorities in science careers.

Constructivism indicates that each human being (learner) must put together ideas and structures that have personal meaning if he or she is to learn. The model suggests that knowing means being able to do or construct something. Research concerning the Constructivist Model continues today at an ever-increasing rate as educators attempt to apply what we know about learning to instructional strategies and curriculum materials in attempts to meet goals better.

The Constructivist Model explains that knowledge can never be observer-independent. In fact, knowledge must be attained in a personal sense; it cannot be transferred from one person to another like filling a vessel. It is not like other physiological processes, which can be described chemically. Instead, it requires a personal commitment to question, to explain, to test explanations for validity.

Although the model indicates that each learner constructs meaning for him/herself, it does not always mean in isolation. Nonetheless, it often occurs without teachers, textbooks, and schools. The classroom must become a place where students offer *their* personal constructions. They can then be encouraged to apply them to new situations where they are useful, adequate, and/or altered. Teachers, other adults, and, even more often, peers can enhance learning by challenging conceptions of a given learner.

Constructivist practices result in students who attain more of the goals typically cited by teachers—certainly those that characterize the STS approach. Among these are demonstrated mastery of basic concepts (in ways other than repeating or recognizing standard definitions); use of basic process skills (again, in new situations); ability to apply, interpret, and synthesize information; enhancement of creativity skills (questioning, proposing causes, predicting consequences); and improved attitudes concerning study, schools, classes, teachers, and careers.

Constructivist practices and the STS approach in science require teachers to place students in more central positions in the whole instructional program. They must question more and their questions must be used as the basis for discussions, investigations, and actions in the classroom/laboratory. They must propose solutions and offer explanations and these proposals must be used in the classroom and form the basis for seeking and using information and for testing the validity of all the explanations offered. This suggests a progression of involvement that starts with the student, moves to pairs and/or small groups of students for more questions and eventually consensus, then to the whole class for similar processing, and finally to what the professional (scientific) community views are. This progression is just the opposite of what typically happens. In traditional classrooms where traditional strategies are used, the textbook, teacher, or professionals (scientists) define what student should know. Typically they are expected to read, to listen, and to repeat the desired information. If students read, listen, and repeat, they are said to have learned. However, this definition of learning is simply not adequate.

Cognitive scientists report that most undergraduate science majors (the most successful K–12 and college students in a discipline) cannot use the concepts and skills they seem to have mastered in solving real-world problems given to them. As many as 90 percent of the engineering students cannot relate what they seem to know to problems in real-world situations. Such learning in typical situations was not "constructivist" and thereby suggests the reason for learning not to have occurred. Measures of successful learning too often include items that require only recall of concepts and definitions and performance of basic skills out of any real world context.

Constructivist teaching practices illustrate needed approaches in STS classrooms. These practices include:

1. Seeking out student ideas before presenting teacher ideas or before studying ideas from textbooks or other sources.
2. Encouraging students to challenge each other's conceptualizations and ideas.
3. Utilizing cooperative learning strategies that emphasize collaboration, respect individuality, and use division of labor tactics.
4. Encouraging adequate time for reflection and analysis.
5. Respecting and using all ideas that students generate.
6. Encouraging self-analysis, collection of real evidence to support ideas, reformulation of ideas in light of new experiences and evidence.
7. Using student thinking, experience, and interest to drive lessons (this means frequently altering teachers' plans).
8. Encouraging the use of alternative sources for information both from written materials and live "experts."
9. Using open-ended questions.

Table 12–2 provides contrasts between traditional and STS classrooms. These are the differences in instruction that characterize the classrooms that provide evidence for the advantages for STS.

TABLE 12–2

Contrasts between Typical Science Classrooms and STS Classrooms

TYPICAL SCIENCE CLASSROOM	STS SCIENCE CLASSROOM
Goals:	
1. Minimal consideration given to human adaptive capacities.	1. Human adaptation and alternative future emphasized.
2. Marginal emphasis on current societal problems and issues and then only as an afterthought (that is, if there is any extra time at the end of a unit).	2. Dealing with societal problems and issues as goals which create a need for learning science concepts.
3. Inquiry skills, if present, characteristic of a generalized model of science (often follows direction-type activities).	3. Inquiry processes unique to each problem.
4. Uncovering a correct answer to discipline-bound problems.	4. Decision making using scientific knowledge in social contexts.
5. Minimal attention to careers; only historical personages highlighted.	5. Career awareness an integral part of learning.
6. Value-free interpretations of discipline-bound problems.	6. Value, ethical, and moral dimensions of problems and issues considered.
Curriculum:	
7. Curriculum is textbook-centered, inflexible; only scientific validity is considered.	7. Curriculum is problem-centered, flexible; culturally as well as scientifically valid.
8. Humankind incidental	8. Humankind central.
9. Textbook controlled; local relevance fortuitous.	9. Multiple sources of information; local and community relevance emphasized.
10. Contrived materials, kits, and classroom-bound resources; use of hands-on materials often only for the sake of keeping students involved.	10. Use of the natural environment, community resources, and the students themselves as foci of study.
11. Information is in the context of the logic and structure of the discipline.	11. Information is in the context of the student as a person in a cultural/social/technological environment.
12. Distorts the nature of science by portraying science solely from an internalist position.	12. Portrays a more accurate view of the nature of science by explicitly making connections between science and society (externalism) as well as the isolated workings of science (internalism).

Instruction:

13. Teacher-centered.	13. Student-centered.
14. Group instruction geared for the average student and directed by the organization of the textbook.	14. Individualized and personalized, recognizing student diversity.
15. Some group work, primarily in laboratory.	15. Cooperative and experiential work on problems and issues.
16. Students seen as recipients of instruction.	16. Students are considered important ingredients in instruction, that is, active partners.
17. Weak psychological basis for instruction in the sciences; behavioristic orientation.	17. Methodology based on current information and research in developmental psychology involving cognitive, affective, experiential, and maturational studies.
18. Teachers ignore students in terms of what they might bring to the instructional process; use of information where success can be measured by rote learning.	18. Teachers build on student experiences, assuming that students learn only from their own experiences.

Reform in science education is at the top of the nation's agenda for action. The President has called for improvements that will make the United States first in the world in mathematics and science. To achieve such a goal will require significant changes in school programs and teaching strategies. Certainly STS represents major changes for many that could provide fundamental reform. We need to be sure that all the changes are also appropriate for females and minorities who are so poorly served with traditional courses and approaches.

D. DATA SOURCES

The Iowa Chautauqua Program is an in-service model designed to assist teachers in changing their goals, curricula, and teaching strategies. The needed changes are indicated in Table 12–2, which contrasts typical conditions and desired ones which exemplify STS programs as defined by an NSF research effort called Project Synthesis (Harms and Yager, 1981).

Although the Chautauqua Program operates on a continuing basis, an annual sequence of events describes its basic features. The sequence of events for the Iowa Chautauqua Program consists of the following:

1. A two-week leadership conference for thirty of the most successful teachers from previous years who want to become a part of the instructional team for future workshops.
2. A three-week summer workshop at each of five new sites for thirty new teachers electing to try STS modules and strategies; the workshop provides experiences with STS instruction (participating teachers as students) and time to plan a five-day STS unit to be used with students in the fall.
3. A two and one-half day fall short course for 30 to 50 teachers (including the thirty enrolled during the summer); the focus is upon developing a monthlong STS module and an extensive assessment plan.
4. A series of interim communications with central staff, lead teachers, and fellow participants, including a newsletter, special memoranda, monthly telephone contacts, and school/classroom visits.
5. A two and one-half day spring short course for the same thirty to fifty teachers who participated in the fall; this session focuses upon reports by participants on their STS experience and the results of the assessment program.

During the course of the year, Lead Teachers are involved in one or more action research projects as well. Much of the data to support the Iowa Chautauqua Model and the STS approach comes from experiments conducted in cooperation with these Lead Teachers who are part of the instructional team for new teachers introduced to STS procedures.

The Iowa Chautauqua Program is an example of teachers helping teachers with new curriculum modules and especially new approaches to instruction. The three-week summer workshop is a time of academic training, when teachers are free of teaching responsibilities. It is a time when they experience new approaches to curriculum and the instructional strategies they are expected to try during the academic year. They agree to try the new approaches for five days after school begins in the fall and before returning for the fall short course. This provides teachers who have tried something new ready to discuss successes, problems, and failures was well as ready to raise questions, suggestions, and ideas for gathering evidence of successes and failures on the part of their students. After the fall short course, pretesting is conducted prior to a four- to eight-week experiment with STS teaching. The spring short course is a time for sharing, analyzing, and planning for even more extensive changes in school programs and teaching strategies. Teachers learn from each other in a constructivist climate/format. Information is provided regarding successes in the domains of science education as well as relative successes and failures of students (and teachers) from underrepresented groups.

Several dissertations (Iskandar, 1992; Mackinnu, 1991; Myers, 1988; Zehr, 1991) and a variety of other studies have been completed which have occurred in over 200 Iowa schools and involved over 2,000 K–12 teachers. Some studies have involved changes in STS teachers and the nature of preparatory programs for science teachers. Many have provided information about the advantages of the STS approach for persons from underrepresented groups. Although the STS approach has been gaining increasing support among science educators (for example, Bybee, 1987; Hurd, 1984; NSTA, 1982), very little empirical support for this approach is available in the literature.

The unique nature of the studies offers even more support to the confidence in the results. The design included a variety of age groups with multiple teachers teaching each of them. This allowed the researchers to note results which were common to all age groups as well as differences among these groups. The participation of different grade levels and the student-centered nature of the STS approach did not allow for teaching identical topics to all classes. This setting unavoidably implied the use of different test items by each teacher in the concept and application domains. However, other instruments were kept constant. Results which were common to all or many teachers, in spite of differences in content and specific activities, may be regarded as reflecting the generic impact of the STS approach and constructivist teaching practices. The basic consistency of results across studies provides even more confidence.

E. RESULTS/CONCLUSIONS

Teachers in the Iowa Chatauqua Program collect data concerning student growth in concept development, process skill development, ability to apply concepts, creativity, and positive attitudes. Not until recently has evidence emerged in relation to the differential gender effects of STS instruction. Blunck and Ajam (1991) looked at the gender-related differences in students' attitudes toward science and science classes and science teachers. Using data collected by 20 exemplary Chautauqua teachers, it was found that female students enjoy STS classes more than male students (Figure 12–1). After STS instruction, female students tend to have more positive attitudes than male students about their science teachers (See Figure 12–2). Male students have significantly more positive attitudes about their science classes. After STS, female students closed the gap and their attitudes became statistically nondifferent from those of male students (see Figure 12–1). Figures 12–1 and 12–2 reflect the percentages of students (male and female) responding on the pre- and posttests. Differences are significant at $p < 0.05$ level.

More recently Mackinnu (1991) investigated the differential gender effects of STS instruction compared to a textbook approach. Over seven hundred students

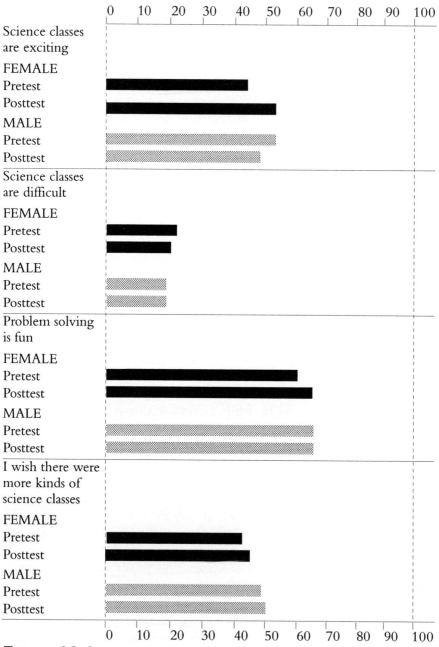

FIGURE 12-1

Areas of Students' Attitudes toward Science Where STS Has Shown a Normalizing Effect Favoring Females: Before STS There was a Significant Difference Between Females and Males, But After STS There Was No Significant Difference in Attitudes With Females Closing The Gaps of Attitude Difference with Males

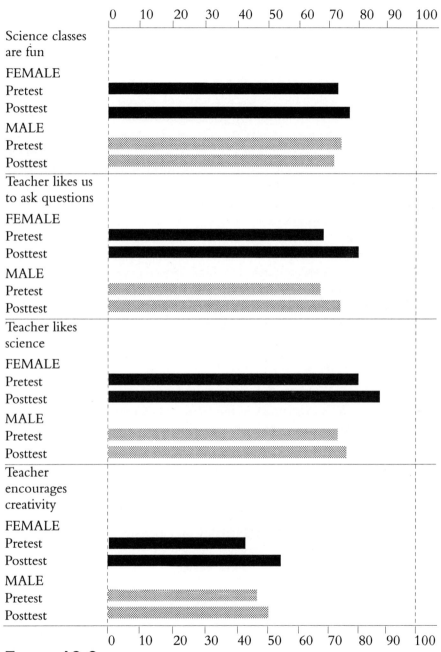

FIGURE 12-2

Questions Where STS Has Shown a Differential Effect on Gender-Related Differences in Students' Attitudes Favoring Females: Before STS There Was No Significant Difference Between Females and Males, But After STS There Was a Significant Difference in Attitudes With Females Showing More Positive Attitudes and fifteen teachers were involved in this study. The experimental design included use of a pre- and posttest scheme with treatment and contrast groups. Mackinnu found that females showed more negative attitudes toward science initially than their male counterparts. Results showed that the attitudes of the female students were improved by STS instruction; the STS approach facilitated more improvement than the comparable textbook approach. "This means that STS instruction does minimize the gap between male and female attitudes toward science for the teachers involved in this study" (Mackinnu, 1991, p. 118). Comparison of the *t*-tests on pretest and posttest scores showed a decrease in the number of classes with significant differences between males and females.

Given the fact that the majority of researchers agree that school science programs must be transformed and restructured to better meet the needs of both male and female students, STS is emerging as a viable alternative to traditional science programs. Given the research that is appearing recently in the professional literature, the hope is that STS will continue to make a difference for both the male and female students in school science programs. The challenge remains for science educators who are using STS to continue to collect evidence on the differential gender effects of their instruction. Too often we are quick to dismiss the idea that gender issues still exist within our science classrooms. It is the sensitivity of the teacher to these issues in the science classroom that will, in the long run, make the biggest difference of all. As we search for more inclusionary approaches to science teaching, STS must be studied carefully in terms of its positive effects on both the male and female learners.

Results with STS instruction in the Iowa Chautauqua Program result in the following changes in all students, including minorities and females:

1. increased attention span,
2. a gradual shift from concrete to abstract functioning,
3. greater ability to comprehend and manipulate abstractions and to see relationships between abstractions,
4. higher levels of abstractions, generality, and inclusiveness,
5. the ability to discriminate between two sets of analogous ideas, and
6. the ability to transfer bodies of knowledge.

Unfortunately, a study of STS and minority students is limited in Iowa. For that reason, plans have been made to extend the studies to Arizona, Oklahoma, New York, and Virginia. However, specific results in STS and non-STS classrooms in Davenport (and some of the other urban centers in Iowa where minority enrollment is in excess of 50 percent) indicate that STS approaches enable minority students to achieve as well as majority students. The results of a comparison of successes with minority and majority students is displayed in Figure 12–3. It is apparent that STS is effective in reducing differences in learning in the five domains tested for minority students.

STS instruction seems to bridge gaps where gender and minority effects are a concern. As we move toward more inclusionary practices in science teaching, STS stands out as a powerful alternative for making science more meaningful for all students.

STS has been shown to be superior to traditional teaching in a variety of studies and in various goal and assessment domains (Iskandar, 1992; Mackinnu, 1991; McComas, 1989; Myers, 1988). In fact, the following generalizations are possible:

1. With experienced high-quality teachers the STS approach yields neither better nor worse attainment in the Concept Domain.
2. In all the remaining domains, the STS approach was found to yield substantially better results. The effect size differences between STS and non-STS are unusually high.
3. The largest effect sizes in Creativity and in the Process of Science were found in the upper elementary grades. In some studies females and minorities scored particularly well in creativity areas with STS approaches.
4. The ability to apply is a most significant finding favoring STS approaches. Apparently, transfer of learning has better chances in all students who use their previous experiences and can relate new experiences to their lives.
5. High-ability students have gained more than their low-ability counterparts in all domains regardless of the instructional approach. For low-ability students, the STS approach yielded more positive attitudes toward science and science learning.
6. The only domain in which gender differences were found in all cases was with respect to the development of more positive attitudes. STS classrooms produced a positive change close to three times as large as that found in the non-STS classrooms.
7. The results when differences are noted between minority and majority students show no major differences. This is striking since majority students are favored in typical science classrooms.

F. IMPLICATIONS FOR BEGINNING TEACHERS AND SCHOOLS

Science education is poised for reform. Of course, it has been so poised numerous times in the past. However, there is great cause for optimism at this

Figure 12-3

Comparison of Growth on Scales in the Five Assessment Areas for Students Enrolled in Textbook and STS Sections Taught by Fifteen Lead Teachers

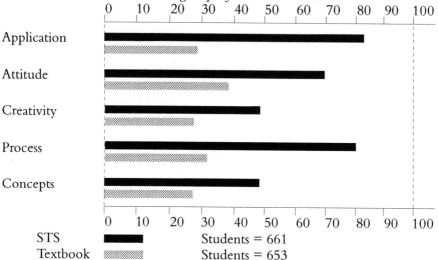

Comparison of Minority and Majority Growth on Scales in Five Assessment Areas for Students Enrolled in Textbook and STS Sections Taught by Ten Lead Teachers

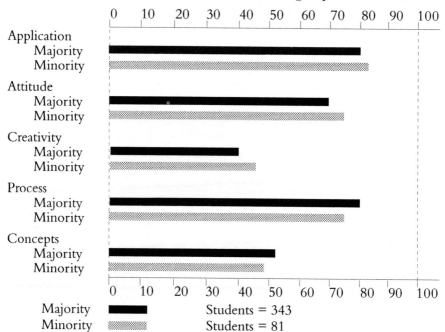

point in time. Never have the calls been so intense, from so many places, the problems more clearly indicated, the sources for funding available, and the research base so broad in scope or so focused upon the changes demanded.

STS offers hope for general reform; the initial results of studies of the STS approach in practice indicate successes with science programs and in science classrooms where typical approaches fail. If attitude and creativity skills are enabling domains for real science learning to occur, typical programs fail, since study after study shows that attitudes and curiosity decline the more students study typical science. STS approaches provide exciting evidence that attitude can be enhanced and that creativity skills (questioning, hypothesizing, and predicting consequences) can be enhanced ever more dramatically.

STS provides the greatest hope for reform in that students who experience science in such a way can utilize the basic science concepts and process skills in new situations, including settings outside the school and laboratory. And this is where typical programs fail—even for the most talented and seemingly successful students (Mestre and Lockhead, 1990). Nonetheless, a problem emerges in this arena: Few examinations rich with application-type items exist and teachers find it extremely difficult to construct such items (two-thirds of the time; Zehr, 1991). Preservice teachers as well as in-service teachers need much more help with assessment strategies. Too often their own success in science classes is based upon their ability to recall information on specific laboratory procedures. It is not surprising, then, that the most common kind of teacher-made test calls for the same skills in their students. And yet, these skills (recall and repeating) are alien to basic science skills.

Teachers must study anew the nature of real science; they must see that it may be unrelated to the concepts presented to them for mastery and the follow-the-direction laboratories they have typically experienced. Whether it is called STS or not, it is clear that improvement in teaching science is necessary. The failure of typical science courses/programs to meet the needs of minority and female students is a growing problem, especially when our need for professionals is growing. We need more and better scientists and technologists if we are to maintain our leadership in the world. It may be necessary for survival of the nation—perhaps humans on the earth. Our current failure to attract and to retain females and minorities in the study of science and ultimately in scientific/technological occupations is a national tragedy.

The time is right; the needed directions seem clear. But change is difficult — even when it is so urgently demanded. Education and educators should be leaders in stimulating needed changes. And yet, it has rarely happened in the past. Perhaps our hope for the year 2000 is in the general agreement that reform is a necessity and in the specific direction for change that STS provides. STS is more than improved science; it provides a way to improve schools and schooling as well. It shows great promise for meeting the challenges provided by underserved and underrepresented groups in science and technology study and careers.

REFERENCES

Aldridge, B. G. (1989, January/February). Essential changes in secondary science: Scope, sequence, and coordination. *NSTA Reports!* pp. 1, 4–5.

American Association for the Advancement of Science. (1988). *Project 2061: Education for a changing future.* Washington, DC: Author.

Anastasi, A., and Cordova, F. A. (1953). Some effects of bilingualism upon the intelligence test performance of Puerto Rican children in New York City. *Journal of Educational Psychology, 44,* 1–19.

Anderson, J. A. (1988). Cognitive styles and multicultural populations. *Journal of Teacher Education, 39,* 2–9.

Anderson, J. A. (in press). *An examination of teaching styles and student learning styles of minority students for science education at the pre-college level.*

Ausubel, D. P. (1950). Negativism as a phase of ego development. *American Journal of Orthopsychiatry, 20,* 796–805.

Ausubel, D. P. (1968). *Educational psychology: A cognitive view.* New York, NY: Holt, Rinehart & Winston, Inc.

Ausubel, D. P., and Ausubel, P. (1963). Ego development among segregated Negro children. In A. H. Passow (Ed.), *Education in depressed areas* (pp. 109–141). New York, NY: Columbia University, Teachers College Press.

Banks, J., and Banks, C. (1989). *Multicultural education issues and perspectives.* Boston: Allyn and Bacon.

Banks, J. A., and Lynch, J. (1986). Multicultural education in western societies. New York, NY: Praeger.

Blunck, S. M., and Ajam, Mo. (1991). Gender-related differences in students' attitude with STS instruction. *Chautauqua Notes, 6*(2), 2–3.

Burgess, B. J. (1978). Native American learning styles. In L. A. Morris, G. Sather and S. Scull (Eds.), *Extracting learning styles from social/cultural diversity: Studies of five American minorities.* Norman, Okla.: The University of Oklahoma Press.

Bybee, R. (1987). Science education and the science/technology/society (STS) theme. *Science Education, 71,* 667–683.

Champagne, A. B., and Klopfer, L. E. (1984). Research in science education: The cognitive psychology perspective. In D. Holdzkom and P. B. Lutz, (Eds.), *Research within reach: Science education* (pp. 171–189). Charleston, WV: Research and Development Interpretation Service.

Clark, K. B., and Clark, M. P. (1950). Emotional factors in racial identification and preference in Negro children. *Journal of Negro Education, 19,* 341–350.

Clawson, T., Firment, C., and Trower, T. (1981). Text anxiety: Another origin for racial bias in standardized testing. *Measurement and Evaluation in Guidance, 13*, 210–215.

Comber, L. C., and Keeves, J. E. (1973). *Science education in seventeen countries: An empirical study.* New York: Wiley.

Czerniak, C., and Chiarelott, L. (1985). Science anxiety among elementary school students: Equity issues. *Journal of Educational Equity and Leadership, 5*, 291–308.

Davidson, H. H., and Greenberg, J. B. (1967). *Trails of school achievers from a deprived background.* New York, NY: City College of the State University of New York.

Gollnick, D. and Chinn, P. (1990). *Multicultural education in a pluralistic society* (3rd ed.). New York, NY: Merrill Publishing Company.

Good, T. L., and Brophy J. E. (1987). *Looking in classrooms.* New York, NY: Harper and Row Publishers.

Hale, J. (1978). Cultural influences on learning styles of Afro-American children. In L. A. Morris, G. Sather and S. Scull (Eds.), *Extracting learning styles from social/cultural diversity: Studies of five American minorities.* Norman, Okla.: The University of Oklahoma Press.

Hardin, J., and Dede, C. J. (1978). Discrimination against women in science education. *The Science Teacher, 40*(3), 18–21.

Harms, N. C., and Yager, R. E. (Eds.). (1981). *What research says to the science teacher* (Vol. 3). Washington, DC: National Science Teachers Association.

Heathers, G. (1969). Grouping. In R. L. Ebel (Ed.), *Encyclopedia of educational research* (pp. 559-570). New York, NY: The Macmillan Company.

Hilgard, E. R., and Atkinson, R. C. (1967). *Introduction to psychology* (4th ed). New York, NY: Harcourt, Brace and World.

Hill, O. W., Pettus, W. C., and Hedlin, B. A. (1990). Three studies of factors affecting the attitudes of Blacks and females toward the pursuit of science and science related careers. *Journal of Research in Science Teaching, 27*(4), 289–314.

Hurd, P. DeH. (1984). *Reforming science education: The search for a new visions,* (Occasional Paper 33). Washington, DC: Council for Basic Education.

Iskandar, S. M. (1992). *An evaluation of the science-technology-society approach to science teaching.* Unpublished doctoral dissertation, The University of Iowa, Iowa City.

Kagan, S., and Madsen, M. C. (1971). Cooperation and competition of Mexican-American and Anglo-American children of two ages under four instruction sets. *Developmental Psychology, 5*, 32–39.

Kahle, J. B., and Lakes, M. K. (1983). The myth of equality in science classrooms. *Journal of Research in Science Teaching, 20*(2), 131–140.

Keller, E. F. (1982). Feminism and science. *Signs, 7*(3), 589–602.

Kelly, A. (1987). *Science for girls?* Philadelphia, PA: Open University Press.

Mackinnu. (1991). *Comparison of learning outcomes between classes taught with a science-technology-society (STS) approach and a textbook oriented approach.* Unpublished doctoral dissertation, The University of Iowa, Iowa City.

Malcolm, S. (1985). The place of minorities in the scientific and technical workforce. *Black Scholar, 16,* 50–55.

McComas, W. F. (1989). Just the facts: The results of the 1987–88 Chautauqua workshops. *Chautauqua Notes, 4*(4), 1–2.

Mestre, J. P., and Lockhead, J. (1990). *Academic preparation in science: Teaching for transition from high school to college.* New York, NY: College Entrance Examination Board.

Miller, J. (1989, April). *Scientific literacy.* Paper presented at the meeting of the American Association for the Advancement of Science, San Francisco, CA.

Moreland, J. K. (1963). Racial self-identification: A study of nursery school children. *The American Catholic Sociological Review, 24,* 231–242.

Mosteller, F., and Moynihan, D. P. (Eds.). (1972). *On equality of educational opportunities.* New York, NY: Vintage Books.

Myers, L. H. (1988). *Analysis of student outcomes in ninth grade physical science taught with a science/technology/society focus versus one taught with a textbook orientation.* Unpublished doctoral dissertation, The University of Iowa, Iowa City.

National Assessment of Educational Progress. (1978). *The third assessment of science, 1967–77.* Denver, CO: Author.

National Assessment of Educational Progress. (1988a). *The science report card: Elements of rise and recovery.* Princeton, NJ: Educational Testing Service.

National Assessment of Educational Progress. (1988b). *The fifth assessment of science, 1986–87.* Denver, CO: Author.

National Science Board Commission on Precollege Education in Mathematics, Science, and Technology. (1983). *Educating Americans for the 21st century: A plan of action for improving mathematics, science, and technology education for all American elementary and secondary students so their achievement is the best in the world by 1995.* Washington, DC: National Science Foundation.

National Science Foundation. (1980). *U.S. scientists and engineers, 1978.* (NSF 80–304). Washington, DC: U.S. Government Printing Office.

National Science Foundation. (1984). *Women and minorities in science and engineering.* Washington, DC: U.S. Government Printing Office.

National Science Teachers Association. (1982). *Science-technology-society: Science education for the 1980s.* (Position Statement). Washington, DC: Author.

National Science Teachers Association. (1990). Science/Technology/Society: A new effort for providing appropriate science for all (The NSTA position statement). *Bulletin of Science, Technology and Society, 10*(5&6), 249–250.

Oakes, J. (1990). *Multiplying inequalities: The effects of race, social class and tracking on opportunities to learn mathematics and science.* Santa Monica, CA: The RAND Corporation.

Packard, V. (1969). *The hidden persuaders.* New York, NY: David McKay.

Payne, B., Smith, J., and Payne, D. (1983). Sex and ethnic differences in relationships of text anxiety to performance in science examination by fourth and eighth grade students. *Educational and Psychological Measurement, 43,* 267–270.

Ramirez, M. (1973). Cognitive styles and cultural democracy in education. *Social Science Quarterly, 53,* 895–904.

Resnick, L. B. (1986). Cognition and instruction: Theories of human competence and how it is acquired. Pittsburgh, PA: Learning Research and Development Center.

Rosenthal, R., and Jacobson, L. (1968). *Pygmalion in the classroom: Teachers' expectations and pupils' intellectual development.* New York, NY: Holt, Rinehart and Winston.

Rosser, S. V. (1990). *Female-friendly science: Applying women's studies methods and theories to attract students.* New York, NY: Pergamon Press.

Rubba, P. A. (1989). An investigation of the semantic meaning assigned to concepts affiliated with STS education and of STS instructional practices among a sample of exemplary science teachers. *Journal of Research in Science Teaching, 26*(8), 687–702.

Rubba, P. A., McGuyer, M., and Wahlune, T. M. (1991). The effects of infusing STS vignettes into the genetics unit of biology on learner outcomes in STS and genetics: A report of two investigations. *Journal of Research in Science Teaching, 28*(6), 537–552.

Rutherford, F. J., and Ahlgren, A. (1989), *Science for all Americans.* New York, NY: Oxford University Press.

Skolnick, J., Langbort, C., and Day, L. (1982). *How to encourage girls in math and science: Strategies for parents and educators.* Englewood Cliffs, NJ: Prentice-Hall.

Sleeter, C., and Grant, C. (1988). *Making choices for multicultural education.* New York, NY: Merrill Publishing Company.

Spector, B. S., and Gibson, C. W. (1991). A qualitative study of middle school students' perceptions of factors facilitating the learning of science: Grounded theory and existing theory. *Journal of Research in Science Teaching, 28*(6), 537–552.

Voelker, A. M. (1982). The development of an attentive public for science: Implications for science teaching. In R. E. Yager (Ed.), *What research says to the science teacher* (Vol. 4) (pp. 65–79). Washington, DC: National Science Teachers Association.

Wraga, W. G., and Hlebowitsch, P. S. (1991). STS education and the curriculum field. *School Science and Mathematics, 91*(2), 54–59.

Yager, R. E. (1991). The constructivist learning model: Towards real reform in science education. *The Science Teacher, 58*(6), 52–57.

Yager, R. E., and McCormack, A. J. (1989). Assessing teaching/learning successes in multiple domains of science and science education. *Science Education, 73*(1), 45–58.

Zehr, E. E. (1991). *A comparison between teacher scores on application posing ability and student gains in the five domains of science education.* Unpublished doctoral dissertation, The University of Iowa, Iowa City.

CHAPTER 13

Addressing the Reading Needs of Culturally and Linguistically Diverse Children

PETER EDWARDS
State University of New York–Plattsburgh

DAVIE TATE JR.
Clarion University of Pennsylvania

PETER EDWARDS is Director of the Reading/Language Arts Center in the College of Education at State University of New York–Plattsburgh. He studies the basic linguistic factors influencing reading-language performance and the application of research into developmental, cultural, remedial and clinical aspects of instruction.

DAVIE TATE JR. is Professor of Education at Clarion University of Pennsylvania. His research interests are related to the law and education. Specifically, he explores recent court cases, state constitution, and statutory laws, as said laws pertain to education.

ABSTRACT

This investigation focused on African-American children, the mandates of Section 1703(f) of the Equal Education Opportunity Act of 1974, and the attempts to teach these children to read using current reading-method textbooks. In this study, the main aspects of Black English were identified and recognized as significant barriers to reading achievement. The study analyzed the most widely used college and university undergraduate reading-method textbooks to determine whether the reading needs of African American children were being addressed. Results indicate that little attention was paid in reading textbooks to the reading needs of African American children, although the plight of these culturally and linguistically diverse children over the last two decades has not changed significantly. Recommendations included a series of positive teaching steps to improve the situation.

INTRODUCTION

Although most children living in a "culture of poverty" are affected relative to academic success, the focus of this investigation is limited to African-American children living in poverty. Over two decades ago, Lewis (1966) estimated that approximately ten million people lived in a "culture of poverty." Lewis further indicated that the largest numbers of the "culture of poverty" group included "Negroes, Puerto Ricans, Mexicans, American Indians, and southern poor Whites." (p. 25).

During the past three decades, attempts have been made to raise the linguistically different child's academic achievement. Focusing on the educational plight of the linguistically different child generally encompasses language diversity; however, the investigators' primary focus will be directed toward African-American children for several reasons. They are at the bottom of the educational barrel when it comes to maximizing educational opportunities and represent the largest minority group in America (Hodgkinson, 1991). The African-American child is also a member of a minority group that is plagued by a culture (the "culture of poverty") that is the genesis of a barrage of barriers that thwart academic achievement, especially in the area of reading.

OBJECTIVES

Three major objectives posed as questions include:

1.   What are authors and publishers of undergraduate reading-methods textbooks doing to provide prospective teachers with an understanding of the rules, consistency, and patterns of nonstandard English that create inherent problems in teaching African-American children to read standard English textbooks?
2.   What are authors and publishers of undergraduate reading-methods textbooks doing to provide prospective teachers with the knowledge and understanding of how African-American children use nonstandard English?
3.   What are authors and publishers of undergraduate reading-methods textbooks including to assist prospective teachers with problems

associated with African–American children's use of nonstandard English and learning to read?

THEORETICAL FRAMEWORK

The recognition of language differences between culturally different African Americans and speakers of standard English is not a new phenomenon. Around 1750, Quaker Anthony Benezet ". . . perceived the necessity of training his black youngsters in what he conceived to be their 'mother tongue' rather than in the classic language, and got reactions from his teachers which closely parallel those from outspoken but linguistically naive whites in the twentieth century." (Dillard, 1972, p. 266). Ironically, twentieth-century teachers, who have been given years of training, still enter inner-city schools only to find their tasks of teaching the African-American child "irksome" and "monotonous." The "irksomeness" and "monotonousness" which exists in today's inner-city classroom are caused by ". . . the same lack of basic information which incapacitated Benezet's teachers in the eighteenth century." (Dillard, 1972, p. 266). In addressing the importance that language plays in the classroom, Hymes (1981) stated:

> The law of the land demands that equal educational opportunity not be denied because of language. "Language" has been understood most readily in terms of "languages," such as Spanish, and structurally definable varieties of a language, such as Black English Vernacular. If one defines "language," as I do, in terms of ways of speaking, as involving both structure and ways of using structure, there are even deeper implications, implications not yet legally explored. One's language affects one's chances in life, not only through accent, but also through action. Access to opportunities in the form of access to schools, jobs, positions, memberships, clubs, homes, may depend on ways of using language that one has no chance to master, or chooses not to master (pp. vii–viii).

In spite of the fact that "the jury is in," relative to the plight of the child who is caught up in the "culture of poverty," viable steps are not in place to address the language needs of the linguistically different child. The academic plight of the linguistically different child has been ignored. In discussing school reform and effectiveness, Passow (1984) expressed the following criticism:

> The reports of the eighties . . . fail to attend to the particular problems and needs of schools with large populations of poor and minority children. . . .

> If there is a real crisis in education, it is in the urban schools. . . . The implicit assumption in many of these reports is that disadvantaged young-sters are really no different from other students and to believe otherwise is both anti-intellectual and anti-democratic. . . . Simply recommending that school personnel set tougher, stiffer academic demands, and crack down on discipline problems without effecting necessary changes in ped-agogy, curriculum, and personnel is an inadequate solution (p. 680).

Of course, there are programs such as Head Start, Chapter I, and state initia-tives that are designed to correct the child's "language deficiencies." The inves-tigators do not lament these programs, but the fundamental assumptions on which some of the programs are based should be questioned. Teachers often base their philosophies and pedagogical approaches on the findings of linguists, psychologists, sociologists, and so on, whose theories form the basis of com-pensatory programs. For example, Bereiter and Englemann (1966) accepted Bernstein's (1961) original hypothesis, which proposes that middle- and lower-class parents employ different child-rearing practices, resulting in different patterns of language and thought between the middle and lower class. Middle-class language is labeled an elaborated code and lower-class language a restricted code (Ginsburg, 1972). Swaby (1989) explained that elaborated code speakers "use language for a wide variety of purposes, such as communication, problem solving, analysis, synthesis, information gathering, play, and meeting personal needs," but restricted code speakers "use language primarily to get things done and to react minimally to the linguistic efforts of others" (p. 308).

The premise of this investigation is that teachers' knowledge of the African-American child's mode of oral and written communication is important if we are to avoid language theories that create programs based on restricted codes and language deficiency theories. On a more formal basis, unless teachers under-stand consistencies (phonetics and phonology, morphology, syntax, and lexicon) of nonstandard English, they will not be prepared to develop activities to help bridge the gap between linguistically different language spoken at home and standard English in school. That is, teachers must be cognizant that linguistically different children are capable of using the elaborate code, but do not often do so because their social environment does not lend itself to long phrases and sen-tences. So the language controversy continues, obscuring the real issue—the importance of an in-depth knowledge of nonstandard English. Further, an in-depth knowledge of nonstandard English, especially as it is spoken by many African Americans, would facilitate an understanding of the child's culture. But most importantly, once teachers discover that the syntactical structures of the linguistically different child's language and standard English are basically the same, many of the controversies relative to nonstandard English theories disappear.

Concerned educators should *not* let the controversy regarding language theories, cultural deficit theory, or cultural difference theory obscure the needs of the linguistically different child. Dillard (1972) was more specific when he indicated that the teacher's knowledge of the African-American child's language structure will not be gained by osmosis, but through training programs designed to assess and train teachers to recognize that the African-American child's language and standard English are both appropriate and viable in his or her particular social setting (p. 272).

Specifically, culturally different African-American children are expected to speak standard English by teachers, but their peers expect them to speak non-standard language on the playground and in the community. Therefore, teachers are expected to understand culturally different children's language, especially if they are going to introduce them to a language program that is substantially different from their dialect.

Unfortunately, most teachers are not convinced that the African-American child's language has structure. They are unaware of the African-American grammatical structure and dialect and, thus, attempt to superimpose standard English patterns on the African-American child's language structure. Labov (1967) called this unfortunate situation *reciprocal ignorance* ". . . . Where teacher and student are ignorant of each other's system, and therefore of the rules needed to translate from one system to another." (Baratz and Shuy, 1969, p. 29).

The investigators contend that teachers may not use nonstandard materials, even if available in abundance, because teachers lack knowledge of the dialect structure's viability and may view nonstandard English negatively. Yet, special projects and programs demonstrate a lack of "know-how" in teaching skills pertaining to culturally different children when the teacher lacks knowledge of the children's language structure. Shuy (1971) demonstrated his argument vividly when he indicated that little evidence to date shows that teachers are trained to adequately recognize:

1. There is relatively little in the way of materials geared to accommodate teachers who attempt to 'correct' the pronunciation of the African-American child, who is assumed to be verbally destitute.
2. There is practically no understanding of the legitimacy of language as spoken by African Americans among teachers or, for that matter, among *textbook writers* (pp. 54–56).

Fasold (1968) demonstrated that standard orthography is appropriate for lower-class African-American children, despite the traditional argument to the contrary. Fasold assumed that teachers know correct sound-symbol relationships that are appropriate for understanding the African-American child's dialect (Baratz and Shuy, 1969). This information is relevant for teachers because it suggests that "threads" of commonalities exist between the two languages, as well as the unique sound-symbol relationships that are appropriate for each language, causing both standard and nonstandard English to be viable tools of communication. Specifically, Ovando and Collier (1985) suggest that teaching effectiveness:

> affirms the importance of home dialect and its appropriate use within the community in which it is spoken while at the same time students are taught the standard variety. Affirming home languages means that students may produce utterances in the classroom in native dialect without being told that they are wrong or that what they say is vulgar or bad. Instead, the teacher analyzes with the students the differences between their dialect and the standard variety: grammatical patterns, pronunciation, vocabulary items, varying social contexts, and so on (p. 70).

In order for this affirmation process to take place the teacher must *accept* as well as *understand* the structure and function of the child's language. However, the literature indicates that teachers often view nonstandard English as "bad" or "wrong" modes of communication.

In essence, the literature reports shows consistently that many teachers are unsophisticated about the structure of nonstandard English, but just how unsophisticated is not known. For example, Stewart (Dillard, 1972) has shown that teachers have difficulties with the language when they try to learn grammatical patterns of a mode of communication that has been firmly established by the time a child enters school. In fact, by the time children enter school they have control over the phonology and grammar of at least one language, regardless of cultural background (Ginsburg, 1972). Interestingly, Bailey discovered in a comprehensive study of 1,409 infants, from one to fifteen months of age and selected to be representative of all infants in the United States, the impact of social class differences on IQ. She concluded that the IQ of Whites and African-American children was essentially the same relative to all social classes during the first fifteen months of life (Ginsburg, 1972).

Only a serious effort directed at restructuring teacher-education programs can provide the needed skills, empathy, and in-depth insights into all aspects of teaching and learning in predominantly urban schools. Such programs must be designed with special emphasis on the African-American child's speech habits and linguistic system. Since educators have not taken the initiative relative to training teachers to teach the culturally/linguistically different child, at least one district court has mandated such training in an entire school district. This mandate emanated from *Martin Luther King Jr., Etc. v. Ann Arbor School District (M.L.*

King v. Ann Arbor School District), a court case involving fifteen African-American schoolchildren whose families brought action against the Ann Arbor, Michigan, Board of Education and various other school authorities. The families alleged that the process of determining the eligibility of students for special education services violated their civil rights as established by the Equal Educational Opportunities Act of 1974. The Act was based upon Section 1703 (f) of The Equal Educational Opportunity Act of 1974, which states in pertinent part:

> No state shall deny equal educational opportunity to an individual on account of his or her race, color, sex, or national origin, by . . . (f) the failure by an educational agency to take appropriate action to overcome language barriers that impede equal participation by its students in its instructional programs.

The investigators contend that the mismatch between what the teacher is prepared to deliver and the culturally/linguistically different child's readiness for fluency in reading thwarts the child's academic growth, not only in reading, but in the academic arena generally. Judge Joiner, in ruling in favor of the plaintiffs, also took a thorough and scholarly approach relative to reviewing the history and academic plight of African-American children, and the barriers to reading fluency, caused by a mismatch in the structure of nonstandard and standard English. He also discussed reading fluency. In his ruling, the judge held ". . . the school district had not taken appropriate action, as required by statute, to assure children's equal participation in instructional programs and the school would be required to take steps to help teachers recognize the home language of students and to use that knowledge in their attempts to teach reading skills and standard English." (*M. L. King v. Ann Arbor School District*, p. 1371).

Viewed from a legal perspective, Section 1703 (f) of the Equal Educational Opportunity Act of 1974 is, in essence, a civil rights bill for the linguistically different child. While the investigators do not subscribe to the term "black English," they are cognizant of the significance and "power" of nonstandard English as well as the barriers posed by persons who are "fluent" only in nonstandard English. (The investigators feel that a more appropriate term for the language spoken by approximately 80 percent of the African-American populace would be simply, "situational English".) This would be a more appropriate term to use, since the children do not speak nonstandard English because they are African American, but because of their environment or "situation." For example, many white Americans, especially southern white Americans, also speak a form of nonstandard English that is mislabeled "Black English."

The goal of this research report is to reignite concern for the speakers of nonstandard English, and to communicate to teacher training institutions, school districts generally, and teachers specifically, the importance of the linguistically different child's mode of communication, and that "situational English" can be used as an instructional tool as the child is taught to bridge the gap between nonstandard and standard English. This is a task that educators and friends of educators must accept: the legitimization of all modes of oral communication.

LIMITATION OF THE INVESTIGATION

This study will be limited to the nonstandard elements set out in *M. L. King v. Ann Arbor, Michigan*. This approach is taken because of the urgency of teaching the African-American child to read by becoming cognizant of the most salient nonstandard barriers to fluency in reading. Only textbooks dealing with reading-methods courses were used in the study. Instructors of undergraduate reading-methods courses were not contacted to determine whether or not they used supplementary material to address the issues under examination.

METHOD

PROCEDURE

In July 1991, the major publishers of college reading-methods textbooks in the United States were identified by consulting specialists in the field and by perusing current E.R.I.C. documents, publishers' catalogs, and required texts for reading courses from a number of institutions. There have been a number of mergers and changes in the publishing sector in recent years and several previously well-known publishers no longer operate under their own trade names. The existing major publishing companies identified from this process were as follows:

Allyn & Bacon
Harcourt Brace Jovanovich (HBJ)
HarperCollins
Holt, Rinehart and Winston (currently HBJ)
Houghton Mifflin
Longman
Merrill/Macmillan
Random House/McGraw Hill
Wm. C. Brown

DATA SOURCE

Representatives from the major publishing companies were contacted and asked to list their best-selling textbooks that were currently used to teach undergraduate reading-methods courses throughout the United States. The listing also required the publishers to include textbooks that dealt solely with a specific aspect of reading as phonics. Texts designed for self-improvement courses such as study skills or writing were excluded in the final list. The following texts emerged from the survey:

TEXTS USED IN THE STUDY

1. Barr, R., and B. Johnson. Teaching reading in elementary classrooms. New York: Longman, 1991.
2. Burns, P. C., B. D. Roe, and E. P. Ross. *Teaching reading in today's elementary schools*. 5th ed. Boston: Houghton Mifflin, 1992.
3. Creek, E. H., Jr., R. F. Flippo, and J. D. Lindsey. *Reading for success in elementary schools*. Fort Worth: Holt, Rinehart and Winston, 1989.
4. Cunningham, P. M., S. A. Moore, J. W. Cunningham, and D. W. Moore. *Reading in elementary classrooms: Strategies and observations*. 2d ed. New York: Longman, 1989.
5. Duffy, G. G., and L. R. Roehler. *Improving classroom reading instruction*. 2d ed. New York: Random House, 1989.
6. Durkin, D. *Teaching them to read*. 5th ed. Boston: Allyn and Bacon, 1989.
7. Harp, B., and J. A. Brewer. *Reading and writing: Teaching for the connections*. San Diego: Harcourt Brace Jovanovich, 1991.
8. Hayes, B. L. (ed.) *Effective strategies for teaching reading*. Boston: Allyn and Bacon, 1991.
9. Heilman, A. W., T. R. Blair, and W. H. Rupley. *Principles and practices of teaching reading*. 7th ed. Columbus, OH: Merrill, 1990.
10. Klein, M. L., S. Peterson, and L. Simington. *Teaching reading in the elementary grades*. Boston: Allyn and Bacon, 1991.
11. Leu, D. J., Jr., and C. K. Kinzer. *Effective reading instruction, K–8*. 2d ed. New York: Merrill, 1991.
12. May, F. B. *Reading as communication: An interactive approach*. 3d ed. Columbus, OH: Merrill, 1990.
13. Vacca, J. A., R. T. Vacca, and M. K. Gove. *Reading and learning to read*, 2d ed. New York: HarperCollins, 1991.
14. Zintz, M. V., and Z. R. Maggart. *The reading process: The teacher and the learner*, 5th ed. Dubuque, IA: Wm. C. Brown, 1989.

ANALYSIS

Initially, the texts were analyzed to determine if they addressed any of the three questions posed in the objectives. Descriptors used to identify the topic in the textbooks included: *African American, Black American, Black English, Black dialect, minorities, language differences, linguistically diverse, culturally diverse, dialectically diverse, bilingual, bicultural, ESL (English Second Language), NSE (nonstandard English), and LEP (Limited English Proficient).* If a particular text addressed concerns surrounding one of the questions, one point was credited. If the text addressed two of the questions, two points were credited, and if the text addressed all three questions, three points were awarded. The results of this analysis are displayed in Table 13–1.

Next the selected texts were examined to determine the proportion of material that addressed the reading needs of African-American children. Percentages are expressed in Table 13–2 for each textbook.

A matrix was then constructed to illustrate the coverage of major categories of nonstandard English used by African-American children as outlined:

TABLE 13–1

Questions in the Objectives Dealt with by Each of the Fourteen Textbooks

NUMBER	TEXTS	PUBLISHER	QUESTIONS		
			1	2	3
1	Tchg. Reading in Elementary Classrooms	Longman	0	0	0
2	Tchg. Reading in Today's Elem. Schools	Houghton Mifflin	0	0	1
3	Reading for Success in Elem. Schools	Holt	0	0	0
4	Reading in Elementary Classrooms	Longman	0	0	0
5	Improving Classroom Reading	Random House	1	1	1
6	Teaching Them to Read	Allyn & Bacon	0	0	0
7	Reading and Writing	HBJ	0	0	0
8	Effective Strategies for Teaching Reading	Allyn & Bacon	0	0	0
9	Principles and Practices of Teaching Rdg.	Merrill	1	1	1
10	Teaching Reading in Elementary Grades	Allyn & Bacon	0	0	0
11	Effective Reading Instruction	Merrill	1	1	1
12	Reading as Communication	Merrill	1	1	1
13	Reading and Learning to Read	HarperCollins	0	0	1
14	The Reading Process	Wm. C. Brown	1	1	1

TABLE 13-2
Proportion of Textbook Content Dealing with African-American Children

NUMBER	TEXT	PUBLISHER	PAGES		
			Afro-Amer	Text	%
1	Tchg. Reading in Elementary Classrooms	Longman	0	513	0.000
2	Tchg. Rdg. in Today's Elem. Classrooms	Houghton Mifflin	18	677	2.700
3	Reading for Success in Elementary Schools	Holt	1	540	0.185
4	Reading in Elementary Classrooms	Longman	0	495	0.000
5	Improving Classroom Rdg.	Random House	13	483	2.692
6	Teaching Them to Read	Allyn & Bacon	1	532	0.188
7	Reading and Writing	HBJ	0	542	0.000
8	Effective Strategies for Teaching Reading	Allyn & Bacon	1	413	0.242
9	Principles and Practices of Teaching Reading	Merrill	16	544	2.941
10	Teaching Reading in Elementary Grades	Allyn & Bacon	1	504	0.198
11	Effective Reading Instruction	Merrill	11	618	1.780
12	Reading as Communication	Merrill	12	590	2.034
13	Rdg. and Learning to Read	HarperCollins	2	589	0.340
14	The Reading Process	Wm C. Brown	14	670	2.090

NONSTANDARD ENGLISH EXPRESSIONS (AS DISCUSSED IN *M. L. KING V. ANN ARBOR SCHOOL DISTRICT*)

1. The use of the verb "be" to indicate a reality that is recurring or continuous over time.
2. The deletion of some form of the verb "to be."
3. The use of the third person singular verbs without adding the "s" or "z" sound.
4. The use of the "f" sound for the "th" sound at the end or in the middle of a word.
5. The use of an additional word to denote plurals rather than adding an "s" to the noun.
6. Non-use of "s" to indicate possessives.

7. The elimination of "l" or "r" sounds in words.
8. The use of words with different meanings.
9. The lack of emphasis on the use of tense in verbs.
10. The deletion of final consonants.
11. The use of double subjects.
12. The use of "it" instead of "there."

TABLE 13-3

Nonstandard English Expressions Dealt with by Textbooks ★

NON-STANDARD ENGLISH EXPRESSIONS	| 1	2	3	4	5	6	7	8	9	10	11	12	13	14
1. The use of the verb "be" to indicate a reality that is recurring or continuous over time.									9		11	12		14
2. The deletion of some form of the verb "to be."								9		11		14		
3. The use of the third person singular verbs without adding the "s" or "z" sound.										11		14		
4. The use of the "f" sound for the "th" sound at the end or in the middle of a word.		2							9		11			14
5. The use of an additional word to demote plurals rather than adding "s" to the noun.												14		
6. Non-use of "s" to indicate possessives.														14
7. The elimination of "l" or "r" sounds in words.									9		11			14
8. The use of words with different meanings.													13	14
9. The lack of emphasis on the use of tense in verbs.									9		11			14
10. The deletion of final consonants									9		11			14
11. The use of double subjects											11			14
12. The use of "it" instead of "there."														

★Table 13–3 illustrates how many of the nonstandard English expressions used by African-American children were treated by the 14 texts used in the study.

RESULTS

Five of the fourteen texts addressed all three questions:

1. What are authors and publishers of undergraduate reading-methods textbooks doing to provide prospective teachers with an understanding of the rules, consistency, and patterns of nonstandard English that create inherent problems in teaching African-American children to read standard English textbooks?
2. What are authors and publishers of undergraduate reading-methods textbooks doing to provide prospective teachers with the knowledge and understanding of how African-American children use nonstandard English?
3. What are authors and publishers of undergraduate reading-methods textbooks including to assist prospective teachers with problems associated with African-American children's use of nonstandard English and learning to read? Two of the texts dealt with the third question and seven texts did not address any of the questions posed in the study.

In addition, the texts were examined to ascertain the proportion of material being devoted to the reading needs of African-American children. The five texts that addressed each of the questions, plus one other text which addressed one question, accounted for eighty-four pages (93 percent) out of a total of ninety pages devoted to the reading needs of African-American children. Five other texts each contributed a page or more to the issue, but did not deal with specifics, and generally referred to the problem as related to ESL, bilingual, or nonstandard English. Overall, from the fourteen texts, only ninety pages out of the combined total of 7,710 pages (1.167 percent) dealt with the reading needs of African-American children.

This analysis shows that the six textbooks that addressed the reading needs of African-American children at some length did not cover all of the aspects of nonstandard English. Only three of these six textbooks treated more than three nonstandard English expressions and one of the six textbooks and seven of the other eight books did not deal with the issue at all.

IMPLICATIONS FOR BEGINNING TEACHERS AND SCHOOLS

First, in addition to the recommendations that were set out in *M. L. King v. Ann Arbor School District*, we suggest that teacher-education programs implement courses designed to inform prospective teachers on how to take advantage of the language spoken by a majority of African-American children to create an enriched learning environment. These programs or courses should be required along with the requisite reading courses. No one would think of sending teachers to teach in a middle-class school environment without proof that they have satisfied the minimum requirement in basic English. Conversely, no teacher should be sent into the urban African-American schools without a minimum level of knowledge about the structure of nonstandard English. The programs or courses should be structured to prepare prospective teachers to teach *urban* African-American children, because an increasing percentage of the nation's teachers, approximately 2,400,000 (Ornstein and Levine, 1989, p. 61), will be teaching in predominantly African-American schools. Hopefully, these programs or courses will be instrumental not only in helping teachers understand the structure of nonstandard English, but in identifying problems that are unique to the urban African-American child.

Second, linguistic concepts should not be taught in isolation. Personal experiences relative to linguistically and culturally different groups and the urban environment are instrumental in creating understanding and democratic attitudes. Urban field experiences are instrumental in transmitting insightful skills for teaching the urban child in all areas of the curriculum. With the recent demand for accountability, classroom teachers must have a better understanding of the African-American child's language structure. Such knowledge can be instrumental in helping African-American children achieve common educational goals that mainstream society demands or deems necessary for status, employment, and the enjoyment of full civil rights.

Educators are aware that our nation is becoming increasingly urbanized, and that the number of African-American children is increasing. Thus, the use of nonstandard English is also increasing. It seems obvious that teacher-preparation programs should give prospective teachers the knowledge, attitudes, skills, and understanding that will make it possible for teachers to reach and relate effectively to the African-American child. This can be accomplished only when language barriers are recognized and accepted as a part of our culture. An understanding of the African-American child's language structure leads to a better understanding of the African-American child's culture.

Third, concerned individuals, action groups, and African-American organizations at the state and national levels should initiate dialogue with educators, authors, and editors of publishing houses to express their need for representation more thoroughly in textbooks being used in teacher-education programs.

Fourth, immediacy is key in overcoming the teachers' lack of knowledge relative to nonstandard language as spoken by many African Americans. Long before this study was initiated, concerned linguists and educators advocated a restructuring of the teacher-education program. We can no longer afford to spend more time giving lip service to this vital concern. We now have the knowledge and physical capabilities to implement professional course work, workshops, and seminars relative to inner-city life-styles, as well as nonstandard language components in the teacher-education curriculum. These programs should be implemented in the context of personal involvement. For example, student teaching could be scheduled on a two-semester basis, with a minimum of one semester spent in selected urban schools and one semester spent in another school setting, such as an Appalachian school setting, a suburban school setting, or a rural setting. Both semesters could be spent in selected urban schools, depending on the student teacher's primary and secondary areas of interest. However, every new teacher should have urban training, because a teaching certificate indicates that the teacher is qualified to teach *anywhere* in the state and most states have urban centers.

Fifth, the prospective urban teacher should be asked to participate in community activities and become personally involved with the life-styles and the setting where he or she participates as a student teacher. The participating student teachers would supplement their field experiences with classroom instructional activities such as studying various dialects, literature, and a plethora of activities designed to prepare them to understand the deep structure of nonstandard urban dialect.

To implement the above recommendations, a call to action is in order. However, this study is not only a call to action, it is also a plea for *expedient* action. The gathering of data for this study was meant to become an instrument of immediate change. A total commitment to teacher education in the areas of reading and language must be made so that learning experiences for all pupils can become meaningful and positive. This commitment must be in the form of a collaborative effort by all educators, not just a handful of concerned citizens.

Finally, more research is needed in the areas of nonstandard English dialects and how they affect not only reading and standard English, but also other areas of the curriculum. The literature reviewed revealed a surfeit of materials addressing the need to recognize nonstandard English as an adequate language with rules, structure, and consistent patterns that should be accepted and incorporated into teacher education. The fact that African-American dialects share many structural features common to standard English has also been emphasized, but little research has been done on the place of nonstandard dialects in the classroom since the 1970s. This lack of in-depth research relative to nonstandard dialect as pedagogical tools is possibly caused by a reluctance by schools to accept a non-white, nonstandard formal language in the classroom. This mind-set bars such studies from being initiated. The investigators, therefore, recommend that concerned educators take a further look at ways to utilize nonstandard English generally, but especially nonstandard English as spoken by many African Americans, the largest minority population in the United States.

REFERENCES

Baratz, J. C. & Shuy, R. W. (1969). *Teaching black children to read.* Center for Applied Linguistics. Washington, D.C.

Bereiter, C., & Englemann, S. (1966). *Teaching disadvantaged children in the preschool.* Englewood Cliffs, N.J.: Prentice-Hall.

Bernstein, B. (1961). Social class and linguistic development: A theory of social learning. In A. H. Halsey, J. Floud & C. A. Anderson (Eds.), *Education, economy and society.* New York: Free Press.

Dillard, J. L. (1972). *Black English—Its history and usage in the United States.* New York: Random House.

Fasold, R. W. (1968). Orthography in reading materials for black English speaking children. In J. C. Baratz & R. W. Shuy (Eds.), *Teaching black children to read* (pp. 68–91). Washington, D.C.: The Center for Applied Linguistics.

Ginsburg, H. (1972). *The myth of the deprived child.* Englewood Cliffs, NJ: Prentice-Hall.

Hodgkinson, H. (1991). Reform versus reality. *Phi Delta Kappan, 73*(1), 8–16.

Hymes, D. H. (1981). Forward. In C. A. Ferguson & S. B. Heath (Eds.), *Language in the USA* (pp. vii–viii). Cambridge: Cambridge University Press.

Labov, W. (1967). Some sources of reading problems for Negro speakers of nonstandard English. In A. Frazier (Ed.), *New directions in elementary English.* Champaign, Ill.: National Council of Teachers of English.

Lewis, O. (1966). The culture of poverty. *Scientific American, 225,* 19–25.

Martin Luther King Jr., Etc. v. Ann Arbor School District, 473 F. Supp 1371 (E. D. Mich. S.D. 1979).

Ornstein, A. C., & Levine, D. U. (1989). Foundations of education. (4th ed.). Boston: Houghton Mifflin.

Ovando, C. J. & Collier, V. P. (1985). *Bilingual and ESL classrooms: Teaching in multicultural contexts.* New York: McGraw-Hill.

Passow, A. H. (1984). Tackling the reform reports of the 1980s. *Phi Delta Kappan, 65*(10), 674–683.

Shuy, R. W. (1971). Sociolinguistic strategies for studying urban speech. In M. L. Imhoof (Ed.), *Viewpoint.* School of Education: Indiana University.

Swaby, B. E. R. (1989). *Diagnosis and correction of reading difficulties.* Boston: Allyn and Bacon.

CHAPTER 14

Curriculum Development: Teacher Empowering and Professional

BURGA JUNG
Texas Tech University

BURGA JUNG is Assistant Professor of Curriculum and Instruction in the College of Education at Texas Tech University. Her current research interests incorporate qualitative methods to study curriculum decision making in professional development schools, curriculum development courses and student teaching.

ABSTRACT

An overview of some current curriculum development practices in public school districts is provided. These practices draw primarily on Tyler's principles of curriculum construction. Characteristics of three innovations receiving recent attention are also described: site-based selection of curriculum committees, reflective deliberation in curriculum decision making, and curriculum as an interactive construct within the school community. Drawing on the findings from an ethnographic case study of a site-based curriculum committee, I illustrate ways in which conventional and innovative curriculum development practices generate a curriculum document. I also point to ways participation in site-based group curriculum decision making empowers classroom practitioners. Lastly, I suggest how school districts can provide an appropriate support system for both new and experienced teachers when appointing them to curriculum committees.

In this chapter, I will present an overview of approaches to curriculum development advocated in the curriculum development literature. This overview includes both conventional and innovative formats. For illustration, I will draw primarily on a case study describing a site-based curriculum committee charged with revising a K–12 mathematics curriculum (Jung, 1991). The committee consisted mainly of classroom teachers; most had seven years or more of classroom experience although two were first-year teachers. The way in which this committee was appointed and the way the committee members chose to fulfill their charge can be traced to both recent and traditional curriculum development guidelines. So, both conventional and innovative curriculum development formats will be discussed.

A Contemporary Textbook Format and Innovations: An Overview

Tyler (1949) is often looked to as a guide to rational curriculum development. Tyler posits four process components in curriculum development: subject matter disciplines, objectives as learning experiences, the psychology of the learner, and objective methodology in evaluation. These four central components are to serve as guidelines for curriculum decision making.

In practice, curriculum development is conventionally a reforming of both subject matter (curriculum content) and related instructional strategies (curriculum delivery). In pre-college curriculum development, curriculum and subject matter specialists working out of a district's administrative offices are typically charged with the curriculum development task. The reforming process is, in this tradition, a formal and carefully structured procedure that begins by positing certain subject matter aims, goals, and objectives as ends and then proceeds to determine the best means to reach these ends as well as their evaluation (Doll, 1992; Posner, 1992; Posner and Rudnitsky, 1991; Tyler, 1949; Wiles and Bondi, 1989). The technical nature of this curriculum development strategy is best illustrated by the central position that detailed behavioral or performance objectives occupy in public school curriculum documents.

The writing of behavioral objectives has come to be an integral and important part of conventional curriculum development processes (Gagne, 1974; Gronlund, 1991; Mager, 1962; McNeil, 1990; Ornstein and Hunkins, 1988; Popham, 1971; Popham and Baker, 1970), as are questions of scope and sequence, learning activities, and curriculum alignment (McNeil, 1990; Ornstein and Hunkins, 1988). Conventionally, the curriculum development process comes to an end when an official curriculum document is produced.

Though this curriculum document is destined for use by classroom teachers, such a curriculum development project usually is neither initiated nor directed by classroom teachers (Doll, 1992; Tyler, 1949; Wiles and Bondi, 1989). In my case study, most of the curriculum committee's time and effort were spent in reviewing and revising behavioral objectives. These behavioral objectives made up the bulk of the curriculum document. In this way, the traditional model of curriculum development strongly influenced the work of this committee.

Though the Tylerian format of curriculum development is the most frequently used by school districts (Doll, 1992; Eisner, 1985; Schubert, 1986; Wiles and Bondi, 1989), curriculum development innovations are appearing nationally and internationally and are receiving an increasing degree of acceptance and support (Eisner, 1985; Grundy, 1987; Marsh, Day, Hannay, and McCutcheon, 1990; Schubert, 1986; Schwab, 1983). One innovation foregrounds the content of the curriculum. A second highlights the curriculum decision makers. A third emphasizes the decision-making process in curriculum development.

The first innovation I discuss draws attention to the content of the curriculum. Insofar as the curriculum is considered all that is made available to students under the auspices of the school, traditional discipline and subject concerns as well as concerns about student activities, reading material, and the 'hidden' curriculum can be included under the curriculum umbrella (McCutcheon, 1982). So, in addition to subject matter content drawn from a discipline (such as history), curriculum development projects have come to include questions of textbook choice, special events (the Science Fair, Book Week), scheduling, cross-grade and cross-subject coordination, major out-of-school experiences (such as exchange programs), and the student's daily part in the construction, reformation, and implementation of the curriculum. In my case study, the committee took account of the subject matter of mathematics; cross-grade coordination; differences in teacher expectations at elementary, middle school, and high school levels; and admission requirements of colleges and universities.

A second innovation in curriculum development involves a site-based (that is, local school or district) focus. This innovation foregrounds the curriculum decision makers who are drawn from local schools, hold their meetings in local schools, and direct their deliberations to the problems and concerns of local schooling. Most of these decision makers are classroom teachers representing building, grade-level, or department colleagues. My case study illustrates this innovative format of curriculum development in two important ways: all of the teachers in the study volunteered to sit on the curriculum committee and all were held in high esteem by their grade-level and department colleagues.

A third innovation in curriculum development involves the decision-making process itself. Thanks to the writings of Reid (1978), Schwab (1969, 1971, 1973, 1983), and others, deliberation as a curriculum decision-making process is an alternative approach to educational problem solving, that is, alternative to the linear approach of conventional curriculum development specialists who focus primarily on the crafting of behavioral objectives. Deliberation is usually understood to include thoughtful discussion, reflection, and a weighing of alternatives while taking account of schooling commonplaces of teacher, learner, and subject matter within the sociocultural milieu. In my case study, members of the committee (especially the facilitator) believed they were deliberating throughout the committee's proceedings.

These examples of innovations in curriculum development include contextual dimensions (such as schooling practices and personnel) and process dimensions reflecting certain views about process, goals, and the means-ends relationship. These views are in keeping with a point that Schwab (1969, 1971, 1973) consistently tries to make, namely that the curriculum decision-making process cannot be reduced to a technical one. Schwab maintains that the curriculum decision-making process is marked by an absence of widespread consensus regarding goals. This is so because responsibility for setting such goals is politically sensitive, and the means for attaining such goals are highly debatable. Also, the decision-making process juxtaposes demands for public accountability with claims of professional autonomy (Bryk, 1983) and support for competing research findings. For all these reasons, Schwab maintains that deliberation rather than a technical means-ends strategy is the appropriate one for small group decision making about educational matters.

CURRICULUM DEVELOPMENT: SOME COMMONALITIES

So, in examining curriculum development formats, some important differences and commonalities are found. Differences were pointed to above; some commonalities also are apparent. One commonality is that each approach takes account of complex forces guiding decisions about the subject matter of schooling. Contextual factors inevitably influence the achievements of any decision-making group (Dahllof, 1971; Lundgren, 1972). The most successful decision-making groups are those who show the most internal harmony and who are in harmony with the larger community of direct or indirect stakeholders (Boyd, 1978).

Another commonality is variations in stakeholders as decision makers. This commonality points to the relationship between curriculum decision making and the interests of the decision makers as stakeholders (Jung, 1991). In studies of curriculum decision making in school systems, the school and community status of participants vary significantly; they may be board member, superintendent, curriculum specialist, principal, teacher, municipal official, student representative, parent representative, civic group representative, or influential individual (Cuban, 1979; Dahl, 1961; Gross, 1958; Jung, 1991). Participants also vary in the amount of attention given to decision-making tasks, length of time spent with the group, the quality of the time spent, and the actual personal stake in the outcome of the decision-making process (Cuban, 1979; Dahl, 1961; Gross, 1958; Jung, 1991).

Donmoyer's (1990) findings based on his work with curriculum decision-making groups as they engaged in deliberation and my research (Jung, 1991) highlight an additional commonality about group deliberation. Conceptual questions (questions of meaning or prior questions) rather than empirical questions are ultimately the ones needing attention. Conceptions of doing science, reading, doing math, writing, and even of education itself are held by all participants, but the meanings and understandings of these concepts are highly variable. Deliberation about such meanings and understandings enriches committee members' understandings in turn.

The relationship between decision making and implementation of decisions at the local school level is still another commonality. The question of implementation has inspired a small but important number of studies (Cross, 1992; Leithwood, 1982; Reid and Walker, 1975; Roby, 1978). These studies focus on the relationship between group curriculum decisions made by site-based stakeholders (teachers, administrators, students) and the implementation of those decisions through practitioners' actions. Particularities of the school and classroom can influence curriculum decisions. Sociocultural, professional, political, and economic factors can likewise influence the process of decision making and the decisions reached (Apple, 1979; Giroux and McLaren, 1989; Kliebard, 1987; Page and Valli, 1990; Rosenholtz, 1989; Spring, 1989; Stevens and Wood, 1987).

Although curriculum development projects differ, recognizing and understanding commonalities may inform and improve future curriculum development projects. So, the commonalities discussed here briefly provide further clues to productive curriculum decision making: (1) that complex factors go into decisions about school curricula, (2) that variability among curriculum decision makers is to be expected and celebrated, (3) that conceptual questions ought to be asked and deliberated, (4) that curriculum deliberation is an educative process for the participants, and (5) that an empowering relationship exists between participation in curriculum decision making and the implementation of curriculum decisions.

CURRICULUM DEVELOPMENT:
SOME PRACTICES

So far, we have probed the rhetoric of formal curriculum decision making and curriculum development with occasional excursions into practice. How are curricula actually developed? Here are some instances. The development of curricula occurs in a number of social, professional, and political settings. A curriculum development project may be self-initiated and self-directed. This was the case for three teachers of French who decided that a different kind of cross-grade subject matter coordination would make more sense than the existing subject sequence given the student population, parental expectations, and district testing practices (Jung, 1992). Their high school administrator not only permitted but also encouraged ongoing departmental self-evaluation (but, unfortunately, could not provide released time or other forms of compensation). These three classroom teachers happened to get along well with each other. They arranged a common meeting time (right after their last classes on Tuesdays) and "got on with" the business of subject matter coordination.

Site-based curriculum decision making seems to be one of the more appealing innovations in current curriculum development projects, at least in the eyes of many classroom teachers (Marsh, Day, Hannay, and McCutcheon, 1990). However, site-based curriculum development is usually not left entirely in the hands of classroom teachers (contrary to the example of the three French teachers). The building principal, an assistant principal, a university curriculum specialist, or a representative from district office may be the facilitator for a school's curriculum development project. When this is the case, it is usually because the district office has determined that a particular curriculum change is called for and wishes at least to oversee the process if not also to direct the process.

To some extent, the curriculum development process will be channeled to fulfill agendas emanating from outside the classroom and may be reflected in subsequent ownership of the curriculum document (Jung, 1991; Marsh, Day, Hannay, and McCutcheon, 1990; Smith, Prunty, Dwyer, and Kleine, 1987). And, to some extent, the teachers will be compensated through released time from classroom duties (though many teachers do not see this as much of a compensation) or through some form of payment for their participation in meetings held after school hours or during the summer months.

Another level of site-based curriculum development is illustrated by those curriculum projects that are district-wide, that call for a number of teachers representing the district's schools to meet under the guidance of district office personnel or invited curriculum consultants (Doll, 1992; Wiles and Bondi, 1989). For example, Ed, Freshwater's Professional Development Coordinator, facilitated all of the district's K–12 curriculum committees

(Jung, 1991). Committee meetings were held over the summer months and teachers were given a set stipend upon completing the committee work.

And last, there are curriculum development projects that are initiated and developed by commercial companies or government agencies independent of public schools, and eventually made available through national marketing or governmental dissemination. Such was the case for the major science and mathematics curricula developed in the 1950s and 1960s.

So What's New?

Two innovations have changed school district curriculum development in dramatic and profound ways. One innovation is site-based curriculum decision making (or curriculum development). That is, school districts develop and periodically revise their own school curricula. A second innovation is in the source of the school district's curriculum development professionals. School districts are drawing directly on the expertise of classroom teachers in developing and revising district curricula.

These two innovations in curriculum development, namely in location and staffing, are not yet widespread. But public school districts are beginning to recognize the advantages in looking to site-based professionals to provide up-to-date district curricula (Grundy, 1987; Kimpston and Rogers, 1988; Marsh, Day, Hannay, and McCutcheon, 1990). These formal curriculum tasks fall primarily to classroom teachers.

So, school professionals are being asked to engage in group deliberation about official curriculum documents. Teachers have always had a considerable moral and professional stake in the content of school curricula, inasmuch as they are expected to implement these curricula. However, such group deliberation involves skills and knowledge not previously emphasized in the education and professional development of teachers. In this sense, classroom teachers now asked to sit on local curriculum committees are novice stakeholders in the process as well as the product of the committee's decision making (Connelly, Dukacz and Quinlan, 1980; Gold, 1983; Greene, 1987).

The case study discussed below underscores normative interests held by teachers and shows their pivotal place in curriculum development. *Normative interests* are dispositions to act for one's own or others' welfare. In the case study, I argue that normative interests school professionals bring to their committee work guide both the curriculum deliberations (or decision-making process) and the content of the curriculum document (the product). First though, a short description of the study's research methodology will help to set the stage for the findings.

FRESHWATER'S K-12 CURRICULUM COMMITTEE

This single case study of a curriculum decision-making group was undertaken in Freshwater, a midwestern suburban public school district, rated as one of the state's best in student achievement.

Participant observation shaped my case study as an ethnographic one (Bernard, 1988; Ellen, 1984) using cultural, naturalistic, contextual, and emic lenses (Bruyn, 1966, 1976; Glick, 1984; Hansen, 1979; Junker, 1960; Jorgensen, 1989; Sarsby, 1984). In addition, all committee members were interviewed. I audiotaped all meetings and interviews (Blacking, 1984). The transcripts supplemented but did not replace my participation at committee meetings and having the opportunity to interact informally with committee members.

Also, I collected documents and records (Bogdan and Biklen, 1992; Lincoln and Guba, 1985) before, during, and after the scheduled set of committee meetings in order to place the discourse and actions of the committee meetings within the larger cultures of school and community. Other records and documents were collected as examples of the written products of these curriculum committee meetings and to better understand the total curriculum document entitled the Graded Course of Study.

The resulting data are comprehensive, systematic, and in-depth, as is characteristic of case studies (Patton, 1990). I developed and applied codes to analyze the data (Bogdan and Biklen, 1992; Strauss, 1987) and 15 categories of group interests were generated. I used these 15 categories to analyze the data from field notes, records and documents, and transcripts of meetings and interviews. Data were compared within and across the field notes, records, documents, and transcripts through the constant comparative method of data analysis (Bogdan and Biklen, 1992; Strauss, 1987). Ultimately, I collapsed the fifteen categories into three overarching categories.

Three normative group interests were found to be compellingly characteristic of the culture of the Freshwater Mathematics Graded Course of Study Committee. These are interests in group process, professional development, and accountability.

1. INTEREST IN GROUP PROCESS

The normative interest in group process was evidenced in numerous ways. Cooperative moves to consensus was one way in which the interest in group process was acted on. In other words, the committee forged consensus by agreeing to include or make room for members' individual interests (such as manipulatives), by agreeing to exclude certain administrative concerns (multicultural and career components), and by reframing the discussion (questions about philosophy statements became quibbles about words).

The Freshwater Curriculum Committee's normative interest in group dynamics and practices also included active listening to colleagues, the avoidance of open conflict, and open cooperation with Ed, the committee facilitator.

2. INTEREST IN PROFESSIONAL DEVELOPMENT

During interviews, committee members reflected on the professional nature of their revision tasks. They spoke of connections with teaching practices, testing standards, the taking of formal courses, and informal colleague-to-colleague sharing of information. During committee meetings, they acted on these connections when justifying revision decisions.

Committee members considered themselves as acting professionally when they represented building and grade-level colleagues' concerns, shared practitioner knowledge informally with colleagues, and improved their understanding of schooling and curriculum subject matter by volunteering for building and district committees such as this one. In addition, a number of committee members were enrolled in university courses leading to a professional graduate degree.

3. INTEREST IN ACCOUNTABILITY

Although the teachers were not contracted to revise a curriculum (and after all, each had volunteered), their tacit and voiced sense of accountability was expressed in perceived obligations toward colleagues and parents. The teachers among the committee members frequently referred to their perception of accountability toward building and grade-level colleagues. For example, they presented the concerns of their colleagues as carefully as possible during committee sessions.

The teachers' perception of accountability toward parents was ambiguous. On the one hand, they believed they had a clear responsibility to the parents of their students and to the wider community. On the other hand, they did not want their classroom practices questioned by parents.

In these ways, these three normative group interests were instrumental in shaping the flow of committee work, the discourse of committee decisions, and the format and content of the Freshwater Curriculum Committee.

CONCLUSIONS

I can point to two conclusions resulting from this study that are potentially significant to school professionals, including beginning teachers and curriculum decision-making groups.

One conclusion is that these shared or group interests are instrumental in important ways for the committee to accomplish its charge. The forming of group interests is at one and the same time a mark of solidarity and a form of cooperation. The group can get its work done expeditiously this way. So a strong unifying and legitimizing sense of cooperation evolved as the revision tasks continued, program goal by program goal.

A second conclusion is that group interests are instrumental in shaping the direction and content of the committee work. In this way the group interests of these stakeholders directly affected the product of the committee's work, namely the revised mathematics curriculum. For example, they cooperatively agreed to revisions of the mathematics curriculum implemented at the elementary and middle-school grade levels, and to include a high school reform plan proposed by the high school teachers.

So, for the curriculum committee to fulfill its charge through group deliberation, certain normative interests disposed the members of the committee to act cooperatively or collaboratively for the good of the group.

PROFESSIONAL IMPLICATIONS

One implication of the findings discussed above is that, given the positive role of normative group interests in accomplishing group tasks, early identification of such interests might make possible more productive group actions in committee work.

A second implication is that appropriate preparations for district-wide committee work in a school district ought to include specific professional development for the teachers selected to sit on such committees. Given that the heart of all schooling practices is the curriculum being taught and learned, what preparation do teachers have for these curriculum development and revision tasks? In the study, only Freshwater high school teachers had any preparation for curriculum development outside of their teaching assignments; this preparation was through graduate courses geared to a reforming of the scope and sequence of high school mathematics.

Is it enough that the teachers are *using* the curricula? Is this the best or only preparation really needed? Is special preparation needed only when there are major changes wanted by parents, the district administration, or teachers? I would answer no to each of these questions. As more and more school districts find ways to develop and revise school curricula by relying on the expertise of classroom teachers, classroom teachers should be given adequate preparation for the group work that awaits them. This is so because group curriculum decision making is sufficiently different from individual curriculum decision making occurring every day in classrooms to warrant a deliberative approach that takes account of the social nature of group work. Beginning teachers can also get a better understanding of the knowledge base and skills they can add to their continuing education as a professional.

CONCLUDING STATEMENT

The work being done by curriculum committees such as the one in the Freshwater school district has so far not been exposed to extensive research of the kind used for this study. There is room for more ethnographic research with curriculum committees. Comparisons would then be possible in ways that are impossible at the present. Teachers would have a chance to look into the curriculum decision-making activities of a variety of groups, select those practices that might be productive in their respective school systems, and contribute to a better understanding of the moral, political, cultural, and professional dimensions of the most important single task of any school, namely, to plan and develop the best and most appropriate curricula for students.

These recent developments in formal curriculum decision making provide avenues for beginning and career teachers to make contributions that are innovative, professionally significant, empowering, and professionally rewarding.

REFERENCES

Apple, M. (1979). *Ideology and curriculum.* London, UK: Routledge & Kegan Paul.

Bernard, H. R. (1988). *Research methods in cultural anthropology.* Newbury Park, CA: Sage.

Blacking, J. (1984). Preparation for fieldwork: Audio-visual equipment in general ethnographic studies. In R. F. Ellen (Ed.), *Ethnographic research: A guide to general conduct,* (pp. 199–206). New York: Academic Press.

Bogdan, R. C., & Biklen, S. K. (1992). *Qualitative research for education: An introduction to theory and methods.* Boston: Allyn and Bacon.

Boyd, W. L. (1978). The changing politics of curriculum policy making for American schools. *Review of Educational Research, 48*(4), 577–629.

Bruyn, S. T. (1976). The methodology of participant observation. In J. I. Roberts & S. E. Akinsanya (Eds.), *Educational patterns and cultural configurations: The anthropology of education* (pp. 247–264). New York: David McKay.

Bruyn, S. T. (1966). *The human perspective in sociology: The methodology of participant observation.* Englewood Cliffs, NJ: Prentice-Hall.

Bryk, A. S. (Ed.). (1983). *Stakeholder-based evaluation.* San Francisco: Jossey-Bass.

Connelly, F. M., Dukacz, A. S., & Quinlan, F. (Eds.). (1980). *Curriculum plannning for the classroom.* Toronto: Ontario Institute for Studies in Education Press.

Cross, B. (1992). *Teachers' practical knowledge and curriculum planning in a Professional Development School.* Unpublished manuscript, The Ohio State University, Columbus, OH.

Cuban, L. (1979). Determinants of curriculum change and stability, 1870–1970. In J. Schaffarzick & G. Sykes (Eds.), *Value conflicts and curriculum issues* (pp. 139–196). Berkeley, CA: McCutchan.

Dahl, R. (1961). *Who governs?* New Haven, CT: Yale University Press.

Dahllof, U. S. (1971). *Ability grouping, content validity, and curriculum process analysis.* New York: Teachers College Press.

Doll, R. C. (1992). *Curriculum improvement: Decision making and process.* (8th Ed.). Boston, MA: Allyn & Bacon.

Donmoyer, R. (1990). Curriculum evaluation and the negotiation of meaning. *Language Arts, 67*(3), 274–286.

Eisner, E. (1985). *The educational imagination: On the design and evaluation of school programs.* (2nd ed.). New York: Macmillan.

Ellen, R. F. (1984). *Ethnographic research: A guide to general practice.* New York: Academic Press.

Gagne, R. M. (1974). *Essentials of learning for instruction.* Hinsdale, IL: The Dryden Press.

Giroux, H. A., & McLaren, P. (Eds.). (1989). *Critical pedagogy, the state and cultural struggle.* Albany, NY: SUNY.

Glick, P. B. (1984). Producing data: Long-term research. In R. F. Ellen (Ed.), *Ethnographic research: A guide to general conduct* (pp. 241–247). New York: Academic Press.

Gold, N. (1983). Stakeholders and program evaluation: Characterizations and reflections. In A. S. Bryk (Ed.), *Stakeholder-based evaluation.* San Francisco: Jossey-Bass.

Greene, J. C. (1987). Stakeholder participation in evaluation design: Is it worth the effort? *Evaluation and Program Planning, 10,* 373–394.

Gronlund, N. E. (1991). *How to write and use instructional objectives.* New York: Macmillan.

Gross, N. (1958). *Who runs our schools?* New York: John Wiley.

Grundy, S. (1987). *Curriculum: Product or praxis.* Philadelphia, PA: The Falmer Press.

Hansen, J. F. (1979). *Sociocultural perspectives on human learning: An introduction to educational anthropology.* Englewood Cliffs, NJ: Prentice-Hall.

Jorgensen, D. L. (1989). *Participant observation: A methodology for human studies.* Newbury Park, CA: Sage.

Junker, B. H. (1960). *Fieldwork.* Chicago: University of Chicago Press.

Jung, N. (1991). *Curriculum decision making and stakeholder interests: A case study.* Unpublished doctoral dissertation, The Ohio State University, Columbus, OH.

Jung, N. (1992). [Curriculum development: Teacher initiated]. Unpublished raw data.

Kliebard, H. (1987). *The struggle for the American curriculum, 1893–1958.* New York: Routledge & Kegan Paul.

Kimpston, R. D., & Rogers, K. B. (1988). Predispositions, participatory roles and perceptions of teachers, principals and community members in a collaborative curriculum planning process. *Journal of Curriculum Studies, 20*(4), 351–367.

Leithwood, K. A. (Ed.). (1982). *Studies in curriculum decision-making.* Toronto: OISE Press.

Lincoln, Y., & Guba, E. (1985). *Naturalistic inquiry.* Beverly Hills, CA: Sage.

Lundgren, U.P. (1972). *Frame factors and the teaching process: A contribution to curriculum theory and theory of teaching.* Stockholm: Almqvist & Wiksell.

Marsh, C., Day, C., Hannay, L., & McCutcheon, G. (1990). *Reconceptualizing school-based curriculum development.* New York: The Falmer Press.

McCutcheon, G. (Ed.). (1982). What in the world is curriculum theory? *Theory into Practice, 21*(1), 18–22.

McNeil, J. D. (1990). *Curriculum: A comprehensive introduction.* New York: HarperCollins.

Mager, R. (1962). *Preparing instructional objectives.* Palo Alto, CA: Fearon Publishers.

Ornstein, A. C., & Hunkins, F. P. (1988). *Curriculum: Foundations, principles, and issues.* Boston, MA: Allyn & Bacon.

Page, R., & Valli, L. (Eds.). (1990). *Curriculum differentiation: Interpretive studies in U.S secondary schools.* Albany, NY: SUNY.

Patton, M. Q. (1990). *Qualitative evaluation and research methods.* (2nd Ed.). Newbury Park, CA: Sage.

Popham, J. (Ed.). (1971). *Criterion-referenced measurement.* Englewood Cliffs, NJ: Educational Technology Publications.

Popham, J., & Baker, E. (1970). *Establishing instructional goals.* Englewood Cliffs, NJ: Prentice-Hall.

Posner, G. J., & Rudnitsky, A. N. (1991). *Course design: A guide to curriculum development for teachers.* New York: Longman.

Posner, G. J. (1992). *Analyzing the curriculum.* New York: McGraw-Hill.

Reid, W. A. (1978). *Thinking about the curriculum: The nature and treatment of curriculum problems.* Boston: Routledge & Kegan Paul.

Reid, W. A., & Walker, D. F. (Eds). (1975). *Case studies in curriculum change.* London: Routledge & Kegan Paul.

Roby, T. W. (1978). Problem situations and curricular resources at Central College: An exemplification of curricular arts. *Curriculum Inquiry, 8*(2), 95–117.

Rosenholtz, S. J. (1989). *Teachers' workplace: The social organization of schools.* New York: Longman.

Sarsby, J. (1984). The fieldwork experience: Special problems of fieldwork in familiar settings. In R. F. Ellen (Ed.), *Ethnographic research: A guide to general conduct* (pp. 129–132). New York: Academic Press.

Schubert, W. H. (1986). *Curriculum: Perspective, paradigm, and possibility.* New York: Macmillan.

Schwab, J. J. (1969). The practical: A language for curriculum. *School Review, 78,* 1–23.

Schwab, J. J. (1971). The practical 2: Arts of eclectic. *School Review, 79,* 193–542.

Schwab, J. J. (1973). The practical 3: Translation into curriculum. *School Review, 81,* 501–522.

Schwab, J. J. (1983). The practical 4: Something for curriculum professors to do. *Curriculum Inquiry, 13*(3), 239–265.

Smith, L. M., Prunty, J. P., Dwyer, D. C., & Kleine, P. F. (1987). *The fate of an innovative school: The history and present status of the Kensington School.* Philadelphia, PA: The Falmer Press.

Spring, J. (1989). *The sorting machine revisited: National educational policy since 1945.* New York: Longman.

Stevens, E. J., & Wood, G. H. (1987). *Justice, ideology and education.* New York: Random House.

Strauss, A. (1987). *Qualitative analysis for social scientists.* New York: Cambridge University Press.

Tyler, R. W. (1949). *Basic principles of curriculum and instruction.* Chicago: The University of Chicago Press.

Wiles, J., & Bondi, J. (1989). *Curriculum development: A guide to practice,* 3rd ed. Columbus, OH: Charles E. Merrill.

Curriculum: Implications and Reflections

GAIL MCCUTCHEON
The Ohio State University

INTRODUCTION

Two reports in this section rest on an underlying set of important assumptions. This response addresses them by questioning what kind of nation we want to develop in the United States of America, the role the curriculum plays in such a matter and potential processes of implementing a change toward a new vision of the nation. Finally, it turns to applying the discussion further by elaborating on processes of curriculum development.

THE NATURE OF THE NATION WE WANT TO CREATE

One of the biggest issues currently facing the nation concerns how to think about the variety of ethnic groups and races comprising this country. Historically, we have considered ourselves to be a melting pot where various immigrants transformed themselves toward a central tendency. However, that central tendency became predominantly northern European and male, reflective of those who held power. As a result, Caucasian male images and thoughts have predominated in American society and, as a result, in the curriculum.

Further, while many immigrants bought into that definition and tried to transform themselves to it, others retained elements of their own language and culture and remained in small isolated communities. This is still somewhat true of many Amish and so-called Pennsylvania Dutch people. However, it is important to remember that many of them have chosen to maintain their unique culture and religion by remaining isolated, rejecting many customs and practices of the wider culture and rarely venturing into it. By contrast, people who are culturally different who *do* desire to engage in life in the wider culture face difficulties under the melting-pot ideology. These people include many women and Asian-Americans, African-Americans, Native Americans and Hispanic-Americans—people of color—as well as Appalachians. The reason for their difficulties is that they have constructed reality differently from how northern European-American men have constructed it.

Further, women and people of color do not have the power that northern European-American men hold, so inequities exist and continue to widen because of the definition of the merit of images and knowledge the nation holds and thus teaches through the curriculum of the schools.

For the nation to reach a high level of success, this sort of inequity cannot continue because it disenfranchises many of the nation's citizens and wastes their potential talent and productivity. Further, the nation loses an opportunity to be truly outstanding by taking into account the varying talents and strengths of all its citizens instead of allowing success to be defined by just one view, which was the initial problem. This issue is particularly troublesome when the population is shifting and people of color are beginning to comprise a larger percentage of the citizenry than ever before. The problem may also be increasingly significant because society has become more complex and interdependent and because of changes in technology and communication. It is clearly time for the nation to reconsider its definition of itself and of what constitutes success.

WHAT ROLES DO SCHOOLS HAVE HERE?

Clearly, several alternative strategies are possible about changing society to celebrate or, at the very least, to tolerate cultural differences instead of expecting everyone to transform themselves to a male, northern European-American norm, and several of the options are not mutually exclusive.

One obvious strategy is to teach students about the nature of various cultures within their country. It is important to understand that this issue is in the nation's interest rather than merely being relevant to the local level. As a result, it is important to consider teaching about various cultural groups within the nation, not necessarily limiting it to those present within a particular community. A second level of teaching cultural diversity would be an appreciation of differences so students could see and act upon the potential strength of a nation comprised of differences rather than a nation comprised of uniformity. As a result, they would be able to redefine what are important and beneficial ways of thinking about defining the knowledge and practices of the nation. Yet another strategy is to teach about issues common to all humans, such as the environment and use of natural resources, because this is *our* nation and *our* planet.

A fourth strategy is to teach about ways to change society so it will not tolerate and support inequity. One issue concerning these four possible strategies is whether to adapt students to fit into society or to teach students how to change society so it can be adapted to fit those students and its other citizens. As a result the citizens would not have to adapt: Should society be changed or individuals within it?

THESE REPORTS AND THE ISSUE

Yager implicitly argues for some of both—changing students and as a result changing society—by teaching both females and males and all cultural groups science and technology in ways aimed at equal opportunities. Science and technology made the nation great and may do so again. While Yager doesn't say so, this idea can obviously be approached in other areas of the curriculum as well.

Edwards and Tate argue for teaching African Americans by accounting for their linguistic differences. They do not discuss linguistic differences of other people of color, nor the potential affects of such a practice on students and society. It is important to recognize that while some African Americans are linguistically diverse, not all African Americans speak the same language; rather, individual differences apply here as they do about other groups of people. For this reason, perhaps the Edwards and Tate proposal is best seen as an example of one sort of individual difference teachers might account for when planning. If so, this implies that teacher education should address a multitude of linguistic differences.

Jung portrays deliberation as a process useful in making curriculum decisions. This process could be particularly helpful in developing policies about matters such as the one addressed in this discussion because the issue is one where certainty about how to proceed is lacking and the rules for knowing whether a good decision has been made are also lacking. The issue is so complex and crucial that deliberation about it seems the best way to proceed in making warranted decisions, for through deliberation a range of opinions can be heard and considered and what appears to be the best decision can best be made after close examination of alternative possibilities.

APPLICATION

Teachers play a central and enormous role in developing the curriculum. They do this on two occasions: As they plan individually and as they work in groups at the grade, departmental, school or school-system level. As humans, we construct reality to make sense of it and to act. In curriculum work, teachers act, observe, and reflect; read arguments about what should be taught and reflect; discuss matters with students' parents and other teachers and reflect; study curriculum materials and policies and reflect. These reflections and teachers' ensuing planning activities are among teachers' most professional activities. This is true because teachers apply professional knowledge about pedagogy and the subject matter(s) they teach while they reflect, plan, and act. As Yager's report intimates, teachers' observing their students' constructions of knowledge and planning accordingly is also among the most important of professional activities. The three curriculum reports have implications for teachers developing the curriculum and for their reflections. One crucial matter for teacher education concerns how to help teachers improve their reflective practices to examine tacit assumptions underlying their views.

TEACHING AND THE CONSTRUCTION OF KNOWLEDGE

One important source of the knowledge educators apply to their planning is comprised of experience before teaching. During that time, they were making sense of the world. They may have vowed privately, for example, never to treat people the way a particular teacher treated people or always to be as fair or as enthusiastic as another teacher.

Because we are born into a particular culture and era, in a sense we are as much "children" of that culture and time as we are children of our actual parents. That is, the culture and era are partly responsible for shaping our thinking and our personal, practical theory of action—just as the ideas teachers have provide a basis for their actions. As teachers, it is important to bring to consciousness our beliefs and assumptions about the world so we can act in appropriate ways and ensure the best education of students under our care. One aspect of this is to examine what we know about teaching children of cultures different from our own. Edwards and Tate argue this with respect to African-American students. I would hope they would extend the argument, as Yager does, to all people of color, whose numbers are increasingly rapidly. That is, I hope that Edwards and Tate would agree that Asian-American, Appalachian, Hispanic-American, and Native American children also need to have equal access to the curriculum. This means understanding what instructional strategies and curriculum materials are most efficacious if we mean to develop a curriculum and schools genuinely fostering opportunity for equity, for they are also linguistically diverse. Moreover, all of these groups are culturally diverse. Yager's report further extends the argument to gender.

Because teachers were born and grew up in a particular culture, they know that culture well, but not the cultures of others comprising our society.

If we mean to develop a nation that is truly multicultural and truly provides equal opportunities, it is important for teachers (and as a result students who are impressionable members of society) to come to understand different cultures within the United States of America. This means much more than merely adopting reading or health textbooks containing African American, Hispanic American, Asian American and Native American people in them and more than merely studying customs by eating food representing different cultures or stringing colored macaroni and making paper-feathered headbands and coffee-can and inner-tube rubber tom-toms, and other similar practices under the guise of multicultural education. These practices are superficial and misleading. Rather, in-depth study and experiences are needed about cultural norms and practices in order for teachers—and as a result their students—to develop genuine understandings and appreciations of cultural and linguistic differences. It further means inquiring into and applying varied instructional strategies and considering which are most efficacious in helping students of both genders and diverse cultures to have the greatest access to the curriculum in and for constructing their own meanings of the world.

CURRICULUM ARGUMENTS

One way to assess the Edwards and Tate and the Yager reports is to examine the basis of their curriculum arguments. Arguments in curriculum and other fields must be supported by reasons and evidence to allow the reader to follow along from their rational foundations (see Toulmin et al., 1984). Some statements are easily understood as they stand, without support, such as when we order a meal at a restaurant.

However, other statements, such as curriculum arguments, need evidence and a clear line of reasoning in order to present a case sufficient to persuade a reader. I can locate no difficulties in either the Yager or the Edwards and Tate arguments with respect to evidence and a clear line of reasoning.

Another way of evaluating curriculum arguments is to wonder what might happen if they were successful. For instance, what if Edwards' and Tate's proposal were accepted, and it worked? One result might be miseducation of African Americans, because in the absence of social change to accept African-American English, graduates might have difficulty in the job market and in getting into college, or technical or vocational schools. Hence, such a proposal in the absence of social change might continue to support inequities. Because social change occurs slowly, such inequity might continue for a long time.

Yager's report does not require social change to implement, but might ultimately yield social change if people were educated equitably and learned about science and technology, which have contributed to our success as a nation and might continue to do so.

While she does not explicitly argue for it, Jung's report might lead to more local curriculum development, which could yield a more diverse curriculum nationally. That is, if curricula were developed this way they would probably be well suited and carefully considered, but we might see a range of differences between communities' curricula.

Yet a third matter some people might find problematic in the Edwards and Tate and the Yager reports is the issue of how their reports constitute a curriculum issue. Both concern curriculum matters on a number of counts.

First, teachers who are interested in developing and enacting an *optimum* curriculum (one likely to reach the most students with the most content), these reports provide clues about teaching people of color and females. They also keep that issue alive, so are important in that right.

Secondly, both comprise examples of what might be problematic in the implicit curriculum. School is not (or *should* not be) just for the heretofore dominant northern European-American students; science is not (or *should* not be) just for boys.

Thirdly, the Yager and the Edwards and Tate reports implicitly question an issue in the overt curriculum. It could easily be argued that overt school knowledge has been dominated by a Euro centric and male view of the world and what is important to know. These reports can be construed as calling into question that definition of what should constitute school knowledge.

Fourthly, and perhaps most importantly, these reports imply and acknowledge that curriculum planning is (or should be) more clearly now than ever before the province and role of teachers, not textbook authors.

TEACHERS' PLANNING

When teachers plan, they take into account several factors, some of which relate to these two reports. They consult relevant curriculum policies and the materials they have, reflect and weigh them based upon their practical theories of action and other factors. They consider the discipline(s) they teach. They also take into account the context in which they teach. What is the nature of the neighborhood? the parents? the likely future prospects for their students? Finally, teachers consider their students. Now, it is important to understand that when teachers plan they do not consider each factor in isolation from the other factors. Rather, teachers relate them to one another as they deliberate about what to teach and how to do so to enhance the opportunity for the most students to learn the most information possible. They further develop images of themselves teaching the lessons while planning and mentally rehearsing lessons so they can envision potential strengths and weaknesses of the lessons, whether they can enact that lesson, and its likely success.

It is also important to recognize that not *all* of this planning occurs before the lesson. Some occurs while actually teaching, and reflections on the lesson influence future plans. The Edwards and Tate and the Yager arguments contribute to the planning by presenting cases that elaborate on thinking about students while planning and enacting lessons. So, teachers might also begin to reflect upon whose knowledge they are teaching. Has the Eurocentric, male view prevailed? This is likely, because they themselves were probably educated through that view and because textbooks present it. (See Black, 1967, for some possible reasons why this is so.) Locating bias in their own teaching and calling it into question could be an important form of professional inquiry and transform education in the ways Yager and Edwards and Tate suggest. They are further related in that their arguments affect both the overt and the implicit curriculum.

GROUP CURRICULUM DEVELOPMENT

In addition to planning lessons individually, teachers frequently work in small groups to deliberate about the grade level, department, school or school-system curriculum. Jung's report portrays a recent case of teachers deliberating about the mathematics curriculum to develop a curriculum policy for their school system. In such cases, teachers socially construct the curriculum. Whether meetings are formal or casual, they offer opportunities for teachers to interact and socially develop a vision of what their classrooms, grade levels, departments, schools, and school systems should be like in terms of what should be expected, done, and created through their work. By developing such social constructions of this, teachers can develop coherency in the vision so it can be well-integrated throughout the grade level department, school, and school system. Secondly, through discussing such issues and deliberating about them, teachers can grow to understand and act on them. Issues such as what and whose knowledge should be contained in the overt curriculum are clearly worthy of group deliberation.

As teachers and curriculum developers we continue to learn throughout our lives and do so, in part, by hearing other people's views. This is the case because society changes, inventions and discoveries appear, and knowledge is continually reshaped to accommodate the changes and discoveries. As a result, the curriculum is continually redeveloped. Without such professional development of ourselves and of the curriculum, we would continue to teach content that becomes progressively more out of date until it is a "saber-tooth curriculum" worthy of a preceding generation but not of present students (see Benjamin, 1939). For example, today we'd see no computers in classrooms if it were not for curriculum revisions over the past fifteen years. AIDS education would not be required in most states, and accompanying sex education would probably not be required in most were it not for the current devastating AIDS epidemic. Nor would we entertain ideas about cultural diversity and try to provide for equal opportunities to both genders.

THE ABSENCE OF ABSOLUTES

While curriculum is a central field in education, it is important to recognize that absolutes simply do not exist about what to teach. This does not mean people do not make curriculum decisions or base them on whim. Rather, it means the decisions are problematic and tentative. Further, the grounds for making curriculum decisions are unclear. As a result, unless educators reflect deeply, reach conclusions about what to teach, consider why they're defensible conclusions and enact them with conviction, virtually anyone can ask, "Yes, but why aren't you teaching *that*?" Teachers need to be able to explain and defend their decisions clearly. Curriculum arguments need to be well conceived and carefully considered in order to answer such questions, which educators frequently encounter.

Because curriculum is not a field of absolutes, it is critical to recognize that teachers take part in the great debates about what and whose knowledge is of most worth and how to enact those decisions in optimum ways. Teachers take part in those debates through reflections, and in small group meetings, but mostly through their actions.

KEEPING THE DEBATE OPEN

The lack of absolutes about what to teach and even about the grounds for making such decisions means that extraordinarily careful attention has to be paid to the question of what teachers should teach. Careful consideration of how to educate with cultural diversity in mind, yet ultimately have a society that can communicate well is an important example of such deliberations, as is the question of how to educate toward enhancing opportunities for gender equity. No easy answers exist here, only careful considerations about how to proceed to develop optimum curricula (see Reid, 1978).

This is further complicated because, as McCaslin and Good note (1992:4), many educational reforms (such as more homework) are supported for political rather than educational reasons and as a result are superficial. School reform, including curriculum reform, must be considered in a broad context, not merely by trying to mandate and apply quick fixes, such as lengthening the school day and year or using competency tests, as a panacea for deeper problems. Needless carping at public schools and the adoption of simplistic answers to complicated problems schools face is not likely to help; rather, the reforms are likely to take time and energy for individual teachers, departments, schools, and school systems to create or adopt and enact with the conviction necessary to have an optimum curriculum. Moreover, it will need to be continually revised so it does not, in the future, become a saber-tooth curriculum meeting the needs of yesterday's students and society. Jung's report provides a glimpse of how this can occur, as does Reid's (1978) book.

One crucial issue to consider here, then, is not only *what* knowledge is most valuable, but also *whose* knowledge. One way of considering this is to consider the relative importance of students' constructed meanings and the importance of objective knowledge. This undoubtedly varies by discipline. For instance, in the arts we would have little creativity if only objective knowledge were taught such as history of the arts, or how to clean paint brushes, set up a palette, sew ribbons on to toe-dancing shoes, or mix potter's clay and glazes. While these may be important skills in the arts, they remain at a technical level. If we taught only objective, technical knowledge, creativity would suffer and we might also ultimately experience a decline in inventions and in the generation of knowledge in many fields.

An obstacle education is currently experiencing might ultimately have such an effect. The difficulty is with the rampant movement toward testing, which typically tests knowledge at this technical, objective level and tests for the northern European-American, male-dominated view of knowledge. All of us who are concerned about education must take part in communicating to the public the importance of forms of knowledge other than those present on competency tests. We are in peril not only of losing the debate, but of having the debate closed about what and whose knowledge should be taught via the testing movement, for it seems the test writers are deciding the answers for us, and legislators are endorsing their conclusions. Using competency tests is probably an example of legislators' adopting the policy for political rather than educational reasons, for by mandating the tests they appear to be doing something about educational problems. Unfortunately, in my view, they are exacerbating them because they are close to shutting off the debate and therefore rigidifying the curriculum.

Summary

This discussion suggests two occasions when teachers deliberate about the curriculum and take into account matters such as the nature of knowledge they make accessible to students overtly and implicitly. One of these occasions is when teachers plan alone using their personal practical theory of action. The other is during group deliberations with colleagues. An important issue for deliberation concerns whose knowledge is made available. Another concerns how particular students learn, and therefore what instructional strategies seem most appropriate.

Rather than only reading about different cultures within the United States of America, in what other ways might people learn about them sufficiently to be able to incorporate the experience into their theory of action and their actions? Small discussion groups, living with families unlike one's own, making a genuine appeal to others to teach one what it's like to be an African American, Hispanic American or Native American are some beginning points. The necessary start, though, is recognizing the existence of the problem and why it is important. This is a major responsibility for teachers to undertake, but I do not see how anything will occur to improve matters unless the case is made to teachers because they ultimately bear the responsibility for the curriculum.

References

Benjamin, H. (1939) *The saber-tooth curriculum.* New York: McGraw Hill (Author pseudonym: J. A. Peddiwell)

Black, H. (1967) *The American Schoolbook.* New York: William Morrow and Company.

Reid, W. (1978) *Thinking about the curriculum.* London: Routledge and Kegan Paul.

McCaslin, Mand Good, T. (1992) Complaint cognition: The misalliance of management and instructional goals in current school reform. *Educational researcher*, 21:3, (April) pp. 4–17.

Toulmin, S., Rieke, R. and Janik, A. (1984). *An introduction to reasoning.* New York: Macmillan.

DIVERSITY AND TEACHING: TEACHER EDUCATION YEARBOOK I

Edited by Mary O'Hair and Sandra J. Odell

Current ATE Commissions on Diversity

ATE Special Interest Group on Multicultural Education
Dr. Sam Spaght, Supt.
Wichita Public Schools
Area III
Four Twenty-Eight Building
428 S. Broadway
Wichita, KS 67202-3910

Commission on Preparing Teachers for Diverse Student Populations
Dr. Edwina Vold, Chair
Dept. of Professional Studies in Education
Indiana University of Pennsylvania
303 Davis Hall
Indiana, PA 15705-1087

Commission on Urban Schools
Dr. Francisco Hidalgo, Chair
Dept. of Occupational & Education Studies
ED 100
California State University
San Bernadino, CA 92407

Commission on Preparing Teachers for Multiple Settings
Dr. Terry James, Chair
Department of Administration & Secondary Education
University of Central Arkansas
PO Box 4917
Conway, AR 72032

Name Index

311

Subject Index

Ability grouping and tracking, 44
Abuse, 4
Accepting Behaviors for Cultural Diversity for Teachers (ABCD), 32-55, 58-59
Accountability, in curriculum development, 293
Achievement motivation
    ethnography of, 217-219
    of Hispanic secondary students, 212-226, 234-236
Administration, in urban education, 16, 18-26
Administrators, teacher-administrator politics, 74-75
Affinity, 170
African Americans. *See* Blacks
AIDS education, 306
Alaskan schools, 52
American Indians
    communication patterns of, 215
    science education for, 248
    workshop for student teachers on, 32, 35-37
Asian Americans, 32

Behavior-alteration techniques, 171
Behavioral objectives, 286-287
Black English, 271-284
Blacks
    communication patterns of, 215
    family of, 216
    language of, 271-284, 301
    racism against, 7-8
    reading needs of, 269-284
    science education for, 248
    workshop for student teachers on, 32
Bureaucracies, and children in poverty, 5, 7

Case studies
    to document developmental changes of student teachers, 98-110, 158-159
    use of, 155, 158-159
CDAI. *See* Cultural Diversity Awareness Inventory (CDAI)
Class dialogues, analysis of, 138-150, 157-158
Cleveland schools, 10-30
Communication
    apprehension and avoidance of, 172

areas of study in, 166-169
children's problems in, 168
educators as communicators, 166
general communication theory, 167
intercultural communication, 169, 172-173, 196
interpersonal and relational communication, 168-169
mass-mediated communication, 168
in multicultural classrooms, 212-226, 234-236
multicultural perspective in basic communication course, 193-207, 232-234
nonverbal communication, 167, 170
organizational communication, 167-168
persuasion and social influence, 169
research trends in, 169-173
teacher plans for managing teacher- and student-owned classroom misbehaviors, 175-189, 229-231
Community, and urban education, 15, 18-26, 84-85
Constantinople test, 115, 117, 118
Constructivist Learning Model, 251-253
Cross-cultural training, 197-198
Cultural Diversity Awareness Inventory (CDAI), 64
Culturally diverse learners. *See also* Multicultural education
    ability grouping and tracking for, 44
    factors associated with school success and failure, 39-41
    and how students learn, 46-47
    individualization for, 46
    reading needs of, 269-284
    relationship between academic tasks and opportunities to learn, 38-39
    science education for, 243-264
    standards for student performance, 44-46
    stereotyping of, 35-38
    and student ability, 47-48
    student teachers' attitudes and beliefs about, 39-48, 50-53
    tasks appropriate for "low" and "high" achievers, 41-43
    teacher education on, 60-69, 86-87
    and teacher expectations for "slow learners," 44
    and teacher roles, 47
    and teaching in English, 48